A brief history of
Trade Unionism
in Mauritius

Rajpalsingh Allgoo. MBE, MSK

पुस्तक भारती
Pustak Bharati
Canada

Author :
Rajpalsingh Allgoo, MBE, MSK

Book Title :
A brief history of Trade Unionism in Mauritius

This book present the history of Slavery and forced labour in Mauritius. It tells us how Mauritius was occupied by the Europeans and was converted in to a colony. When slavery was abolished in 1833, the British started a new system called 'Indentured Labour.' The Indian Indentured Labour were brought in Mauritius in 1834. This book presents an overview of the Trade Union movement in Mauritius from its beginning in the 1930s to the present day. It gives a brief description with images and roles played by several people involved.

Published by :
PUSTAK BHARATI
    Division of PC PLUS Ltd.
    Toronto, Ontario, Canada, M2R 3E4
    email : pustak.bharati.canada@gmail.com
    Web : pustak.bharati.canada.com

A Lost Historic Treasure Recovered and Restored
  with the request and permission from the author :
By Prof. Ratnakar Narale, Toronto, Canada

ISBN 978-1-897416-16-7 NBZI

Copyright ©2019
ISBN   978-1-897416-16-7

9 781897 416167

Dedicated

to all labor forces of Mauritius

Mr Rajkeswar Purryag, GCSK, GOSK
President of The Republic of Mauritius

Mr Rajpalsingh Allgoo, MBE, MSK
President of MLC Addressing the ILO, Conference 1993

FOREWORD

It is a tradition in our country that, in a book written by a politician, or a biography devoted to former Prime Ministers or presidents of the Republic, no allusion is ever made to the struggle of the trade unions leaders. In fact, it is "natural" in Mauritius to forget those who paved the way, so that other generations could enjoy a better life.

Fortunately, when I decided to write a brief story of trade unionism in Mauritius, I chose to distinguish myself far from the madding crowd of politicians. From my reminiscences, we will thus be able to know that a Harryparsad Ramnarain is also a great figure of this country. And that every political leader, whatever may be his party, should continuously pay homage to this great man, who
deserves to be remembered.

I was influenced by this man and my uncle Partab Allgoo the ex-General Secretary of the Labour Party. And this is why I deem it necessary to devote an entire chapter to late Harryparsad Ramnarain. This year, in February 2014, the trade unionism movement saw the demise of Farook Auchaybar. He died at the age of 65. The former president of the General Workers Federation, of the Union of Bus Industry Workers and Secretary of the National Trade Union Confederation was also an adviser at the Ministry of Labour. He was appointed to this job by Minister Sowkatally Soodhun, himself a former Trade Unionist.

Suffice to say that I pay homage to Emmanuel Anquetil, but also to all freedom fighters that, through their struggle, made it possible for all workers of our country that their rights be respected by employers and by Government. This is why I begin his book on trade unions with a chapter on slavery, maroonage and Indentured labour. In fact, the struggle began in those years when man ill-treated his neighbour. In these harsh times, emerged names like Ratsitatane, Adolphe de Plevitz, and Manilal Doctor.

I also remember that it was Emmanuel Anquetil who created the Artisans and General Workers' Union (AGWU), in year 1938. Considered as the father of Trade Union movement in Mauritius, Anquetil has been forgotten, particularly by politicians. And even if his name has been given to a building in Port-Louis, it is ironically known that the Emmanuel Anquetil Building has been subject of gross neglect!

When I became president of AGWU, I stressed on the fact that "throughout its years of existence, the Artisans and General Workers' Union has striven hard to uplift the general standard of living as well as conditions of work for the working class. I shall not say that there have been no setbacks but rather that, having outlined them, the union has each time come out even stronger."

Today, the Trade Union Movement in Mauritius is on the modern way. And much progress has been made, thanks to all the leaders of this movement. But, be it in the port area, in the sugar cane fields or in the private and public sector, challenges are still there. And it is up to the trade union leaders to get along with evolution, with a united force and be prepared to face the multiple challenges occurring with the global labour market every day in our country.

As rightly said by Mr Marcello Malentacchi, former General Secretary of International Metalworkers' Federation, "at such at time, it is good to look back and assess the developments which have shaped the organisation. Those who have the strength of character to create a trade union where non previously existed are very special people, and we should never underestimate the difficulties they had to overcome, or the personal sacrifices they were prepared to make, in order to establish a trade union, and to be of service to their fellow workers."

This is why no one of us shall forget the vivid image of me, handcuffed on a hospital bed. I was arrested by police, just because I was true to the philosophy I adopted. I was jailed under false charges, under the section 102 of Industrial Relations Act 1974. And I was arrested because I refused to call off the strike at Sinotex textile factory, where 3000 workers were involved, prior to negotiation with employers of Sinotex (Mauritius Ltd). During lock up period, I fell sick in the cell and was handcuffed on my hospital bed!

Eventually, Sir Gaetan Duval, then in "alliance" with Mouvement Socialiste Militant and Labour Party in Government, chose to leave Government. Did Sir Gaetan do this move because Allgoo was also an inhabitant of Grand Gaube, like him? Nobody knows. But Sir Gaetan Duval was a special politician. And he never condoned "politik dominer". He publicly presented his apology to me, following his arrest. Sir Gaetan Duval, truly a man for eternity!

It was in July 1988, and three years later, MSM would part away from Labour Party and general elections were held in 1991, with MSM/MMM gaining power and Labour Party and PMSD in opposition.

For all the future readers of this brief story of the trade union movement in Mauritius, we deemed it important to recapitulate all these facts so that everyone, from politicians to civil servants, employees from the private sector, and particularly the youth and Mauritians at large, may cherish all the memories linked to the glorious struggle of trade unionism in our country!

Like everywhere in the world, the Mauritian economy is based on money, which is subject to inflation and rise in cost of living. Periodically, wages have to rise in order to catch up with the loss suffered in the standard of living. In such a situation, employers benefit and a redistribution of income is imperative. Labour is an essential factor of production. It has its share in the total revenue earned by all four factors. Workers are generally engrossed in their functions and they are not well aware of the proper returns they deserve. They only become conscious when they face real life situations and see that their earnings do not suffice to make both ends meet. Somewhere somebody is taking the lion's share. Collective effort is then needed to claim the increases they deserve. Here comes into play the role of the trade union.

Mauritius has always been a rich and prosperous country in Africa. The "Sugar Bowl" of the XIXth century with its hundreds of sugar mills at one time brought revenues that were mostly wasted in European capitals or exhibited in castles, churches and other buildings at home. There was no proper redistribution of profit, so that workers toiled and died in misery. The evils of industrialism had reached the shores of Mauritius leading to the enrichment of a few only. The trade union movement emerged forcefully at the beginning of the XXth century and the battle cry of Karl Marx in "Das Kapital": "Workers of the world, Unite", resounded far and wide, bringing hope in the hearts of the downtrodden. As employers controlled the economic machinery and exploited workers better, socialism was out to compel changes through unity and political control.

First, the writings of Langland, the poet of the poor, then Robert Owen, the socialist and, later Marx, the communist, were precursors of trade union movement. In Mauritius, Adolphe de Plevitz and Manilal Doctor sought improvements in the workers' lot through Royal Commissions, although not always successfully. Labour associations emerged painfully through employers' and Colonial government repressions, resulting in house arrest of Maurice Curé, banishment of Emmanuel Anquetil and imprisonment of Hurryparsad Ramnarain. The latter lost his physical health behind the bars. As a government minister in 1972, he would remember those days when young MMM leaders were imprisoned. He asked for their liberation and resigned from his post when his demand was rejected. The 1930s and '40s were the hot years of unionism with riots, even deaths, but the movement held its ground under the leaderships of Anquetil, Ramnarain, Jugdambi, Guy Rozemont and others.

Maurice Curé in politics started the Labour Party in 1936. Repression galore fell upon him from all quarters. Ramnarain used to hide his bicycle in cane fields and enter his house from the back door in secrecy to communicate news of happenings among labourers in the North and sought advice from him. Workers became aware of the injustices they were undergoing. They responded to the call of their representatives and leaders. The Hooper Commission of 1938 authorized the setting up of trade unions. Devoid of formal education, labourers were prone to violence in the claims for their rights. A few of them even died or got wounded in their efforts. It was during those years of labour unrest that I joined the fray.

The North was very active in the setting up of unions as it was the home of pioneers in the field. It was also the playground for budding politicians. I got directly involved in trade union activities. I rubbed shoulders with all the great personalities of the time gaining inspiration and experience from them. I also went through the ups and downs of life in the trade union movement, even losing my job and facing arrest, handcuffed to a hospital bed.

As a retired union leader, I thought it would be a praiseworthy effort to share my experiences with the public at large because I had my say in the history of the movement. This book depicts the life of the barefooted and naked-handed worker to the one in boots and gloves and protective garments of the late XXth century. I have been directly involved in bettering the day to day lives of the most downtrodden beings that are workers whose just contribution to production and revenue is overlooked.

Employers study how to exploit labour at university level in terms of productivity through all kinds of promises but little money in return. Workers have always in mind two things: work and money. They know little about their rights and do not even know how to make proper tax returns.

Workers' education through training programmes for union leaders themselves in local and foreign institutions had been a laudable initiative and I participated in what I conceived as the enhancement of workers. This book which is in fact an autobiography is a document that will appeal to all workers. Research students will find in it answers to many questions of interest, even the direct intrusion of politics in the movement that is a stepping stone to parliament. It goes without saying that I have my own political bent but I have always put the interests of union members first.

I also pay homage to Jean Jaurès, who died 100 years ago. He was the one to "se bat très tôt pour la création de retraites ouvrières. Sa première proposition de loi sur le sujet, cosignée par deux députés modérés, date d'avril 1886." He was the one, who had known « l'émergence des premiers syndicats ouvriers autorisés par la loi Waldeck-Rousseau ». As rightly pointed by the Newspaper Le Monde, in the Hors-Série dedicated to the Memory of This Great man," il plaide pour une action de masse et rassembleuse". Unity in the trade union movement is of utmost importance. The International Trade Union organisations, the International Confederation of Free Trade Union (ICFTU), and World Confederation of Labour (WCL) which were separated in 1949 due to Cold War had deemed it important and necessary in the global world to merge together to form the International Trade Union Confederation (ITUC), in November 2006 in the interest of the working class despite more than 50 years of separation. Even the International Trade Secretariats are following the step. I humbly suggest our Trade Union leaders to put emphasis on the urgent need to think seriously in line with the International Trade Union Organisations, to face the unique Mauritius Employers' Federation and better protect the working class!

Rajpalsingh Allgoo

ACKNOWLEDGEMENT

After having retired from trade unions activities, I have often been solicited to write a book on "Trade Union Activities" as being doyen in the Trade Union with a good experience. I started collecting information through my writings and Press clippings which I had gathered since long, to write a second edition of My Book "Le Mouvement Syndicale à l'Ile Maurice" which I had written to the Founder of the Mauritius Engineering & Technical Workers' Union (to be known as Artisans & General Workers' Union) in the context of the Birth Centenary on Trade Unions in Mauritius on the 18th August, 1985.

In the meantime, a team of lecturers from the School of Management of the University of Mauritius, came to my office at the National Remuneration Board, and requested me to help them to write, to write a book on Trade unions in Mauritius, commissioned by the Mauritius Research Council. I gave them all the documents I had already gathered, in the hope that they would produce a complete history of Trade Unions, which could serve as reference.

A ceremony was held in January 2008, to present the Report on "Trade Unionism in Mauritius" at the MRC. But unfortunately, for unknown reasons this book has not yet been published.

Sometime in 2012, after the meeting of GOPIO Mauritius, my good friend Mr Vinay Cheewan Dookhony had gathered Afzal Delbar, Kiran Ramsahaye and few other friends to encourage me to write a book on the Trade Unions in Mauritius. A few weeks later Mr Kiran Ramsahaye, the Editor of Le Matinal, wrote a long article on my trade unions activities. This really triggered me to write this book.

I wish to seize this opportunity to thank my two late friends namely Mr Vellah Soobrayen, who was a teacher (later retired as School Inspector) for helping in doing administrative work at the office Sundays only, and Mr Vinod Ramdhary, who was the Assistant General Secretary of the MLC, was helping in writing important documents as General Secretary of the union had no time off for union work. I would also like to thank the President Mr Chandrassensing Bhagirutty and Mr Dan Cunniah the General Secretary of the MLC for supporting me in my job as Director of Organisation and also the Executive Members of AGWU.

The documents of this book are my collections during my trade union career, including the interviews of Mr Hurryparsad Ramnarain OBE and Mr Mohunparsad Jugdambi both Former Presidents of the Mauritius Labour Congress with whom I got the opportunity to work.

Last but not least, I express my warmest thanks to my Daughter-in-law Sangeeta (Kavita) Allgoo BSc, MSc, MA and my two collaborators: Mr Bhishmadev Seebaluck O.S.K. and Mr Sedley Richard Sedley Assonne, Producer at the MBC/TV, for their valuable contributions and several persons who in one way or other helped me.

TABLE OF CONTENT

Dan Cunniah
Former General Secretary of the MLC
Former Director of the Bureau for Workers' Activities of the ILO
Currently Senior Adviser to the Deputy Director General of the ILO
for Field Operations and Partnerships. "

particularly in "Le Mauricien", and I told him that what he had heard about the MLC's intention to create problems in the EPZ was false and that the workers could no longer bear the harsh conditions of work with compulsory long hours of overtime etc, which prompted them to go on strike. He did not want to hear that but was determined to "donne ène léçon" banne "fouteurs désordre". He wanted to use Allgoo as an example to silence the trade union movement.

I leave you to read the whole story as being told by brother Allgoo in this book. But just to illustrate how it was difficult and dangerous to be a trade unionist at that time. The day before I was to go to meet the workers, who had decided to gather at the Pamplemousses Gardens to demand the release of Allgoo and the other trade union leaders, a policeman from the Special Branch was waiting for me at my house. As soon as I arrived at home, he told me that he was carrying a message of warning from the Commissioner of Police and that if I were to address the workers on strike, I would also be arrested. That did not deter me to go and meet the workers but I did not address them collectively.

I am grateful to Raj for writing on this difficult episode of our trade union history. Raj's struggle to improve the conditions of work and living of poor workers and their families is exemplary. His life is one of commitment, of sacrifice and selfless devotion to the ideals of trade unionism.

I think it is not improper for me to express a personal regret and sadness to see the condition of the MLC today. Without criticising or condemning anybody, I must recall that when I left the MLC in 1991, after eleven years as its General Secretary, the organisation had 65,000 members and several thousands of rupees in the banks, four vehicles and a new building in Rivière des Anguilles, a full-fledged and running Workers Education Centre in front of its current seat. I cannot fail to recall the work and sacrifice of trade unionists like Hurrypersad Ramnarain, Sharma Jugdambi, Chandersendsing Bhageerutty, Hassam Patel, Narainsamy Pillay and Rajpalsingh Allgoo and others in building the MLC into a strong and viable institution.

I commend Raj Allgoo for this laudable initiative of not letting this portion of trade union history go into oblivion and to put it in words for posterity. I recommend this book to all, old and young, because only the lessons of the past can help us carve our future with courage and determination. Long live the trade union movement.

Dan Cunniah

~ Chapter 1 ~

SLAVERY
AND
FORCED LABOUR

THE island of Mauritius was not permanently inhabited before its "discovery" by the Dutch, but in 1638 established the first Dutch settlement in Mauritius with a garrison of twenty-five men. He thus became the first governor of the island. In 1639, thirty more men came to reinforce the Dutch colony. *Gooyer* was instructed to develop the commercial potential of the island, but he did nothing of the sort, so he was recalled. His successor was , who began the development in earnest, developing the export of wood. For that purpose, *Van Der Stel* brought 105 Malagasy slaves to the island. Within the first week, about sixty slaves were able to escape into the forests; only about twenty of them were eventually recaptured.

Slaves were not particularly well-treated by the colonists, and revolts or the act of organizing one was severely repressed and punished. Some punishments consist in the amputation of various parts of the body and exposure in the open air for a day as a deterrent to others, eventually culminating in the condemned slaves' execution at sunset.

As rightly pointed by Jacques David, in his book entitled "The slave legacy", Mauritius is specially renowned for its "brutal slave regime", which make Mr David evoke Bernardin de Saint Pierre's "Voyage à l'île de France", where he depicts the cruelty against the slaves: *« Pour l'ordinaire, ils se réfugient dans des bois, où on leur donne la chasse avec des détachements de soldats, de nègres et de chiens ; il y a des habitants qui s'en font une partie de plaisir. On les relance comme des bêtes sauvages » lorsqu'on ne peut les atteindre, on les tire à coup de fusil ; on leur coupe la tête, on la porte en triomphe à la ville, au bout d'un bâton… »*

FRENCH SETTLEMENT

The first permanent settlement of Mauritius was effected in the year 1722 by the French Governor Denis de Nyon, who brought African slaves to work on the sugarcane plantations. The French developed the island and renamed it Isle de France.

The British Royal Navy realized the problems arising as long as this island would be under French control. The trading routes to the Indian Ocean became blocked. The British captured Mauritius in 1810 for economic and strategic purposes. After the capitulation, a pact was signed by British with the French Governor Charles Decaen that the British will keep French language and it culture and the French law codified under the Napoleon's regime. And the French Colonists did work hard and make the Island fruitful in many ways.

However, in Mauritius and elsewhere, the sugar plantation economy since its inception had depended, for its success and profitability, on plentiful, cheap, coercible and disciplined labour force. Slavery labour had, for centuries, been the backbone of the plantation colonies of Mauritius and the Caribbean.

After the abolition of slavery on 1st February 1835, the Indentured labour system was introduced. In subsequent decades hundreds of thousands of workers arrived from India. Mauritius was the first British Colony to embark on the 'Great Experiment' of importing an indentured labour workforce from India, to replace the local labourers liberated from slavery by an indentured workforce. This workforce later became a majority population group after the abolition of slaves on 1st February 1835. Around 360,000 Indentured labourers were brought to Mauritius. The Indian labourers came to Mauritius mainly through the Port of Calcutta.

It was a pity the slaves were uprooted from their original countries to Mauritius and elsewhere. They lived in a piteous state and frightful conditions. Slaves were not paid like the indentured labourers, furthermore they were not properly treated by the Colonists and any act contrary to the laws was severely repressed and punished.

At a certain point in time, the slaves began to exert a certain form of resistance which was expressed in a number of ways: (1) rebellions; (2) refusal to reproduce new-born; (3) suicides; (4) refusal to work and above all "maroon slaves" which was an act of running away and living on the Mountains and in the woods.

Le Code Noir

According to researchers in Mauritius, it was not easy to evaluate exactly the output of the labour force, their wages, frequency of punishments and their gravity, the rate of births and deaths. The census carried out prior to the abolition of slavery gives a rough idea of its importance.

From Mgr Nagapen's book "Le marronage a l'Isle de France–l'Ile Maurice", it is to be noted that the masters of that time feared insurrection, after the evasion of Ratsitatane: "La nouvelle de l'évasion se propagea graduellement parmi la population. Port-Louis céda à une véritable psychose de peur, la population ayant toujours redouté ce genre d'évènement du fait de son infériorité numérique face à la population d'esclaves Noirs. Il s'agissait du "syndrome de Saint-Domaingue". Car à cette époque, il ne faut pas l'oublier, la population comptait environ 80,000 esclaves et 20,000 hommes libres dont à peine un dixième étaient des Blancs."

Ironically, The Code Noir, compiled by Jean Baptiste Colbert in 1685, and which was meant to do justice to the slaves, in fact turned into a Bible for masters to lord it over the slaves. The punishments were extremely severe and even inhuman. The fugitives had one ear cut for a first offence, thigh cut for the second and fleur de lys stamped on shoulders. It tried to establish the vital minimum masters had to comply with. At that time, Father Jacques Désiré Laval thought that better treatment would have yielded better and more positive results. Slaves were given 1 kilo of maize per day or the equivalent in rice, manioc or sweet potatoes. No roots were allowed. The slaves supplemented their meal by vegetables they cultivated on a square plot of land allotted to them. They also reared pigs and poultry and could eat meat periodically. They received a set of dress per year. The men were given a pair of trousers, a shirt and sometimes a waistcoat, while the women received a shirt, and a kerchief. A few masters even gave them a sheet of linen they used as cover in winter.

Slavery received a boost from Mahé de Labourdonnais as he devised some very efficient and effective methods to treat the slaves. He trained them as sailors and soldiers and used them to fight against the British in India. He also trained them as policemen to track runaway slaves and to ensure peace and order. He sometimes visited them and spent a few hours with them. Dr Charles Telfair was another humane master who treated his slaves in a humanitarian way. He provided them with decent living conditions, schooling for their children and medical treatment on his estate at Bel Ombre.

Rémy Ollier, son of a french soldier and a woman slave, would later be the spokesperson for the Creole and Coloured Community, through "La Sentinelle", the newspaper he founded. On every 1st of February, since 2001, the Mauritian State celebrates the African heritage in the region of Le Morne, where many maroons lived. This mountain has been inscribed on Unesco World Heritage since the 7th July 2008.

Chapter 2

THE INDENTURED
LABOUR

After slavery was abolished by the British in 1834, the Sugar magnates, feeling the need to get labourers to work in the sugar canes field, turned to India.

Caption

FROM 1834 to 1870 approximately 362,150 immigrants (289,763 males and 72,387 females) were imported to Mauritius from India. The immigration of the indentured labourers was supposed to be on a temporary basis. However, once on the island, the small planters and the sugar estates found all sorts of reasons to manipulate and retain them for longer than what was stipulated in their contracts. In 1847, the State also judged that the quota of female indentured labourers be not less than 25%. This is how short term immigration turned into lasting one. This was a strategy used by the government and planters; firstly to discourage the male immigrants to return to their country of origin and secondly give them reasons (women and money) to stay in Mauritius. The immigrants settled on the plantation fields. With this massive labour force working on the sugar cane fields, the economy of the country was boosted. This form of exploitation turned out to be very profitable for the sugar barons and small planters.

THE PLIGHT OF THE INDENTURED LABOURERS

The workers were forced to work like machines and made to live as animals. The working, living and social conditions were as follows:

* They had no fixed hours of work. Starting before sunrise they were required to go on responding to the whims and caprices of their supervisors;
* They had no set time for lunch. Some days, it could be as late – 2.00 p.m.
* The wages varied between 30 & 40 cents per day;
* They were forced to give certain a percentage of their earnings to their supervisors;
* They were often abused and ill-treated by the foremen and Supervisors, and dismissed on flimsy grounds even without any reason;
* They lived in small thatched rooms with only one door and no other openings;
* They wore tattered rags;
* They had few utensils, two wooden beds or mattresses made of grass and used as bed sheets and covers;
* Their food consisted of some boiled rice, or farata and one dholl or vegetables;
* They could not do anything to have a satisfactory social status as they received meagre wages which were not enough to buy food and clothes let alone a about decent living. In cases of sickness, they could not even afford to buy medicine. They thus used traditional medicines.
* Education was not a priority, their children were to help the father and mother in the sugar canes fields. No one told them about the working conditions.
* A ruthless capitalist system was set up to crush the wishes of the workers who had begun to think that the rich had been sent by God to enjoy all the good things. They had been made to believe it that was their sacred duty to serve the rich planters.

Indian Family – Indentured Labourers – Mauritius – 1920s

THE INDENTURE SYSTEM ABOLISHED

While active Indian immigration came to an end in 1924, it certainly did not mean that the indenture system was abolished and this practice officially took place only between 1938 and 1939. In November 1938, the local British government replaced the Labour Law of 1922 with the Labour Ordinance of November 1938. This new labour law brought the protection, regulations for payment of wages as well as working hours and all matters concerning the Mauritian workers under the control of the Labour Department.

It became law in January 1939 and during November of the same year, through Ordinance No.47, the title of the Office of the Protector of Immigrants and Poor Law Commissioner was changed to that of Director of Labour. In effect, the Protector of Immigrants was officially replaced by the Director of Labour. Without doubt, these actions brought an end to a system which had existed for a century in British Mauritius.

During the 1840s and after, the old immigrants, or those who had served their five-year contracts and remained in Mauritius, had saved some money and began to settle outside the sugar estates. They either bought or squatted on small patches of land in the rural areas and some even married ex-slave women and others settled in Port Louis. Gradually, between the 1840s and 1860s, a small rural Indian peasantry was emerging as they acquired small patches of marginal lands and became small cultivators and raised domesticated animals. At the same time, others became small traders and hawkers.

Aapravasi Ghat, where the Indian immigrants landed, their descendants

It was only really between the 1870s and 1920s that a large and important class of rural Indian landowners began to emerge in Mauritius. During the last thirty years of the nineteenth century, with the stagnation and gradual decline of the sugar industry, many of the sugar barons sold their marginal lands which were located on the fringe of their sugar estates to thousands of old Indian immigrants and a few Indian merchants and traders in what became known, according to Richard B. Allen, an American historian, as the 'Great Morcellement Movement'.

Today, through the Aapravasi Ghat, where the Indian immigrants landed, their descendants pay homage to the memory of those hard workers, every 2nd of November. Thanks to Mr Bikramsing Ramlallah, a former member of Legislative Assembly and Journalist, this date has been a landmark in the remembrance of indentured labourers' legacy in Mauritius. But now the time is ripe to also remember all those who fought for the rights of the Indian immigrants.

As a militant for the cause of the workers of this country, I have dedicated my whole career to the fight for their rights. I have been at the forefront of several important workers' actions and devised acceptable solutions to knotty industrial disputes.

I have always been inspired by the early fighters like de Plevitz, Moutou, Curé, Anquetil, Ramnarain, Jugdambi, my uncle Pertab Allgoo and others. Workers' struggles of the 30s and 40s often come to my mind. Those were difficult days indeed. But thanks to the efforts of those pioneers, a wind of change had started blowing over the workers' world.

It is with fond nostalgia that I recall some of the early fighters and the periods of unrest often punctuated with strikes:

The first fighter that comes to my mind is Adolphe de Plevitz. De Plevitz was not a union leader but his fight in favour of the downtrodden indentured labourers has been written in golden letters in the pages of our turbulent history.

Chapter 3

ADOLPHE DE PLEVITZ, IMMIGRANTS' MESSIAH

I<small>T</small> is common knowledge that the White planters of the 19th century meted out a very cruel treatment to the Indian indentured labourers. In 1867, Governor Henry Barkly introduced a Labour Law which, he said, was going to bring "a new era of social improvement." However in real fact, far from the pretended era of social improvement, or improving the conditions of the labourers, it only helped to push them further down into the quagmire of misery and desolation.

The callousness and depravity of the White masters was severely condemned by a young White estate manager, Adolphe de Plevitz, who arrived in the colony in 1858. He was sickened at the plight of the labourers. He was simply disgusted by the way they were treated. The White behaved as if these workers were not human beings but a batch of objects to be used.

Adolphe de Plevitz was born in Paris in August 1837. At the death of his father in 1850, he was sent to live with an uncle in Germany. A few years later he came back to Paris where he joined the French army and became a Lieutenant at the tender age of seventeen.

He is also reported to have adopted the British nationality and enrolled himself in the British army. He had postings in Africa, India and Madagascar, thus getting the opportunity to learn the languages of the countries where he served, including Hindi. He landed in Mauritius on September 4, 1858 at the age of 21. He soon obtained a job as a Forest Ranger, a position which he kept for two years until 1860. The same year he got married to Marie Emilie, daughter of Francois Rivet. After their marriage the couple lived at Cassis until 1869, when they moved to Nouvelle Découverte where Adolphe took charge of the plantation of his father-in-law.

The 175,000 Indian indentured labourers found a saviour at last, as Adolphe de Plevitz started militating for better working and living conditions for them. The afflictions of the labourers were consolidated by the Labour Law of 1867 which was efficiently enforced by the Inspector General of Police. Adolphe de Plevitz saw the hardships of the labourers and empathised with them. He championed the cause of these downtrodden and oppressed underdogs.

In a bid to erase some of their hardships and miseries, De Plevitz addressed a petition to the Governor of the day, Sir Arthur Gordon, exposing the grievances of the labourers and pressing for reforms. The petition contained 9,400 signatures and thumbprints and was submitted on 6th June 1871. It had been drafted by Godfrey Soobhanee, a Headteacher, Stevens, a retired soldier, and Professor Rajurathnam Mudaliar of Royal College, Cure pipe. The petition was addressed to Queen Victoria, with copies to the State Secretary, the British parliamentarians, the London press and the authorities in India. It gave a vivid description of the execrable ordeals of the sugarcane workers.
On 30th October of the same year, the capitalist class sent a counter petition with 900 signatures expressing their approval of the conduct of the authorities and requesting the Governor to order the immediate expulsion of the "alien," Mr. de Plevitz, from the colony.

The Governor, Sir Arthur Gordon, did not pay much heed to this petition, although a question was addressed to him in the Legislative Council by Sir Virgile Naz as to the steps His Excellency was intending to take in order to "prevent the falsehoods and calumnies of Mr. de Plevitz from being propagated here and abroad."

As luck would have it for de Plevitz and the indentured labourers, the Chamber of Agriculture unwittingly committed a catastrophic blunder at a meeting on November 13, 1871. It unanimously adopted a motion which offered the Governor either of two choices: (i) "To take the earliest opportunity of refuting the malicious assertions contained in the libel, in order that the Home Government and the Indian authorities should be made acquainted with the truth:" (ii) "In case His Excellency the Governor should not find reason to accede to our request, Her Majesty may be prayed to name a competent Commission to inquire fully and fairly into all the circumstances, and report on the conditions of labourers employed in the colony."

The Governor was also requested to "express repudiation of the aspersions made on the planters by a foreign adventurer" and to discredit "the miserable libel written by Mr. de Plevitz". By asking a Commission of Inquiry, the Chamber of Agriculture was anticipating the appointment of a Commission made up of members selected locally, that would clear the planters of all blame. But that was counting without the sagacity of Sir Arthur who took them by surprise by acceding to their request and asking the Secretary of State, Lord Kimberley to appoint a Royal Commission.

The Royal Commissioners, Frere and Williamson, arrived in Mauritius on April 7, 1872 and were given offices at the Line Barracks in Port Louis. They had several sittings and also went all over the island. They visited 51 sugar estates and interviewed hundreds of people.

In the course of the inquiry, de Plevitz put up a very strong fight in favour of the labourers. He was not a lawyer but he acted as counsel for the immigrants.

The Commissioners were fully satisfied that the points raised in de Plevitz's petition reflected the truth. Both the police and the Protector of Immigrants were severely censured. The police were blamed for their high-handedness towards the immigrants, while the Protector of Immigrants was rebuked for turning a deaf ear to the complaints of the labourers. It came to light that just in one year some 5,000 complaints had been made but the Protector feigned ignorance of any complaint.

The Commission of Inquiry also recommended, among others, that the "vexatious and arbitrary" Labour Law of 1867 be repealed and replaced by another.

However the new laws didn't completely change the plight of the labourers who continued to suffer the whims and caprices of the planters. The labourers were considered as the private property of the estate, just like slaves were before them.

From time to time labourers and artisans came together to fight for their rights and for the betterment of their working and housing conditions. But the mobilization of the working class was slow. An impetus was needed: And it came from a man named Manilal Doctor.

Chapter 4

CONTRIBUTIONS OF
MANILAL DOCTOR
TO INDIAN IMMIGRANTS

WHO WAS MANILAL MAGANLALL DOCTOR?

MANILAL MAGANLALL DOCTOR was an Indian from the Baroda State of Gujarat, his father, Dr Maganlall, was a Medical Doctor in charge of the state Mental Hospital. Manilal was the eldest son followed by three brothers and two sisters. The surname "Doctor" was derived from their father's profession. Manilal Doctor did his B.A. LLB in 1903 and the following year he completed his M.A. in Philosophy from University of Bombay, his core subject were Economics, Political Science, Logic, Philosophy and had an option subject of Sanskrit.

After completing his B.A., LLB, and M.A. Manilal Doctor went to London with the financial help of Dr Pranjiwandas Metha who was Philanthropist and a friend of M. K. Gandhi, for further advance study in Law. Manilal Doctor was brilliant student at the Middle Temple and completed his Bar-at Law Examination in 1906. In early month of 1907 he went to New York and Boston.

On his way back to London Manilal Doctor was personally recommended by Mohandas Karamchand Gandhi who had just came from South Africa in a delegation to discuss the Indian Immigrants problems in Natal with the Secretary of the State for the Colonies. During their meeting Gandhi request Manilal to proceed to Mauritius as there was great need of an Indian Barrister.

Manilal was an avid reader and he had keen interest in history and Philosophy. He was a linguist and acquired admirable knowledge in two classical languages, Sanskrit and Latin. He had a sound knowledge of English, a working knowledge of French and half dozen of Indian languages.

The custom in India was very common of child marriage in 19th century, so Manilal was married in his adolescence. His wife was from Surat, unfortunately she passed away in 1902 leaving a daughter who died in infancy when Manilal was at the University for his Degree Studies.

Manilal Doctor's Mauritian Experience

Manilal arrived in Mauritius on 11th October 1907; he was a widower of 26 years, very energetic he took lodging at 8, Desforges Street, Port Louis. Only six days after his arrival, on 16th October 1907, he was called to take the usual Oath at the Supreme Court. On that very day he was asked to remove his turban, but he refused and challenged the Authority either to remove his shoes or his turban while entering a Court of Law. This had created a stir and Manilal wrote articles and also sent petitions to the Governor on this subject.

On the 19th November 1907 a meeting was organised where 200 hundred people of Indian origin were assembled at Tahar Bagh under the Chairmanship of Mr A.S. Hossen, where Manilal moved a motion to sympathize with the arrest of Lalalajpat Rai and Ajit Singh in Calcutta. On the same day several issues were discussed and it was decided to organise a public meeting in Mauritius and to pass resolutions of sympathy for the nationalist Indian charged for sedition, meant that Manilal was directly involved in active politics.

In those days the workers living conditions were very poor, the salary earned was not enough to buy basic food. Due to this sometime the workers were forced to steal manioc (cassava). Manilal Doctor very offen defended the poor Indians in the District Courts. The Magistrate was giving very unfair treated the Indians with severe penalties. An Indian was given a 3 months jail for stealing 4 kilos of Manioc by the magistrate of Rivière du Rempart; the same magistrate sent another Indian to prison for 3 months for stealing 30 pieces of sugarcane from the estate. The Magistrate of Grand Port had condemned 3 months imprisonment for stealing a pig. Manilal Doctor as a lawyer considered the penalties to be harsh; he wrote a long article to expose the miscarriage of justice, and his innocent client was dismissed through his intervention, although he had already spent nine days in the custody before his action was taken in court.

Manilal Doctor intensified his activities in 1908 by effecting regular visits to the far-off villages and sugar estates, organised meetings, delivered exciting speeches in Hindi, the language of the people, passed resolutions for their demands and submitted petitions to the authorities on behalf of individuals and also of any particular groups within Indian community.

In 1908, Manilal Doctor organised a group of literate Indians in Port Louis and founded a society, "the Young Men Hindu Association (Y.M.H.A.) which was registered in 1910 and a primary school was inaugurated which the help of its members. Besides, he also attended the historical meeting to launch the foundation of Arya Samaj in 1911. This was a reformist movement among the Indo-Mauritians. He also arranged to invite Dr. Bhardwaj from Rangoon, who got the new society registered in1913. When Manilal decided to leave Mauritius, he entrusted his printing press and his newspaper "Hindustani" to their care.

THE "DOUBLE CUT" AND "CORVÉE" SCHEME FOR LABOURERS

Manilals' presence in the colony had served as a catalyst to end the reprehensible law of the "Double Cut" and the "Corvée" which was a tool in the hands of the sugar magnets if absent or refused, they used to declare the workers as vagrants and the help of the district magistrates, the workers were sent to prisons handcuffed in batches. Out of this evil system the big planters were making huge financial gains.

In the year 1909 was the most crucial year for Manilal Doctor because he had shown his legal acumen and judicial capacity while defending the nine arrested Indians, who were accused of "Attempt to Murder" and through Manilal able and effective defence six were declared innocent and released and the remaining three accused received light sentence of two years each. Only H. Tinker had commented favourably on the judgement – "By the harsh standard s of Mauritian Justice, they were treated leniently for a crime of killing."

The publication of "The Hindustani" on the 15th March, 1909 was another contribution of Manilal Doctor to the Indo-Mauritian community because it was first Indo-Mauritian newspaper that was published mainly in English and Gujarati thus breaking the monopoly of the well-establish Franco-phone press in the colony. It was meant to defend their rights, privileges, socio-cultural and politico-economic interests of the Indians in Mauritius. Thirdly, it became the forerunner of the Indo-Mauritian newspaper like" The Mauritius Arya Patrika" and the "The Oriental Gazette" that were started in 1911 and 1912 respectively.

MANILAL DOCTOR
DEPOSED TO THE SWETTENHAM COMMISSION

One of the most important works of Manilal Doctor was in favour of the Indians of Mauritius was to depose before the Royal Commission in1909, as said by several historians have gone so far in their speculations that they have said: (a) Manilal Doctor had militated for the appointment of the Royal Commission in 1909; (b) The Indo-Mauritian had no one among to depose before the Commission on their behalves, so Manilal became their spokesman. All these are unfounded assumptions.

As Manilal Doctor was a foreigner, he had not received the three sets of questionnaires sent by the Commission on their arrival to the three categories of persons, namely the big planters, Mill-owners and merchants; the heads of department and a few potential members of the colony. As Manilal did not form part of any group, the question of summoning him did not arise, and so what was the reason behind this?

According to Mr P. Ramsurrun up till today, nobody has revealed that before the appointment of the Swettenham Commission for Mauritius, The Sanderson Commission had already instituted in U.K. and it had already started its work in March 1909. Strange as it may seem, the first deponent was no other than Mr Louis Souchon, the proprietor of Labourdonnais sugar estate, where a serious industrial unrest had just erupted a few months back.

Tinker has said that the Sanderson Commission did not go deeply into the Labourdonnais unrest case. But had the historian delved into the case deeply, he would have understood that the incident in connection with the Labourdonnais case was in fact revealed in dept, when Souchon has said "if you would allow me to relate a personal case, we just turned out an employee from the estate because he had given a slash to an Indian." This refers to Maxime Morel, the administrator of Labourdonnais who was found guilty in Court for ill-treatment, and fined by the Magistrate. In the most indirect way, but sometime later Louis Souchon had also indirectly accused Manilal for instigation unrest when he said, "We have had a great fuss and a great row now made over these things in Mauritius because the Indians are being given ideas that they are badly treated by some people who have an interest to lead them in that way. Not only this, when the Swettenham Commission began it work in June 1909 in Mauritius, the Colonial Secretary, Sir Graham Bower, had said that Manilal Doctor was in touch with the agitators in Bengal and he was here (in Mauritius) giving ideas to the Indians to agitator for better treatment.

Success in the Activities of Manilal Doctor

Manilal Doctor's success in 1909 was because out of the five Court cases emanating from Labourdonnais S.E. unrest won three, lost one and was to be tried later. The starting of the Newspaper *Hindustani* was looked down upon by his opponents because its existence was detrimental to their interest. His interventions before the Swettenham Commission were considered harmful to the plantocracy, and holding public meetings with small planters, this move was not approved by the reactionary press.

Hence in 1909 and 1910, a machinery comprising of a few Government officials, big planters and the francophone press was set up to counteract and out to do the work of Manilal Doctor in the country. An anti-Manilal group within the Indian Community was form with the financial and moral support of the oligarch, and whenever a meeting was organised in which Manilal was to be present, trouble-mongers were sent to create trouble.

Journeys and Activities

Manilal Doctor second father-in-law was a very kind gentleman, who helped him financially from time to time. Shrimati Jaya Kunvar Devi was a good wife and self-respecting lady. Once she underwent a three months' jail term in South Africa but she stuck to her stand.

Manilal Doctor went on many journeys and performed many great deals of works for which he will be remembered in history. This profound thinker went to South Africa, Fiji, and Aden, Mauritius other countries as he sowed the seeds of revolution in religious, social and political fields. This tireless worker drilled home the message of the awakening, keeping in mind the place and time, and challenged the Hindus to rediscover their identity. He travelled first to many cities and towns in India and had first hand field experience, which he used throughout his life.

The motto of Manilal Doctor through his Newspaper "The Hindustani" **Liberty of Individuals! Fraternity of Men! Equality of Race!**

Manilal Doctor and Action Liberal

In the early 20th century, changes in the economy have not put an end to the resistance and the struggle for workers' absenteeism, and desertion. Vagrancy among the labourers continues. Planters in turn, ignore the law of Labour 1878. The "double-cut" is applied in its entire rigor, labourers revolted: August 17th, 1903 at Mon Désert, October 21, 1905 in Bel Ombre. These revolts are still isolated. Due to the slow pace of reforms and the indifference of the government, the labourers were impatient. There are thus spectacular actions (making crush to touch the rails, for example) to draw the Government's attention to their plight. Exasperated, they set fire to fields, a symbol of their misery and exploitation. In despair, many commit suicide.

It is in this context that Mr. Manilal Doctor arrives in Mauritius on October 13th, 1907. Mauritius, at that time, is severely affected by a financial crisis. The Chamber of Agriculture formulated for a loan worth 600.000 with the Government Council supports. The Council requested an additional loan of Rs 200,000. The Liberal Action, founded in 1907 and comprising Dr. Edgar Laurent (leader), René Mérandon, Anatole de Boucherville and others, campaigned against the hegemony of the sugar bourgeoisie. Representatives of the latter are the bogeyman of "endangered Asian" seeing developing collaboration between the leaders of the Action Libérale and Manilal Doctor. The Liberal Action calls for a Royal Commission to investigate the finances of the island and its sugar industry before loans are granted through the meetings that it organized. Before the commission Swettenham, Mr. Doctor pleaded the cause of small farmers and labourers. They claim taxation 'of' luxury goods instead of basic necessities (rice, dholl and Mantègue).

The historian Dayachand Napal wrote that such situation were harshly, and was criticized in the same columns of the conservative papers as enemies of the people, progress and prosperity, and also opponents of the colony'.

Manilal Doctor was personally recommended by Mohandas Karamchand Gandhi himself. The man who will later be known as the Mahatma sojourned in Mauritius for 18 days in year 1901, and he saw in what condition lived his fellow citizens. Meeting of Manilal Doctor in London in 1906, Gandhi had urged him to come to Mauritius "to safeguard their interests in court", as written in Mr Pahlad Ramsurrun's book:"Manilal Doctor-his political activities in Mauritius".

Manilal Doctor stayed for four years in Mauritius, from 11th October 1907 to 9th December 1911.Ramsurrun rightly says that "Manilal Maganlall Doctor was one of the greatest Nationalist Indians who gave the Indo-Mauritians a new insight in life, a sense of respect, and guidelines for living peacefully and harmoniously in a multi-racial and multi-cultural society".

Thus, despite opposition from conservatives and reactionaries, the government, under pressure, introduced a bill abolishing the "double-cut" and drudgery. After general election of 1911, there was a violent campaign against the leaders of the Action Liberal. They shout at risk in Asia. Workers recognize part in the keynote address of the Action Liberal. The thing was democratizing politics through workers meetings. January 19, 1911, riots broke out in Port-Louis after rumours about an alleged assault of Dr. E. Laurent. Action Liberal movement wanted democratic and unitary workers recognized the different segments in the ideology of the Action Liberal Democratic and Popular content. Anti-oligarchic consciousness with all its contradictions and limitations and new born.

Chapter 5

WILLIE MOUTOU –
A BORN FIGHTER

WHITE supremacy has thrived for long in this country and has used the blood, sweat and tears of the workers to reinforce itself. However, God has never completely forsaken His people on earth. From time to time He has sent people here to deliver the downtrodden from the clutches of oppression. Willie Moutou must be remembered as one who tried to unite the workers of the sugar industry, both labourers and artisans, in their struggle for better conditions of work and housing.

Although an employee in the printing sector, he had the plight of the sugar industry workers at heart; a man with faith and determination he fought relentlessly for the cause of the oppressed labourers and artisans. He knew that the workers had to be united in order to stand together against the oppressor, and fight for their rights. In a way, he was one of the precursors of the Trade Union movement in the country.

He started his activities in this field in 1921. The Retrocession movement had suffered a thorough defeat at the general elections held in January of that year. Public opinion could not be aroused in those days and people were not motivated to create a Trade Union movement. Willie Moutou was too early for his time, but he did tour the island and he organized public meetings in the four corners of the colony and talked to the people about the need for unity among the working class.

In 1924 he became the editor of a publication entitled "Le Drapeau Ouvrier." He also created the National Trade Union of Mauritius, but he encountered a barrage of opposition and couldn't get it registered. Moutou submitted a draft proposal of the constitution of the National Trade Union, based on the British Trade Union Legislation, but it was disregarded. In order to get the consideration of the Government Council, the draft proposal had to be tabled by a member of the Council. But he could not persuade any Council Member to come forward with such a motion as all of them belonged to the conservative class and fiercely opposed the workers. How could they encourage the creation of a Trade Union?

Moutou, however, was a man of mettle and couldn't accept defeat so easily. He adopted another approach. He organised a public meeting on 6th April, 1934 and presented the following resolution for approval by those present:

"In view of unanimous refusal of the elected members of the Council of Government to present a private bill in order to authorize the establishment of trade unions in Mauritius, the workmen seek the intervention of the State Secretary for the Colonies in order to allow the incorporation of projected trade unions in Mauritius."

The resolution met with a certain measure of success as Governor Herbert Read was instructed by the State Secretary to make a statement in Government Council on 26 May 1926, about trade unionism and the obligation for employers to provide compensation to employees injured on duty. Two draft conventions prepared by the International Labour Bureau had been submitted to the Governor for consideration. However, the Conservative members of the council were unwilling to discuss trade unionism and workmen's compensations.

Chapter 6

DR JULES MAURICE CURE
FOUNDER OF
THE MAURITIUS LABOUR PARTY

A lot has been written on this great man by different persons, but I still feel it is important to write on his achievement and failure, especially regarding politics and Labour Movement. Dr Jules Maurice Curé had been defeated in the General Election of January 1921; he was the leading member of a Progressive Group. In Mr Roger Pezanni resigned from the Council of Government, leaving his seat vacant in 1934. Dr Curé succeeded in getting himself elected in the by-election (1934 -1936). But due to an aggressive campaign by his opponent he was defeated in the general election of January 1936. However nothing could stop from moving forward in the direction to do something for the working class, who were suffering a lot, they were not even treated as human being. He bore already in mind to claim the recognition of Trade Union in Mauritius.

Slavery was earlier abolished long ago and the importation of Indenture labourers from India was stopped more than a decade. He approached the Colonial Government, so as to eradicate the suffering of the working class, but unfortunately no authority listened to him. When he was an elected member of the Council, he had pleaded in favour of better working conditions of the working class.

Dr Curé also raised the question to amend the constitution of Mauritius so that the working class could elect their Representatives in the Council of Government.

After being unsuccessful in different ways to protect the working class and small planters, Dr Curé and his close collaborators (Pandit Sahadeo Rama, Dr Hassenjee Jeetoo, and Barthélemy Ohsan) decided to alert the public opinion and especially the British Government by organising a mass meeting. He organised a mass meeting at Champ de Mars, which were attended by more than 30,000 persons, including labourers, artisans and small planters on the 23 February 1936. The main object of the meeting was to sensitise the people for economic and Constitutional reforms on behalf of the working classes. The following resolutions were voted:

(1)   Minimum Wages;
(2)   Unemployment Benefits
(3)   Old-Age pension
(4)   Universal suffrage for labourers, artisans and small planters;
(5)   Freedom to organise Trade Unions
(6)   Workmen's compensation and protection against accidents and illness;
(7)   Safeguards for women and children.

A petition was signed by 330 planters of Bon Accueil and Brisée Verdière and was given, over to Dr Maurice Curé on the 6th August, 1936, which was despatched to the Governor. The grievances were as follows:

(1)   15% cut by the Union (FUEL) Sans Souci and Riche Fund estates on the Uba cane;
(2)   the insufficiency of their wages which, according to them, varied between 40-60 cents daily during crop season and a maximum of 40 cents during intercrop;
(3)   the treatment they received at the hands of Sirdars and the recruiting and paying agents.

PROTEST MARCH AND POLICE INTERVENTION

As there was no positive response, a crowd was determined to proceed to Port Louis despite the persuasion of the Commissioner of Police to the contrary. Hence, Colonel Deane decided to call a magistrate to be present in case of trouble, though the crowd was peaceful. The magistrate, M. Legras, came and tried to persuade the labourers to go back home but in vain. The Commissioner of Police threatened to make use of the armed police to disperse the crowd. Meanwhile Colonel Deane had arranged for a special train to take the labourers and small planters back home from Terre Rouge.

As a result of this, a number of riots followed on several Sugar Estates regarding low wages, ill treatment of workers and the small planters:

1.   On the 9 august 1937, a procession reached Port Louis – complaint 15% cut on price of Sugar canes and insufficient daily wages

2. On 10 august there was another trouble at Mon Désert S.E., St. Pierre, where labourers had assembled and they stated their grievances to Asst. Commissioner of Police, Captain Coombes.

    (i) Again for the reason of low wages and ill treatment from the Sirdars, the following day there was a procession from Camp de Masque Pavé to Port Louis. They were however stopped by a Police superintendent at Verdun who persuaded them to cancel their march to Port Louis. They insisted and were allowed to move up to Plaine Lauzun, from where they had to march back home. At Camp de Masque Pavé, officers of the Protector's Office were informed of the complaints, which were:

        (i) Low Wages

        (ii) Lack of confidence in the entrepreneurs or recruiters of labour by whom labourers were paid,

        (ii) Lack of provision for checking the weight of canes at the weighbridge.

It was Hurryparsad Ramnarain who introduced Emmanuel Anquetil to Dr Maurice Curé, in December 1936. In March 27th, 1937, Anquetil accompanied by Hurryparsad Ramnarain went to Camp de Masque Pavé, where Dr Curé and his "lieutenants" were to hold a meeting. On that occasion, Anquetil addressed the gathering and gave a short speech, as he was not used since long to the local language as he was just back to Mauritius after an absence of around 35 years.

The Leaders of the labourers and artisans and the Labour movement associations organised a number of public meetings in different villages and sugar factories areas with the intention of sensitising the sugar workers to the need for Trade Unions. During those days, there was gross exploitation. Labourers and artisans were afraid of the sugar barons and showed indifference to the Trade Union movement. Most often they held private meetings which were followed by public meetings, where resolutions were voted "viva voce" i.e. by acclamation. The workers and small planters were being encouraged and motivated to organise trade Unions.

The leaders explained in a simple way, that they were like the two wheels of a carriage running side by side. Without one the other becomes useless. The decision was reached at the office of the movement, which was situated in the Surgery of Dr Jeetoo "near rue du Vieux Conseil – Port Louis" that labourers and artisans should start organising themselves and form trade unions and fight to bring changes in their working conditions on the sugar estates. Improvement should be brought in the estate camps, where there existed no sanitation and potable water.

Strikes of Labourers –
Artisans & Small Planters

Such prevailing conditions led to the strike of 1937, during the crop season. According to Dr Curé, workers should have recourse to strike so as to change the slave-master mentality of the arrogant sugar magnates. He explained to the agents the implications of the strikes to which plantation workers of Trinidad had had recourse in order to find a solution to their problems. Strike was said to be the last resort for redressing grievances when all other means failed.

The first strike was called at Chebel on 19th July, 1937 on a sugar estate situated at Beau Basin, followed by several strikes in a number of sugar estates.

On 12 August of the same year, workers and small planters were on strike. Mr A. Gujadhur asked for police protection, for which he was ready to pay, against the trouble makers. However, the Police Commissioner could not be of any help as there was a shortage of manpower and informed Mr Gujadhur that in case of serious problems he should stop the mill and mobilize them and inform the police of the situation without any delay and assured them of police protection. Mr Gujadhur gave the advice he had received to his brother, Deonarain Gujadhur the factory manager, who in his turn relayed the advice to members of the staff.

However, it seems that there was misinterpretation of the word "mobilize" which he thought meant – "prepare" for any trouble that might occur, to defend themselves in case of trouble, to see that they would be ready with rifles and guns if any trouble occurred. The consequence of such an interpretation was fatal. Deonarain Gujadhur gave instructions in the light of the advice of col. Deane to J. Ross, the estate overseers, to fetch rifles and purchase ammunition so as to mobilise themselves in case of an emergency.

When Police Inspector Lavictoire arrived at the factory yard, he ordered the crowd to disperse. The general staff of about thirty to forty members were standing some hundred metres away, one of whom with a rifle ready for action. One of the labourers in the crowd told Mr Lavictoire to ask the armed men to go away with his gun. The crowd hurled stones and various missiles at the staff. The arrival of driver Ross worsened matters. The labourers recognised in him as the driver who, on that very morning, had made an attempt of driving the lorry on them. When Ross heard that, he ran to join the general staff, he was panic-stricken.

While Mr Lavictoire was asking the labourers to choose their representatives to discuss with the Manager, another group rushed in with sticks and stones. Their arrival was so sudden that they could not be checked in their movement. The group started their attack with cry of solidarity while the staff members gave themselves to firing at the aggressors who did not show any intention of retreating. Despite the order of Mr Lavictoire not to fire, orders had been given in the morning to Lallah Gujadhur, the manager's brother.

Manslaughter at Union Flacq

The manslaughter had taken place on August 13, 1937 in the factory yard. There were four victims, of who two died in the hospital. They were – Noor Dilmohamed, Nundoo, Mardaymooto Ismael and Brizgobin. There were also two who were wounded. Mr Lavictoire had asked Deonarain Gujadhur , the permission to carry the casualties to hospital on a lorry belonging to the estate. There were three Lorries available in the factory premises but he refused to oblige, alleging that he needed the Lorries as a means of defence against further attacks. Later when the deputy commissioner arrived, the two dead and the five wounded persons were transported to the hospital in a lorry. Then he dispersed the crowd. In the afternoon a hundred angry labourers marched towards the factory premises with sticks as usual. They were asking for the release of their comrades, five of whom had been arrested as trespassers. The men were released the next morning.

In the light of the Report of the Hooper Commission of Inquiry into the unrest of the sugar estates in Mauritius in 1937, a Labour and Social Welfare Department was set up with the help of H.T.W. Oswell, who was an officer of the Malayan Civil Service and who had been deputed to Mauritius for 18 months. Laws were also passed to allow the formation of trade Unions of both employees and employers.

Chapter 7

THE DOCKERS' STRIKE
OF 1938

Emmanuel Anquetil

THE year following the labour unrest and manslaughter of 1937, the Dockers' strike started on the 1st September 1938. According to the employers, this strike had been a result of the fiery language of Anquetil. The Port Louis harbour was completely paralysed. The immediate cause of the strike was the dismissal of a docker, at a time when there were a few ships waiting to be loaded with sugar. The dockers wanted their colleague to be re-integrated before they agreed to resume work. According to the Commissioner of Police, Col Deane, it was Anquetil who had instigated the strikers. What appears strange is that Anquetil was different from the man he was when his collaboration was needed to help put up an industrial association in the late 30s'.

In addition to the immediate cause, the dockers also attached to it their grievances, which in itself was a serious mistake. The dockers had asked for an increase in their wages. The law did not authorise a strike before other methods had failed. They ought to have asked for their increase in wages which would have been referred to conciliation board within thirty days. The Director of Labour failed to bring them to an understanding. Six strikers were arrested on the 5th September and they were brought to Court for trial. Their legal defence was assured by Mr Jules Koenig while the Procurer

General pleaded mercy in their favour on condition that they agreed to resume work. The accused did not wish to commit them before consulting their colleagues.

Magistrate Antoine Legras and the Registrar of Associations, Maurice Ramsancar, parleyed with the strikers but they did not succeed. Then Procurer Hooper had also intervened with the Director of Labour, but it was also a failure. Finally it was through the intervention of Anquetil, in the presence of Lewis Gerard and Lionel Collet, the Protector of Immigration at the association that the dockers agreed to resume work.

On September 4th, at a meeting held at Mahébourg under the aegis of the Labour Party, Anquetil had violently attacked the sugar barons, calling them by all sorts of names. Eventually at Trianon, labourers had attacked the sugar factory. Immediate police intervention brought the situation under control. Seven persons were arrested and brought to Court before Magistrate Raoul Brouard and they were sentenced according to law but the condemned appealed against the verdict and as a result they were acquitted. Their defence was undertaken by Jules Koenig and Harilall Vaghjee.

On the 6th September, the Governor decided by a proclaiming of a state of emergency to stop the situation from becoming worse. Sir Bede Clifford considered Anquetil to be a very dangerous man, a firebrand, and had to be moved from the scene. Anquetil was arrested at his residence in Rose Hill, on September 7th at 01.00 hour together with his son. They were taken to the Line Barracks, Port Louis. Thence, both father and son were conveyed to Rodrigues on exile. The Secretary of the Dockers' Association was persecuted to such an extent that he was forced to refund a sum Rs 68.99 which was found to be missing in the fund of the association.

Bede Clifford had been able to break the strike and simultaneously bring to disrepute Anquetil and Antoine Sandivi, the Secretary. The governor had invited the sugar estates to send able-bodied labourers to replace the dockers who had been on strike. He wanted to show that the dockers were not indispensable.

After Bede Clifford had through his strategy divided the dockers from the Labour party and had broken up the strikers, he decided to scare the life out of the leaders of the Labour movement. A Labour Agent had been arrested while he had been collecting union subscription from labourers. He was brought for trial at the Mahébourg District Court. His defence was assured by Barthélemy Ohsan but he was found guilty and fined Rs 100.

But Emmanuel Anquetil, mistreated under the Colonial rule, would be rightly rehabilitated years later, when Government officially paid homage to him.

Chapter 8

Une Page
de l'histoire du
Syndicalisme Mauricien

Maurice Curé raconte la déportation
d'Anquetil à Rodrigues

Le fondateur du PTr refusa un siège de nominé au conseil législatif et Anquetil, lui, un poste avantageux au Bureau du Travail.

Doctor Maurice Cure narrates the arrest and deportation of Emmanuel Anquetil and sent by his son:

Le 7 septembre 1958, le Dr Maurice Curé, fondateur du Parti Travailliste mauricien mais avec lequel il s'était déjà brouillé à partir de 1942, fait publier ses mémoires dans *Zamana*, un petit journal fondé par M. Bucktowarsing afin de véhiculer les idéaux de Sookdeo Bissoondoyal et son parti, l'Independant Forward Bloc (IFB). Mais, en attendant d'entrer dans les détails, Maurice Curé ne voulut pas rater l'occasion, ce 7 septembre, de rappeler que 20 ans de cela, Emmanuel Anquetil fut déporté à Rodrigues en raison de son engagement syndical. Et c'est dans le journal *Le Mauricien* qu'il choisit de publier une lettre à cet effet. C'est un document d'archives qui permet de comprendre combien furent ardues les luttes des pionniers du syndicalisme mauricien durant la période pré indépendance.

Après avoir rappelé que 20 ans de cela Emmanuel Anquetil fut déporté, docteur Curé poursuivit sa lettre dans le sens suivant : «Un comité d'organisation a tenu un meeting dimanche dernier pour commémorer cet anniversaire en même temps que le souvenir des victimes des troubles de l'Union Flacq. Il m'a demandé de rappeler les circonstances de cet événement qui fit une grande sensation pendant cette période de notre Histoire.

Dans la nuit du 7 au 8 août, des dispositions importantes furent prises par le gouvernement pour contre carrer la grève des dockers qui avait éclaté quelques jours plus tôt. Pour comprendre les raisons de ces mesures qui procédaient d'une véritable panique de la part du gouvernement, il faut passer en revue les événements des quelques mois précédents.

Conformément aux conclusions de la Commission d'enquête de 1937 où j'avais présenté les revendications des classes laborieuses, le Conseil du Gouvernement avait voté diverses ordonnances, notamment un Code du Travail et une ordonnance ayant trait aux associations industrielles et reconnaissantes le droit de grève sous certaines conditions. Le premier meeting de la Fête du Travail, le 1er mai 1938, que j'avais organisé, avait démontré la force des travailleurs et leur solidarité presque complète. Jamais une procession politique où de nombreuses pancartes étalaient des slogans n'avait eu pareil succès, au point d'arracher au capitaine Coombes, qui faisait l'intérim d'inspecteur général de police, ce cri : «*It is fine Doctor, it is fine !*»D'où la peur qui s'empara du gouvernement, qui ordonna, quelques semaines plus tard (le 28 mai), la suspension des activités de la Société de Bienfaisance des travailleurs de l'île Maurice. Dès ce moment, un conflit très dur mit aux prises le Parti travailliste et le gouvernement. Je raconterai les épisodes de cette lutte dans mes mémoires que publie en ce moment dans le journal de l'Hon. Bissoondoyal, *Zamana*.

Au cours d'un meeting que je tins au marché de Mahébourg vers la fin du mois d'août, Anquetil, entre autres, se montra très violent et les esprits s'échauffèrent, ce que dut noter la police. Mis au courant du rapport de la police, le gouverneur me convoqua au Réduit et me demanda d'user de modération ainsi que mes amis, ajoutant qu'il comptait sur nous pour faire des associations industrielles un complet succès et se montrant disposé à nous faire des concessions au sujet de la Société de Bienfaisance. En ce qui me concernait, il me dit qu'il serait très heureux de me voir siéger au Conseil avant la fin de l'année. À cela je lui répondis que si c'était comme membre élu d'après une nouvelle Constitution, ce serait pour moi une grande satisfaction. Il ne l'entendait pas ainsi. Son idée était de m'offrir un siège de nominé que je lui dis ne pas pouvoir accepter.

Anquetil, de son coté, avait décliné un poste très avantageux que lui offrait le directeur du Travail, Oswell, dans le Bureau du Travail, et il était très occupé à organiser les associations industrielles d'après la nouvelle loi, notamment l'association des dockers. Ceux-ci se remirent bientôt en grève et un Board de Conciliation fut nommé où siégea Anquetil, pour représenter les dockers. C'est vers ce moment que les choses empirèrent. À onze heures de la nuit du 7 septembre, environ 14 jours après mon entrevue avec le gouverneur, je fus réveillé pour recevoir de deux officiers de la police, un ordre du gouverneur me privant de la liberté de mes mouvements.

Le lendemain, je vis ma demeure entourée des policiers. Les territoriaux en armes circulaient dans les rues voisines. Des nouvelles contradictoires circulaient au sujet d'Anquetil. J'appris par les journaux qu'il avait été, ainsi que son fils, déporté à Rodrigues. Plus tard, je sus que Pandit Sahadeo, Mamode Assenjee, membres de mon comité, mes agents demeurant loin de Port-Louis où la grève avait lieu, Seewoolal à Rose Belle, Bhattoo à Rivière des Anguilles, Delaître à Curepipe et d'autres encore de mes agents, avaient été mis en résidence surveillée. Le colonel Deane, qui cherchait de se faire valoir, avait organisé une mise en scène que les circonstances n'indiquaient certainement pas.

La maison d'Anquetil fut fouillée et nombre de documents et de livres, qu'il ne devait jamais revoir, furent emportés. Voici quelques extraits des lettres qu'il m'écrivit de Rodrigues:

LETTER OF ANQUETIL FROM RODRIGUES TO DR MAURICE CURE

«I feel ever so sorry for one thing, the most important price of work that would have shown the advantages of the Industrial Association and the usefulness of the Conciliation Board in dealing with a dispute as seen from the workers' stand point.»

«Yes, my dear Doctor. I was not only confident but I was definitely certain to win for those poor fellows a substantial increase in wages and an appreciable reduction of their working hours. I have implicit trust in Mr. Oswell that he will award them if not all what I would succeed to wring out of the employers, but a reasonable share».

- «I am ever so thankful to my son for his great devotion to me as he refused all offers to stay in Mauritius to that of even accepting to be locked up in a cell».

- «I am well cared for here (in Rodrigues). I have no complaints about the way I am treated and also I must say that Colonel Deane treated me in all justice as a true British officer».

- "I shall be pleased to have some news of things in general also, if any what are the explanations given concerning my deportation".

Immédiatement après la déportation d'Anquetil, nous mimes notre représentant à Londres, M. Jomadar, au courant de la situation. C'est ainsi qu'il s'adressa au Trade Unions Congress, au Parti travailliste britannique et à plusieurs membres éminents de la profession légale. Ceux-ci nous conseillèrent de demander un Writ d'Habeas corpus à la Cour suprême mais, ici à Maurice, on nous fit comprendre l'inutilité de cette procédure.

M. Reginald Bridgman et le National Council of Civil Liberties allèrent en députation auprès du Secrétaire d'État pour les Colonies. M. Creech-Jones rencontra Lord Dufferin au cours d'une entrevue orageuse à propos du renvoi des dockers.

Anquetil retourna à Maurice le 30 novembre 1938. Sans doute, l'intervention de nos amis de Londres avait eu pour effet d'écourter son exil, qui avait duré moins de trois mois. Quand le *Tegelberg*, sur lequel il avait pris place, mouilla à Port-Louis, notre comité exécutif, nos agents, quelques fidèles allèrent à sa rencontre. Dans la rade, quelques dockers lui firent une ovation. Le gouvernement avait fait une démonstration de force, sans raisons sérieuses, qui avait eu comme résultat de décourager beaucoup de nos partisans. Nous continuâmes à lutter. Les associations industrielles avaient subi un coup dont elles ne devaient se relever qu'après l'arrivée à Maurice de M. Ken Baker, en 1945.»

Effectively, we think it is important for all Mauritians, particularly the youth, to take cognizance of this episode in the political life of Emmanuel Anquetil. Thanks to Week-End for publishing this admirable but sad piece in the history of trade unionism and politics in our country, under colonial rule. (An Article Published in of 4th May, 2014)

Chapter 9

DISTURBANCE
IN THE NORTH

M. Jagdambi

AFTER the serious disturbances and manslaughter in the District of Flacq and Moka, the unrest continued in the North region; several strikes and protest marches were organised, to protest against low wages and living conditions.

Before the crop season started, the Director of Labour recommended to the Chamber of Agriculture to look into the working conditions of the labourers and suggested to increase the bonus rate to 30% which was to be conditional for those who work 6 days per week. Some estates followed the advice and implemented it while others did not. The employers' Association was not bound to follow the suggestion of the Director of Labour. They considered that there existed some legal machinery to deal with trade disputes. At the start of the harvest in July 1943, the wages in most of the estates were below the minimum prescribed rates. Moreover, the wages fluctuated from one estate to another. Consequently, in some estates there was an increase in the basic wages of Re 1. - Monthly and ten cents daily for overtime work. To mitigate the malnutrition problem, some estates offered sweet potatoes and manioc at a cheaper price.

The St. Antoine estate factory labourers had made their complaints registered, but nothing was done to raise their wages. Their grievances remained the same. Consequently, on July 28, hundred and sixty factory labourers went on strike but, after the appointment the Board of conciliation was set up they resumed work on 29th July. Agreement was reached on August 5th. However, they went on a one day strike on September 8th, due to a misunderstanding as some factory labourers had been short paid. The matter was soon put right and work resumed the following day, as usual. The Manager of St. Antoine Factory had roused communal feelings towards the Hindu labourers who had been on strike. Alleging that if the factory did not work, the small planters would be the losers, he employed outsiders who were non-Hindus despite the advice of the Director of Labour that such action would deteriorate the situation and lead to trouble.

Consequently, the Administrator agreed to send away the non-Hindus and the strikers agreed to resume work on September 11. They promised to abide by the Award of the Conciliation Board of Belle Vue Harel and Solitude estates while their grievances concerning medical treatment and sanitation were referred to the Medical and Health Department. On September 22nd, an agreement was reached but the labourers of Belle Vue Harel considered it unacceptable. On the same day the labourers of St. Antoine again went on strike. There was hooliganism and damage was caused to the factory while telephone lines were cut off. The Conciliation Board was called to meet on September 24, but the estate representative refused to attend, alleging that the strike was illegal. The Trade Unions Representatives intervened to have the dispute referred to an Arbitration Tribunal. Finally, the matter was referred to the Minimum Wage Advisory Board.

LABOUR UNREST

The 30s and 40s witnessed an uprising of the workers in all sectors of employment. These workers often resorted to strike actions in their struggle for better conditions of work. They were now better organized as new leaders emerged and grouped them in Trade Unions.

On the political front two things were moving fast. Dr Maurice Curé had been defeated at the general elections of 1921, but he continued his action in favour of the workers. As we have stated earlier, together with his close collaborators, prominent among whom were Pandit Sahadeo Rama, Dr. Hassenjee Jeetoo and Barthélemy Ohsan, a lawyer, he called a mass meeting of workers at the Champ de Mars on 23 February 1936. A huge crowd of some 30,000 workers from all over the island attended the meeting and gave birth to the Mauritius Labour Party. The main objective of the new party was to organize the people to press for economic and constitutional reforms on behalf of the working classes.

At the meeting of the 23rd February 1936, the following resolutions were voted:

(1) Minimum wages (2) Unemployment benefits; (3) Old-age pension; (4) Universal suffrage for labourers, artisans and small planters ;(5) Freedom to organise Trade Unions; (6) Workmen's compensation and protection against accidents and illness; (7) Safeguards for women and children."

The workers maintained their pressure and sent a petition to Dr Curé with 330 signatures from the Bon Accueil and Brisée Verdière region. The petition was sent on the 6th August 1936 and Dr Cure dispatched it to the Governor. The following grievances were formulated: (1) Protest against the 15% cut practised by Union, Sans Souci and Riche Fund sugar estates on the "Uba" variety cane;

(2)   The insufficiency of wages which varied between 40 cents and 60 cents daily during the crop season and a maximum of 40 cents daily during intercrop;

(3)   The treatment meted out to them by *Sirdars* and recruiting and paying agents.

As their petition fell on deaf ears, the labourers and small planters decided to organize a protest march to Port Louis. A magistrate, Mr. Legras, unsuccessfully tried to persuade them to call off their march. The Commissioner of Police threatened to send the armed police to disperse the crowd. A special train had also been arranged to take back the labourers and small planters from Terre Rouge.

I remember Pt Ramnarain saying that "a number of other demonstrations were organized on several sugar estates to protest against low wages, ill-treatment and small planters' plight."

Chapter 10

TRADE UNIONISM
IN MAURITIUS

IF in Europe, trade unionism was a reality since 1888, it was only on 28 March 1945 that Kenneth Baker came to Mauritius with an appointment as "Trade Union Adviser." As soon as he arrived, he set himself to work, assessing Trade Union and Industrial Relations in the colony. The terms of reference of Baker's engagement here were "To advise the Governor on Trade Union methods and procedure, with a view to establishing sound industrial relations in the country." According to his own admission, he was greatly helped in his work by the fact that he had relations in the island. "My mother's sister married a Mauritian and this, I believe, has helped to break down considerably the barriers which otherwise I might have found erected. I have been invited socially to meet estate managers and estate employees – some of them distant relatives of mine – who have made the industrial picture so much clearer," he wrote in a report.

Kenneth Baker was greatly touched by the general desire to know about Trade Unionism. "I have experienced on all sides a desire to learn more about Trade Unionism and industrial organization. From the workers' side, those mainly engaged in Port Louis and in sugar factories have been very eager to hear and know about Trade Unionism; they have been very desirous of learning how the British Trade Unionist acts."

He found that the committees of the various associations were doing their utmost to become sound and solid organizations and he was, like Major Orde Browne before him, "impressed with the business-like way in which proceedings were conducted."

A Brief History Of **Trade Unionism** In Mauritius

The workers, he, however, found had a considerable amount to learn as their idea of Trade Unionism was very vague and they were "very easily aroused by irresponsible people." As for Trade Unions in Mauritius, he found they were "only in their embryonic stages," and maintained that the Trade Union movement would have" "to work out its own destiny" and that it would be unwise to force it along certain fixed ideas".

Soon upon his arrival, Kenneth Baker had made it known that he was prepared to meet anybody in Mauritius on the subject of Trade Unionism which would aim at the betterment of industrial relations in the island. This led to an influx of different people going to meet him, specially representatives of defunct Industrial Associations, representatives of those in operation or just recently formed, and people who were desirous of forming new Trade Unions or Associations. The fact that a Trade Union official from Great Britain had come to advice Government did create a great interest in Trade Unionism.

Baker found that the industrial Associations already in existence were, with very few exceptions, operating on unsound lines. He decided to put them back on the right track and also to guide the new ones that were springing up spontaneously. He thought that without guidance the new associations would be formed on unproductive lines, and would prove a menace to sound industrial organization and hamper to a considerable extent the future development of Trade Unionism.

He therefore advised all those interested in Trade Union organization and attended their meetings of inception in order to give them proper guidance. He noticed that in the various associations in the island there were leaders who were quite capable of looking after the affairs of their organizations, but who needed his help and experience to be able to carry on in an industrial democratic manner.

However, he found that the agricultural labourers were in a different category. He considered that the organization of these workers was a difficult one that required a lot of time and attention. He proposed to deal with that at a later stage but prepared a leaflet on Trade Unionism in simple terms. He got it translated into Hindi and distributed copies to all the *baitkas* round the island and requested the *baitka* leaders to acquaint their members with the subject.

Kenneth Baker visited many of the 37 existing sugar estates and discussed the issue of Trade Unionism with the Managers of those estates. While most of them welcomed the idea and said they had no objection, they also showed some reluctance at the same time. They declared that their relationships with the workers had always been very cordial and therefore there was no need for Trade Unions.

Suggestions & Recommendations of
Mr Baker for a Sound Trade Unions Movement

Mr Baker was in permanent contact with different classes of people; for instance he gave an actual illustration of fear occurring in the island among workers: A clerk, working in one of the banks of Port Louis, approached him with the view of forming an association for bank employees. He suggested that they should come and see him at the Labour Department accompanied by one or two friends from the other banks. This he was not willing to do because "he feared they might be seen coming to meet me. Mr Baker then suggested that they could come and have tea with him at his house in Quatre Bornes but this they declined too. Finally he met them separately at their own house. They were afraid that should they be seen meeting him they might lose their employment in the bank for attempting to form an association. He said that "as usual, most employers deny the existence of victimisation. I am certain that the majority in the estate adopt this hateful practice. But there are still a number of employers who by various methods use pressure on their employees to renounce organisation more often than not, the threat of discharge is made."

He visited the employers for the purpose of discussing Trade Union organisation and industrial relations were to help in eradicating this practice.

Mr Kenneth Baker made few suggestions in order to make the Trade Unions run on a professional principle: He therefore, suggested that trade Union classes be set up for union officials. The Labour Inspectors should also attend a series of classes on Trade Unionism and its functions. To achieve the required aims, Mr Baker further suggested that the director of Education be asked to help, the Commissioner of Labour and/ or the Trade Union Adviser should select a minimum of two teachers with necessary qualifications, who could be trained by the Trade Union Adviser to take over the control of these classes. The teachers who take over this work should be paid on the same lines as adult educational teachers in Great Britain. Mauritians winning scholarships and being sent to England, especially those being sent for Social Welfare Instruction should also be invited to take short-term courses on Trade Unionism from one of the recognised adult educational associations.

Mr Baker visited various Trade Unions, saying that "it becomes increasingly evident to me that the white employee trends to hold himself aloof from the other sections of the community in the sphere of Trade Union organisation. This is indeed, unfortunate, and still further helps to keep apart the various races on the island which in itself militates against sound organisation. The Trade union Movement in most countries, especially the European countries, organises workers irrespective of race, colour, creed and sex, and this fact has been one of the reasons why they have been successful."

Therefore he recommended that a series of Trade Union lectures be given to the final year student in Government and, if possible, in other Secondary schools. If we want the Trade Unions as a part of the social machinery of State, as they do in Great Britain, then the question of Trade Unionism become as important to the young mind as other aspects of social significance. In view of the importance of agriculture on the economic life of the island, lectures on trade Unionism could also be given to students at the Agricultural College.

Mr Baker's services were requested by the estate managers and fortunately, they were very keen in putting forward that he should stay here for a considerable time, and that other Trade Unions officials UK should also be brought to the Island.

Following from these meetings, Mr Baker met the president of the Chamber several times, and suggested that the Sugar Interests recognised the Engineering and Technical workers' Union, which had by this time organised branches of members from among artisans in every sugar factory in the Island. Also the Union had officially applied to the Chamber for recognition. No advance was made, but the Conciliation Board appointed by the Commissioner of labour between the committee of the estate Managers and the Engineering and Technical Workers' Union precipitated a change. It is doubtful whether this Conciliation Board should have ever been appointed, but this will be dealt under the heading, Conciliation Board.

"This Conciliation Board raised a number of doubts in the mind of the Chamber of Agriculture, was the estate Managers' committee entitled to enter into agreements affecting the sugar estates owners who were members of the Chamber? After discussion, the representatives of the Chamber said that while the Chamber under its present regulations could not recognise the union, they were prepared to set up temporary machinery with the union, and when the regulations were finally revised then permanent machinery could be set up. A legal deed was drawn up between the owners of the estates and the Chamber appointing representatives and confirmation was sent to the union (METWU). Further, the Chamber agreed to recommend to all estate managers with factories that machinery for the settlement of minor disputes was set up with the union branch in the factory. The Voluntary conciliation committee will have already met by the time this report is received. The Chamber has suggested and I have accepted, with the Commissioner of Labour's permission, the chairmanship of the Committee. I feel that matters have turned out satisfactorily and a substantial advance has been made towards the betterment of Industrial relations and Industrial peace."

THE MECHANICAL ENGINEERING AND TECHNICAL WORKERS' UNION

The Mechanical Engineering and Technical Workers' Union was set up with a view to fighting for rights and welfare formed from the artisans on the sugar estates and was under the Chairmanship of Mr J.E. Anquetil. Every attempt was being made to run this organisation on proper Trade Union lines. It has already been stated that there was a branch in every sugar factory, but not every branch had its committee with appointed officers. This was rapidly being remediated. On estates Mr Baker visited, he endeavoured with the Managers' permission to contact the President and Secretary of the Branch and find out whether they needed advice and help. At the same time, where it had been possible, he introduced Mr Anquetil to the Managers. This has been very useful in most cases, and had often led to further visits, and the setting of disputes. He had also suggested to the Labour Inspectors that they could be of help to the Branch officials of the union by giving them advice on procedure and the functioning of their committees. Mr Baker had also prepared a general leaflet which has been translated into French, giving details of Branch committee organisation, which was to be distributed to every committee. The union was functioning very well and was close to 4,000 members. Mr Baker found the Executive Committee was far too large, comprising 70 members. He felt it necessary to cut down this number considerably, but it would be wise to do this right away. Furthermore, he recognized that the trade unions were organising steadily and satisfactorily. Thus, the general tightening up of the organisation could come later.

One of the largest branches of the Engineering and Technical Workers' Union was situated in the shipping repair yards of Messrs. Taylor Smith & Co. The management of this company had always been interested in the welfare of their workers, and had actively encouraged them to form their own Industrial Association. Unfortunately the Shipping Association, as it was called, did not function as trade Union very well, and the members lost their faith in the Association. Mr Baker suggested that as the employers were closely related to the docks employers generally, the association should amalgamate with the General Port and Harbour Workers Union. Of course, the members themselves did not agree. In the early stages of organisation it was unwise to put too much pressure on people whose minds were made up. So, he gave his sympathy to the amalgamation with the Engineering and Technical Workers' Union instead. A further point which reinforces this moves, was that, if artisans leave Taylor Smith's yard, they usually find work at the estate factories and vice versa, so they still maintain contact with their own work...

Before leaving aside this union he said he should like to refer to Messrs. Forges Tardieu Ltd. The Union had a Branch in this establishment which had not been recognised; indeed the management denied any knowledge of its existence. Unfortunately, the Branch Secretary of the union was discharged, the union alleging victimisation, with the management talking of breach of discipline. This caused a dispute to arise, and the department and Mr Baker were called in to advice. At first the management were entirely uncompromising, but relations improved and a successful conclusion was reached. The management refused to reinstate the discharged secretary but offered him a very substantial sum as compensation. They had set up a works council between themselves and Union Branch and in the event of a deadlock had agreed to set up relations with the officials of the union. They also advised all non-members in the works to join the Engineering &Technical Workers' Union. The artisans generally are among the most intelligent workers in the Island, and the union is progressing well.

Chapter 11

THE REGISTRATION OF METWU

T HE ordinance No. 7 of 1938 brought a new era in the trade union movement in Mauritius; this was first marked by the creation of industry associations among which is the "Mechanical and Industrial Technical Workers Association." Other regional associations of artisans started emerging such as "Plaines Wilhems and Black River Artisans SE IA" the "Grapefruit Mechanical and Technical Workers IA of Moka." etc..

The Ordinance on industrial associations, however, imposed severe limitations and constraints. Nevertheless, certain associations continue to exist and function. Strikes broke out in the north in July 1943 and ended in the killing of 3 workers, at Belle Vue Harel S.E. Following the various amendments made to the industrial Association Ordinance in 1944 and which was recommended by S. Moody, E. Anquetil founded the Mechanical, Engineering and Technical Workers Union, in August 1944. He became President. The Secretary General was B. Grassy, a close and loyal collaborator of Anquetil. Bertin Herbu, a worker at St Aubin S.E. as Treasurer, suffered repression because of his union involvement. At one time the manager was angry and removed part of the roof of his house on the sugar estate camp. Despite these acts of retaliation and threats, Herbu continued to campaign within the trade union movement.

In 1945, METWU had approximately 4,000 members. The following year, after the death of Anquetil, Guy Rozemont became President, several industrial conflicts at that time ending in "dead locks". Guy Rozemont launched campaigns across the island, for instance that workers should enjoy the economic recovery after the war. Agreement was signed with some employers and in case of non-satisfaction, strike actions were triggered.

Before Guy Rozemont died he changed the name of the union to "ARTISANS AND GENERAL WORKERS UNION".

From 1956 to 1958, Abel Cloridor assumed the presidency of the union. Annual Agreement was signed with employers. Philippe Ducasse was president from 1958 till 1961. During his term of office, more precisely in 1959, a dispute broke out between the MALA and AGWU on one side and employers on the other. The dispute was referred to an arbitration tribunal which gave workers a wage increase of 15%.

François Vincent took over the position of President from Philippe Ducasse in 1961 and would remain General Secretary of the union until 1977, for 16 years. During this period F. R. Vincent faced the politicization and the division of the labour movement. He, however, managed to keep the torch of AGWU, fighting hard to depoliticize AGWU. This action was necessary because some political parties attacked the union and presented it as being associated to the Labour Party, and this started to affect the union. The merit of such an action returns to Vincent. It was under his leadership that AGWU was affiliated to ICEF in 1963.

caption

From left to right:
G. H. Favori, Eddey Melisse, F. R. Vincent, Roger Laviolette,
Joseph Lucien Pierre, a. Kunniah

In May 1975, I re-joined the AGWU as Negotiator and Organiser. By the end of 1977 the union had succeeded in increasing its membership which was around 1,100. In March 1978, I became the President of the Union and started an aggressive organising programme. After the refusal of the NRB to accede the legitimate demands of the Union, the Delegates of the Union decided to launch a strike on 23-25 July 1979, with the Collaboration of MLC affiliates and the strike was successful and workers obtained some satisfaction. The effect of the strike made the AGWU stronger and reached a membership of around 2,800. The following year, I created the AGWU Provident Fund for the Artisans, with the help of Professor Charles Cambridge of Harvard University. In 1983, the AALC financed an Actuary work, which was done by Prof Popalathan of SICOM. The AGWU Provident Fund has been enormously helping its members by providing loans for productive projects, retire benefits and grant to the family of the deceased worker, etc. This Provident Fund still exist, continues providing several facilities to its members, but due to the closing down of a large number of sugar factories and by introducing the VRS I and VRS II membership considerably reduced.

I feel particularly happy for having been able to construct a big office of one storey, for the AGWU and Its Provident Fund at Smith Street - GRNW-Port Louis, on 30 perches land, bears the name of the founder and the father of Trade Union Movement in Mauritius **"EMMANUEL ANQUETIL LABOUR CENTRE"**, which comprises several Offices including a Workers' Education Centre, this was achieved before I completely retired from Trade Unions activities.

Chapter 12

THE MAURITIUS AGRICULTURAL LABOURERS' UNION

Pandit Sahadeo

THE Mauritius Agricultural Labourers' Union was established early in the year 1945. Pt. Sahadeo and Mr Partab Allgoo had solicited advice quite frequently from Mr Baker and he had attended several of their meetings. They formed a number of district committees and a Central Executive Committee, and endeavoured to set up a solid organisation. Pandit Sahadeo had now been elected President and Partab Allgoo the General Secretary. A Labour Department official Mr Baker inspected the books, accounts, etc., of the Union and found a genuine desire to act on recognised Trade Union principles. Several criticisms were made, but nothing of a serious nature. Following his visit to the office of this Union, he had no hesitation in recommending to the commissioner of Labour that the registration of the Union should be granted. He did suggest, however, that the membership rule of the Union should be drafted as follows: "To secure the complete organisation in the union of all labourers employed in Agriculture except those in the North and Central Rivière du Rempart, and the vicinity of St. Pierre and Camp Fouquereaux". This was to prevent any suggestion from other organisations that the Agricultural Labourers Union was encroaching upon their territory. This rule conforms more or less to article 4, ordinance 7 of 1938. He had tendered.

Rampartab Allgoo

Later Mr Baker was informed that two or three departments had decided to take the lead and form a new Government Servants organisation and apply for registration under Ordinance No. 7 of 1938. The new association of workers to organise all regularly employed Government servants and employees into one Association (except Railway, Police, Teachers, Printers and Government Sack Factory workers). Although this was against the advice he had tendered, he felt the promoters were not fully aware of the difficulties and he agreed with this course. Therefore the new association was formed under the title of the Mauritius Government Servants and Employees Association. They consistently sought the advice of Mr Baker and he helped them to draw up their rules which conformed in many respect to the British Trade Union model. The members of a majority of the departments joined this association and had formed departmental committees and also the Executive Committee of the Association had now been registered under ordinance No. 7 of 1938 as the "Mauritius Government Servants and Employees Association."

Following the report of the Whitley committee at the end of the 1914-18 war, recommending that Joint Committees should be set up between employers and workers, for the improvement of relations between the two sides, the national Whitley Council was established. This Whitley Council was established by agreement between Government and the Civil Service Staff Association, to deal with matters common to the whole Service and with wages and conditions of classes employed in two or more Departments. Both sides, staff association and Administration, had equal representatives on the council, decisions were reached by agreement, both sides voting as a unit. Agreement on being reported to the Chancellor of the Exchequer became operative subject only to the overriding power of parliament. In respect of failure to reach agreement by negotiation on questions affecting emoluments, weekly hours of work and leave to certains categories of civil Servants, a Civil Service Arbitration Tribunal was set up in 1936. He therefore recommended the setting up of a Whitley Council between Government and the Government Servants and employees association, with the possibility to recourse to arbitration, should the need arise.

Chapter 13

HARRYPARSAD RAMNARAIN AND THE LABOURERS INDUSTRIAL ASSOCIATION

Harryparsad Ramnarain

HARRYPARSAD RAMNARAIN had been a member of the labour movement since its inception in February 1936. On August 1938 with the help of Emmanuel Anquetil, he founded an industrial union at Cottage. The first meeting of these estates industrial labourers had taken place under a jackfruit tree in front of the village "Baitka" which was situated near the village shop. The meeting was organised by Harryparsad and it was attended by Anquetil and labour Inspector G. Ramgoolam.

In those days an industrial union could not embrace the employees of several estates because small unions were allowed to enlist the membership of only the employees of the neighbouring estates. The Central Rivière du Rempart labourer's Industrial association was founded on September 30, 1938. The North Rivière du Rempart Labourers' Industrial Association was founded at Goodlands on April 21, 1939. In 1941, the associations, the Central and the North Rivière du Rempart Labourer Industrial Association merged into the North and Central Rivière du Rempart labourers' agricultural Association.

In his biography "Father of the Nation", historian Anand Mulloo writes: "Once more on September 27, 1943, another strike led by Ramnarain and Jugdambi of the Central

Rivière du Rempart Industrial Association, erupted in the North, leading to more shooting at Belle Vue Harel including three labourers, a boy of ten, a pregnant woman, Anjalay, now honoured as a martyr, a symbol of sacrifice"…

Mulloo adds that "according to Ramnarain, Anquetil showed little sympathy for the agricultural workers and he had refused to support the 1943 labourers' strike as his focus was mainly on the urban Creole Dockers…"

Ramnarain, in the fifties, spoke in meetings all over the island, being both on the political and social forefront. At a public meeting in Rose Belle, attended by some 2500 persons, he said, as published in Advance 23th January 1950, he said:

"M. H. Ramnarain dit qu'il a fréquenté tous les députés, il a suivi de près leur travail, mais il ne voit que seul M.S. Bissoondoyal qui peut faire quelque chose pour les travailleurs. Il ajouta que les travailleurs doivent choisir entre M. Seeneevassen, le Dr Ramgoolam, le Commissaire du Travail et lui-même, et il conclut en disant que les travailleurs devraient le suivre. »

Manilal Doctor was also to address the audience, but he didn't come. In fact, in those days, Sookdeo Bissoondoyal and Manilall Doctor were not on speaking terms. In his book dedicated to Doctor, Pahlad Ramsurrun even writes that "a powerful clique (the Bissoondoyal brothers) had emerged as from the nineteen forties. They were very active to throw mud on the works and achievement of Dr S. Ramgoolam, H.E. Dharam Yesh Dev, High Commissioner of India, and although Manilal Doctor was the invitee of the former and the guest of the latter, he was not to be spared of intense blame from them. It is unfortunate that the Bissoondoyal brothers, disregarding the protocol of both Governments(India and Mauritius) and the authority responsible for inviting Manilal Doctor in January 1950 tried their best to grab and get political capital out of Manilal Doctor's presence by sending stooges to him…"

According to Ramsurrun, "it was then onwards that a Machiavellian strategy was devised by the Bissoondoyal to indulge in character assassination of Manilal Doctor."
Hence, if the name of Manilal Doctor is engraved in Mauritian history, it is good to note that he was not liked by all Indo-Mauritians!

TRADE UNIONISTS THROUGHOUT HISTORY

I shall now pay homage to trade unionists whose base of operation was in the port area. Names that come to my mind are those of Gaëtan Pillay, Mario Flore, Moorgesh Veerabadren, Paul Raymond Bérenger, Michel Gérard Nina, also known as Ti Moignac, Aurélie Perrine and Eliézer François.

As I said at the very beginning of this book, few politicians pay homage to trade unionists. It is to be regretted that this omission-attitude persists even today among our politicians. But fortunately, there are some exceptions. After his death, Government paid homage to Aurélie Perrine, who was a front figure of the Port-Louis Harbour and Docks Workers Union(PLHDWU), a movement regrouping stevedores and henchmen working in the port area.

As in the sugar cane fields for labourers, the conditions were also harsh for the port workers. And everyone agrees that it is in this area that Paul Raymond Bérenger made his name as a trade unionist and a future politician. It was because of his great influence on the workers that Minister Eliézer François, at that time a member of Parti Mauricien Social Démocrate, was sent there to thwart Bérenger's popularity among the port workers.

Aurélie Perrine, of Chagossian origin, became president of PLHDWU, and at his demise, his name was given to the landing station for passengers in the port area.

Mario Flore, Moorgesh Veerabadren and Ti Moignac were closely linked to the Mouvement Militant Mauricien (MMM), and if the latter are still members and diehards of Bérenger's party, this was not the case for Mario Flore. Unhappy with Bérenger, on the eve of the MMM/PSM 60-0 victory in the 1982 General Election, he left MMM and became an opponent to Bérenger. Subsequently, he moved closer to Labour Party and Dr. Navinchandra Ramgoolam. Mario Flore will be remembered for having struggled for a pension to widows of stevedores and henchmen, particularly those who were sacked, after the introduction of Bulk Sugar Terminal. It was after the victory of Navin Ramgoolam party at the elections of 2005 that his Government considered Flore's proposed and made it become a reality.

It must also be noted that Editor and News Reporter Dharmanand Dhooharika, who recently won his Case before the Privy Council, in a case of "scandalising the Court", also publicly paid homage to late Mario Flore, who died in 2011. The former leader of Muvman Morisien Kreol Afrikin (MMKA) always fought for the downtrodden, particularly the drivers of "taxis marrons", the widows of deceased stevedores, for the poor Creoles and for all Mauritians in general.

The name Ajum Dahal needs to be remembered also. As written in Sir Abdul Razack Mohamed's biography by Moomtaz Emrith, "Ajum Dahal, was a charismatic trade unionist, who first stepped on the political stage in August 1948, when he had unsuccessfully sought election to the Legislature and had since kept a low political profile although he continued to show interest in the political issues facing the Muslim community. He was concerned with the issues that faced the Muslims as a community when the Electoral Boundaries Commission began its work in Mauritius." He would later become the co-founder of the Comité d'Action Musulman(CAM), when Abdul Razack Mohamed left Parti Mauricien to form his own party, and collaborated closely with the Electoral Boundaries Commission for the setting up of the Best Loser System, in 1968. He later left CAM, due to dissenting views with Mohamed on the Independence issue.

He afterwards joined PMSD and was elected in Belle Rose/Quatre Bornes constituency and served the House till January 1973, date of his death at 57 years old. Ajum Dahal is said, as emphasized by Moomtaz Emrith, to "be the first to have proposed the creation of an Export Free Processing Zone in Mauritius, a project which, when it materialized in the mid-seventies, became a key-factor in helping Mauritius climb out of its economic rut with rising unemployment and soaring debt, and put it squarely on the road to eventual full employment and economic prosperity…"

As trade unionism and politics are closely linked in Mauritius, we must also remember the name of Guy Rozemont. Although he died at the young age of 41in 1956, his memory is still vividly cherished by all Labour Party members. It was Rozemont who proposed a motion in Parliament that the 1st of May, Labour Day, be a public holiday. We cannot forget Jack Brizlall, Former Honourable member of Legislative Assembly in 1976. As a Mouvement Militant Mauricien (MMM) representative, he left this party, in the wake of dissenting views with his leader Bérenger. Bizlall left the political world to become one of the most respected trade unionists in Mauritius. Today, though involved on the political front with his Mouvement Premier Mai, Jack always lends a hand to trade unions, whenever his services are solicited.

In fact, the press reported about the clash between him and Ashok Subron, the leader of Rezistans and Alternativ, who is also a trade unionist. Originally a Lalit member, Sobron left this party, led by Dr Ram Seegobin, to form Rezistans. In Lalit, Ashok used to help trade unions and workers, and he continued this social and political pattern. And he proved his power when he overcame Brizlall's influence in the port area. Ashok Subron is also to be remembered as the one who forced the Government of Navin Ramgoolam to present a White Paper on Electoral Reform, due to an appeal made by Rezistans and Alternativ before the Human Rights Commission of United Nations.

Faizal Ally Beegun, Amba Lutchoomanen and Yusuf Sooklall need also to be mentioned. All of these trade unionists have been active in the Export Procession Zone (EPZ) sector. And the former has even been quoted as an example in the foreign press for his laudable work in favour of foreign workers in Mauritius, particularly workers from India, China and Sri Lanka.

As there are more than 300 trade unions in our country, it will not be possible to list all the names of their presidents, secretaries and treasurers. We can only publish some names, particularly those who are well known to Mauritians, and still very active in the private and public sector: Radakrishna Sadien, August Follet, Malleck Amode, Naidoo, Rashid Imrith, Toolsiraj Benediny, Serge Jauffret, Pottaraj Kuppan, Georges Legallant, Bagooaduth Kallooa, Rajiv Roy, Veena Dholah, Haniff Peerun, Awadh Balluck, Deepak Benydin, Bidianand Jhurry, Reeaz Chuttoo, Atma Shanto, Jane Ragoo, Devanand Ramjuttun, Cassam Kureemun. Late Ashik Junglee is also to be remembered. He was very active in the education field. All the workers of the country, who are members of a trade union, need also to be congratulated. Without their support, the trade union movement would not have existed. In fact, they are the soul of trade unionism in Mauritius and form the backbone of the "peuple admirable" of our country.

Paul Bérenger himself was a trade unionist and negotiator. If his political opponents usually said that he was an "agitateur politique et un contestataire social à la base de grèves sauvages dans le pays", history will remember him as the man who fought for better working and conditions of service for port and transport workers. He also grouped all unions close to MMM under the umbrella of General Workers Federation, and he literally shut down the port with the strike of the Port-Louis Harbour Workers Union. We were in the seventies and this period would later be known as "les années de braise", when Prime Minister Dr Seewoosagur Ramgoolam declared a state of emergency, and got Bérenger and other MMM leaders arrested and jailed. It is in that particular period that the coalition Government, led by Labour party, PMSD and CAM voted tougher labour laws against strikes and the public demonstrations. Thus were born the notorious Industrial Relations Act and the Public Order Act. Suffice it to say that the struggle for more freedom became the main objective of trade unions in the country. Ironically, Yousouf Mohamed, son of Abdul Razack Mohamed, then Minister of Labour & Industrial Relations," had a hectic mandate".

Another politician who became trade unionist was Sir Gaëtan Duval. In "Le droit à l'excès", by Alain Gordon Gentil, Sir Gaëtan reminds that "Paul Bérenger et moi, nous avions, à l'époque, des activités syndicales. Après la rupture de la coalition, je me lance à fond dans le syndicalisme et les Syndicats Populaires connaissent un certain success. C'est alors que Bérenger demande à me rencontrer. Il voulait que nous fassions cause commune. Bien plus tard, j'ai appris qu'il avait voulu me rencontrer parce qu'il avait peur d'une hémorragie au sein de ses syndicats. Certains commençaient déjà à nous rejoindre..."

When Alain Gordon Gentil asks him « comment abordez-vous la conversation avec Bérenger ? Vous venez directement au sujet ? »

Duval answers « oui, nous parlons stratégie syndicale commune... »

-« Vous ne parlez pas stratégie politique ? »

-« Non, mais il est bien compris que dans un deuxième temps, nous allons en parler. Ca, je crois que Bérenger l'avait bien compris. Comme moi d'ailleurs. Il était convenu que si l'alliance syndicale marchait, rien n'allait nous empêcher d'aborder l'aspect politique des choses. Je découvre en face de moi un homme affable, clair, précis, en un mot, intelligent...

Mais l'avenir me prouvera, hélas! que j'avais tort. Il y a une chose qui m'a profondément déçu chez Bérenger. Quelques semaines plus tard, nous sommes ensemble pour défendre les travailleurs de l'industrie du transport... »

I cannot obliterate the immense contribution of my friend and mentor Chandersensing Bhagirutty, who himself got in the trade union movement due to the great Hurrypersad Ramnarain. Born in 1936, in the village of Poudre d'Or Hamlet, Chandersensing lost his mother at the young age of seven. Brought up by his father, who died when he was 14 years old, the young man became a social worker, and will afterwards become one of the most influential trade unionists at the head of the Plantation Workers' Union and Mauritius Labour Congress.

Moreover, it must be noted that if many politicians were frequently solicited by trade unionists, it is because there were many lawyers in the local political parties. This is why many of them offered help to trade unions, so much so that afterwards, their parties could benefit from a «coup de main» from the members of the unions.

Showkutally Soodhun, like late Harryparsad Ramnarain, became a Minister after having served as a Trade unionist in the Fédération of Travailleurs Unis. As a former trade unionist, he was well aware of the problems affecting the working class. This is why when he became Minister of Labour and Industrial Relations; he chased a trade unionist, Mr Farook Auchaybar, as adviser in his Ministry. Last but not the least the trade union movement has been honoured in December 2014, by the nomination of Hon Showkutally Soodhun as Vice Prime Minister and Tulsiraj Benydin another Trade Unionist with a long Trade Union career became Parliamentary Private Secretary (PPS).

JANE RAGOO,
A TOUCH OF FEMINISM IN TRADE UNIONISM

Let us be frank. The trade union movement has always been dominated by men. In fact, women were always there, but they were confined to administrative work. And thus only men are remembered as trade unionists. Fortunately, there is one Jane Ragoo today to demonstrate the will of women to show that they too can negotiate in the name of workers, be they men or women.

Jane Ragoo

I do not know Jane Ragoo personally, but I must say that I admire very much what she does in the name of the working class. She is a matter of great pride for the trade union movement in Mauritius, and even in Africa. It is good that Jane has put the gender issue on the table, and that she has fought for the rights of women, but also of their male contrary parts too. This is what makes this woman so special.

Mother of two children, and married to a man who supports and encourages her in her act ivies, Jane has the great chance to have had wide press coverage, and thus is well known by all Mauritians, even those not familiar with the trade union matters.
But this was not always the case for women in the past, which probably explains their absence amidst men in the trade union movement. Even in the literary field of our country, researchers always emphasized on male writers, forgetting for instance Marie Leblanc and Danièle Tranquille, respectively in two papers presented in July 2002 at a colloque on « Les discours littéraires sur l'océan indien » threw light on this great figure, author of novels, short stories and poems. Robert Furlong, literary critic and actually president of the Malcolm de Chazal Trust Fund, rightly says that "Nous disons, au contraire, que Marie Leblanc a été une grande dame de notre littérature, à la fois écrivaine sensible, une traductrice de talent, une gestionnaire efficace sachant rassembler autour d'elle des talents réels."

In a prologues to the book « Les femmes ou les silences de l'Histoire », by Michelle Perrot/ Eileen Lohka» Il subsiste bien des zones muettes et, en ce qui concerne le passé, un océan de silence, lié au partage inégal des traces, de la mémoire et, plus encore, de l'Histoire, ce récit qui, si longtemps, a « oublié » les femmes, comme si, vouées à l'obscurité de la reproduction, inénarrable, elles étaient hors du temps, du moins hors évènement… »

It is quite deceptive that this trend has for long subsisted in the pages of the history of our country. Thus, it was difficult to see men mentioning the presence of women at their sides. If I pay homage to my wife Sunyo Devi, who supported me throughout my career as a trade unionist, this was not always the case for the numerous women who fought side by side with men to change the course of history in favour of their peers. Among the numerous fights she led, the one she helped to save Rehana Ameer's job, employee and trade unionist at the Mauritius Broadcasting Corporation, is to be remembered. Together with Jack Brizlall, on Friday, 18th November 2011, Jane Ragoo said: "we like going back to square one." Front "Anti-Repression, composed of several trade union movements, starts a series of actions to demand the reinstatement of Rehana Ameer to her post at the MBC. The union council met the press on Friday 18 November, the headquarters of the Government Servants' Association, Port-Louis. It's been one year that the union calls "justice *to be done*", to Rehana Ameer. Mrs Ragoo said "the Mauritius Broadcasting Corporation sacked Mrs Ameer on an unjustified reason, after 25 years of service."

This is why it is important to remember the names of not only Jane Ragoo, but also those of Veena Dholah, Lindsey Collen, Rajni Lallah, Dany Marie, Rajni Kistnasamy, Anne-Marie Sophie, women engaged every day in the struggle for the right place of women in our society.

Chapter 14

MAURITIUS
LABOUR CONGRESS

T HE labour movement was diversified in the 60s'. In a study devoted to industrial relations, P. Hein lists the reasons which, according to him, explain this diversity: the multiple problems of ethnic and cultural interaction between strong unions and political parties leading to the departure of leaders and thus leaving a void, the usurpation of the social agenda of unions by the State, high unemployment, labour market, the influences of large international federations like World Federation of Trade Unions (WFTU) and the International Confederation of Trade Unions (ICFTU) for instance, and the lack of a formal framework within which the Union is supposed to operate. The study of P. Hein is in the context of the analysis of Crozier (the theory of actors and the system).

This allows P. Hein to write that this diversity, which hovers round personalities, ideologies or strategies, and that underlie unions in general, are very poorly structured. To support its analysis, P. Hein cites the report of a committee of inquiry: "The unions are torn inside by fratricidal struggles. We have had both during public meetings and our official hearings, taken notice of violent accusations made by the base against trade union leaders and the leaders among them."

Caption

Caption

Caption

Mr Dan Cunniah, Mr Chand Shagirutty, Prof. Charles Cambridge, Mr Raj Allgoo, AALC Rep. Mr Dan Maraye at a MLC/AALC– Residential Seminar September 1981, on Labour Economics - Hotel Ile de France - Grand Baie

THE CREATION OF MLC

In 1963, despite all these problems, Mauritius Confederation of Free Trade Unions (MCFTU) of Pakiry, F. Vincent and Descann and Mauritius Trade Union Congress (MTUC) were grouped within a single central Confederation, the **Mauritius Labour Congress**. Outside the MLC, there was the Mauritius Labour Federation (MLF) of L. Badry. The regrouping of forces within the Trade Union was then MLC's hope.

With a view to further strengthening the Trade Union movement in Mauritius, the leaders of two of the most important federations of Trade Unions of the island, namely the Mauritius Trade Union Congress and the Mauritius Confederation of Free Trade Unions, took one of the boldest decisions in the history of local Trade Unionism. They decided to merge these two unions to form one unified, more solid body, which they called the Mauritius Labour Congress, to better defend the workers against the exploitation of the employers and the Colonial Government.

This was made possible through the vision, tenacity and arduous effort of Hon. Hurryparsad Ramnarain. The MLC was launched on 16 July 1963 and became the most powerful trade union organization of the country, with a remarkable contribution to the emancipation of the working classes.

At the time of the merger, Hon. Augustin Moignac was the President of the Mauritius Trade Union Congress (MTUC), founded by Emmanuel Anquetil, while the Mauritius Confederation of Free Trade Unions was under the leadership of Mr. K. Descann. Mr. H. Ramnarain was the Vice President of the MTUC and the other important leaders were Mr. Orcel Lacaze, Mr. Sharma Jugdambi, Mr. Marcel Mason, Mr. Gabriel Louison and Mr G. L'Aimable. Mr. Descann had Mr. Paul Pakiry and Mr. Chand Kowlessur as principal collaborators. The leaders of the newly formed MLC unanimously decided to appoint Hon. Ramnarain as their first President, since he had been the main motivating force behind its creation.

The unions affiliated to the MLC were operating in all the important sectors of the economy: Sugar, Transport, Docks, Tea, Aviation, Banking, Insurance, Construction, Textile, Public Service, Para statal Bodies, Local Authorities, etc.

The MLC was soon affiliated to the International Confederation of Free Trade Unions, the strongest Trade Union Organisation in the world representing some 85 million workers in 91 countries at that time. It also became the only local Confederation to be recognized by the International Labour Organisation.

On the local front, the MLC was the strongest organization of workers with 57 unions affiliated to it, including the Federation of Civil Service Trade Unions which was compelled to terminate its affiliation in 1974 with the promulgation of the Industrial Relations Act of 1973. The MLC was represented on the following boards and committees:

1. Labour Advisory Board
2. Employee Welfare Fund
3. Occupational Health and Safety Committee
4. Workers Education Advisory Board
5. National Pensions Fund Board
6. Termination of Contract Service Board
7. Advisory Committee on Price and Consumer Protection
8. National Tripartite Committee
9. National Solidarity Fund
10. Sugar Industry Labour Welfare Fund
11. Mauritius Sugar Authority
12. National Remuneration Fund
13. Sir Seewoosagur Ramgoolam Foundation
14. IVTB

One of the first tasks to which the MLC dedicated itself was the amendment to the hours of work and general conditions of service of the working classes in general. It also played an important role in the economic and social development of Mauritius, as well as in the struggle for the independence of the country from colonial rule.

In 1965, an important delegation of Trade Union Leaders affiliated to the MLC, together with two Government Ministers, Hon. Kher Jagatsingh, Minister of Economic Planning and Development, and Hon. Jomadar, Minister of Labour, met the Secretary of State, Mr. Anthony Greenwood, then on a mission in Mauritius to study whether the country was ripe for independence. The delegation included H. Ramnarain, S. Jugdambi, Marcel Mason, Chand Kowlessur, C. Bhagirutty, K. Descann, P.C. Pakiry, Malleck Amode and F. R. Vincent.

Since its foundation, the MLC has always remained a democratic organization based on socialist principles. Some of its earlier achievements include the acceptance by Government to proclaim a public holiday on 2nd January on the occasion of the New Year. The publication of the first Wages Order in 1963 in the sugar industry was a result of the efforts of the MLC. The Wages Order provided the guidelines for workers in other fields of employment. The MLC also caused the institution of the Termination of Contract Service Board; the 35 - hour week for labourers engaged in piece work; a law guaranteeing the security of employment in the sugar industry; the payment of severance allowance; an increase in the Workmen's Compensation in cases of accident, among other achievements.

Through its assiduous efforts and indefatigable work, the MLC got recognition from a number of international bodies and was affiliated to organizations like the International Confederation of Free Trade Unions (ICFTU), the Organisation of African Trade Unions Unity (OATUU) established by the OAU, the Commonwealth Trade Union Council (CTUC) and collaborated with the following organisations: the African-American Labour Centre(AALC), the British Trade Union Congress (BTUC), the Force Ouvriere de France (FOF), the Afro-Asian Institute for Cooperative and Labour Studies (AAICLS) the Scandinavian Trade Unions, the Institute of Cultural Affairs of Nairobi and others.

The relationship forged with these international bodies has allowed a number of Mauritian Trade Union leaders belonging to the MLC to obtain training at prestigious centres abroad, like Kampala University of ICFTU; the ILO Torino in Italy, the Ruskin College, University of Oxford, Harvard University, the Institute of Labour and Social Studies, Geneva, the ILO.

With 57 Trade Unions affiliated to it, the MLC soon became the main organization of workers in Mauritius. The need for workers' education was becoming badly felt and the MLC was the first to launch a programme of education for workers through seminars, workshops and conferences.

MLC Leaders meet Mr Anthony Greenwood

It was a matter of pride and satisfaction for the MLC leaders that they had the privilege of forming a delegation consisting of two Ministers and Trade Unionists: Pandit H. Ramnarain, Honorary President of the Mauritius Labour Congress and former Minister of Labour and Industrial Relations; the Hon Sharma Jugdambi President of the MLC; the Hon Kher Jagatsingh Minister of Planning and Department; the Hon Marcel Mason; Brother Chand Kowlessur; Brother Chandrasen Bhagirutty; Brother K. Descann the President of MLC; Brother P.C. Pakiry; Brother Malleck Amode the President of GSA; Brother F.R. Vincent General Secretary of AGWU and Hon Jomadar. They met the Secretary of State, Mr Anthony Greenwood for the discussion which preceded the granting of Independence to Mauritius.

According to Brother Malleck, he had the opportunity of making a plea in favour of the Civil Servants and handed over a memorandum to Mr Greenwood in which contained the views of Civil Servants regarding their right to organise themselves and to bargain collectively, and the setting up of an Arbitration Tribunal, the need of consultation over the nomination of members of the Public Service Commission.

Deregistration of Trade Union Federation

The Industrial Relations Act of 1973, had brought a lot of discontent among the Trade Union movement and also destabilised its proper functioning, contrary to the ILO Convention Nos 87 and 98.

The Industrial Relations Act no 67 of 1973 had denied the rights to build strong Union and Confederations in Mauritius, according to section 9- (1) (d) (e) (2) which read as follows:

(1)   Subject to subsection (2), a trade union shall not be registered if
    (d)   there exists a registered Trade Union which is sufficiently representative of the interests which are intended to be safeguarded by the trade union seeking registration;
    (e)   except in case of a civil service union, its membership is open to public officers;

(2)   Subsection (1) (e) shall not apply in relation to the registered federation comprising a federation of civil service and other trade unions.

This piece of legislation reflected the laws, which were made in 1944. Now it is worth pointing out that rights were denied to the unions or federations of public sectors to join a Federation or Confederation of private sector according to the above law. The GSA was denied the right to form part of Mauritius Labour Congress (MLC), to which it was already affiliated, though the Government Servants' Association (GSA) was a founder member. Since this law was anti-constitutional and against the ILO Convention no 87, on freedom of Association, both MLC and the GSA met Sir Seewoosagur Ramgoolam, former Prime Minster and urged him to remove that restriction; this was done by an amendment to the Industrial Relations Act (IRA). It was only as from 1979, that the GSA, GTU and FSSC joined the MLC again.

A New Team takes over the destiny of MLC

That said I did not remain a passive spectator while the MLC was in action. I was very much involved in several capacities in many fields of activity, being a full time trade Unionist. In fact I joined the MLC executive committee in 1976 and became its Assistant General Secretary in 1978. Mr. Chandrasensing Bhagirutty was the President and Mr. Dan Cunniah was the General Secretary. The MLC had a membership of 20,000 workers, an all-time low since its creation. The new management decided to restore to the MLC the position of pride it occupied at the time of Hurryparsad Ramnarain and Augustin Moignac.

A vast campaign was launched and the MLC leaders started by approaching its former affiliates like the FSSC, the GSA, the GTU and others, urging them to come back to the MLC fold. But they encountered one important stumbling block on their way. The MLC was perceived as being too close to the Labour Party. Some even thought that it was affiliated to that party.

The perception was justified to a certain extent for two main reasons: one of its affiliates, the Plantation Workers Union (PWU), was also affiliated to the Labour Party, and most importantly, the MLC President, Chandrasen Bhagirutty was also the first Vice President of the Labour Party.

It took me and my colleagues a lot of tact and persuasion to get Chandrasen Bhagirutty to resign from the Labour Party's top position for the benefit of the MLC. This brought back the image of the MLC as a neutral workers' organisation and boosted its membership.

It must be said that owing to a number of adverse circumstances on the political and employment landscapes in the country, particularly with the advent of and advancement of the MMM on the political and Trade Union scenes, the membership of the MLC had started dwindling. I must say that with the help of members of MLC, we undertook the uphill task of redressing the situation.

The MLC's relations with International Organisations

The sacrifice of Chand Bhagirutty on the political plan paid dividends in the Trade Union field. He represented the MLC on the ICFTU and was subsequently elected as member to the Executive Board, a position which he kept until his demise in 1993. He was greatly instrumental in re-establishing relations with the African American Labor entre (AALC), AFL-CIO, BTUC, Force Ouvrière (FO) and other international organizations.

In 1979, the AALC dispatched a representative, Mr. John Gould, to the MLC to advise on its plan of action for the short and long terms, as well as on the recruitment of new affiliates for the MLC. Mr. Gould was particularly helpful in the launch of a regular newsletter to disseminate trade union news among members and other unions for which he negotiated some equipment from the AALC. He also helped me Director of Organisation of the MLC in getting two very strong trade unions, namely the GSA with 14,000 members and the GTU with 4,500 members to join the MLC.

With the coming of the GSA, the MLC executive underwent some changes. Mr. Malleck Amode became the 1st Vice President, and Mr. Torul replaced me as the 1st Assistant General Secretary. I then became the Director of Organisation.

In 1980, the ICFTU provided funds to activate the MLC's action plan, based on workers' education and also provided funds to purchase a Volkswagen car to help the MLC in its organising campaign. I organised seminars and courses for workers throughout the island after we purchased a second hand car bearing the number AT322. Needless to say working hours on a daily basis, often took me to faraway places in the South and West of Mauritius. I sometimes came back home after 22.00 hrs. But I was greatly assisted in my job by Mr. Goal Bhujun.

MLC Relations with
Hon Paul Bérenger Leader of MMM

In 1982, after the landslide victory of the MMM/PSM (60-0) Hon Paul R. Bérenger, Minister of Finance in the New Government, had invited Mr Chand Bhagirutty the President of Mauritius Labour Congress, to discuss the future relations between the Government and the Mauritius Labour Congress. Hon Bérenger welcomed the MLC President and had a cordial discussion. He promised the MLC President that he would not change the previous arrangement regarding the nominations of MLC members to different institutions. After some discussion Mr Bérenger asked Mr Bhagirutty to consider withdrawing the objection made by two MLC unions namely Plantation Workers Union and the Artisans and General Workers, regarding objection on recognition made with the Industrial Relations Commission, of two trade unions SILU & UASI affiliated to the General Workers Federation (GWF).

First Mr Bhagirutty thanked Hon Bérenger for his consideration for MLC, but on the second point regarding the recognition he remained undecided. Mr Bérenger reminded him that this matter had been dragging for more than 10 years and the Industrial Relations Commission had rejected the recognition on previous occasion on ground that the two unions concerned were not sufficiently represented in the Sugar Industries. Mr Bhagirutty told him that he needed consultation. Hon Bérenger was not happy with the response of Mr Bhagirutty, saying that "you need to give a reply at the earliest possible otherwise I'll bring changes in the legislation so that the SILU and UASI will be automatically recognised."

In spite of the goodwill the team had targeted, they had to face huge problems in the recruitment programme. It was decided to put the MLC on the right track. Because the public conviction was that the MLC was affiliated to the Mauritius Labour Party. In fact the MLC was never affiliated to the Labour Party. It was one of its affiliates, the PWU, which was affiliated to Mauritius Labour party. But nevertheless the MLC had good working relations with Labour Party. So the Congress had to campaign hard to prove that the MLC was independent to Political Parties.

MLC Co Operative Credit Unions and
Job Creation Scheme

As mentioned earlier, the MLC was not concerned solely with trade union matters, but as a caring organization it also played a tremendous role in the uplift of the society in which the workers evolved.

In 1984, MLC launched the Co operative Credit Unions and a Job Creation Scheme. It initiated 14 credit union societies among its affiliates with the help of Mr. Maureemootoo; Mr. Laval Zephyr; Mr Dev Luchman and Miss Shakuntala.

Unemployment was rife and the MLC tried to find ways and means to alleviate the situation. With the help of the Mauritius Cooperative Bank it set up a scheme giving loans of up to Rs 20,000 to affiliated members who wanted to start a business for them or their children. Over one thousand members benefited from such a loan.

In 1983, after Blanche Birger closed down its carpentry workshop, some 30 workers became redundant. The MLC negotiated for space in the sack factory, which had ceased its operations, and opened a workshop for those employees. The workshop operated along cooperative lines and became successful overnight.

In the meantime, the MLC had succeeded in getting the Textile Clothes Manufacturing Union of Mr. Yusouf Sooklall, one of the strongest affiliates of the GWF, to join the MLC. So did the FSSC of Mr. Rashid Emrith with a very consequential membership. The MLC became the largest central organization of workers in the country with over 85 affiliates representing some 85 individual trade unions with a membership over 68, 000 out of a total of 105,000 organised labour force. The remaining unions were affiliated to two federations, the GWF and the FPU. There were also several individual unions which were not affiliated to any federation. The MLC was thus the only national confederation representing workers from practically all the sectors of the economy.

The Leaders of the MLC had a fighting spirit, dedication, integrity, hard work, sense of sacrifice, and the former top leaders remained in the Office until they themselves decided to leave, and doing so only after ensuring that the successor was also animated by the same spirit. This has resulted in a continuity of policy which has helped towards the sound development of the MLC up to 1994 in the overall development of the island.

THE MLC WORKERS' EDUCATION & WORKERS' PARTICIPATION POLICY

It is a well known fact the ICFTU was against the policy of Nationalization, Research that people particularly in the Eastern Bloc were not better demonstrated off and no proper democracy existed. In those days they were prevented to know what was happening in other parts of the world.

To prevent the Marxist policy from propagating in Mauritius, the ICFTU and its strong affiliates were helped; its affiliates in developing countries. In this connection the ICFTU was sending Experts in the field of Workers' Participation and Profit sharing, I am of opinion that they were considering workers' Participation as Industrial Democracy. In those days' the MEF and the MSPA had started the " Comite Entreprise" in the sugar industry.

The first high level seminar on the theme "Workers' Participation" was organised for Top Officials of the MLC at the University of Mauritius in 1981, conducted by

Professionals from ICFTU, such as Mr Wolker Jung a German Economist and Prem Fakun of ICFTU Education Department; lectured on the experience of German and Scandinavian Counties on workers participation. The Seminar was officially open by the Prime Minister Dr Hon Sir Seewoosagur Ramgoolam in the Presence of Hon Kher Jagatsingh, Minister of Education, the Vice-Chancellor of the University of Mauritius, MEF representatives and Mr Prem Fakun from ICFTU Head Quarters – in Brussels.
I remember the Prime Minister said: *"it is of paramount importance that the social partners, i.e. the employers and employees should adopt a positive attitude in their approach to Participation and Industrial Democracy, they should show the utmost goodwill in their daily rapport. It is only when such conditions prevail that the system of Participation through "Comite d'Entreprise"* can be successful.

Sometime later the ICFTU made arrangements to send two Experts in the field of Workers' Participation and Industrial Democracy, for nearly three months to train the Trainers and also the Shop stewards of the affiliated unions. The Educators together with the MLC officials helped in conducting seminars and workshops in nearly all the sugar estates and Para-Statal Bodies and Municipalities etc. This project was a success in terms of training. It was only after the split of MMM/PSM in 1983 that Anerood Jugnauth Government favoured the workers' Participation as an antidote to Nationalization.

The MLC continued its struggle to introduce Workers' Participations and profits sharing. High level Seminars were organized in November 1984, conducted by Mr. Jorgan Hassen, a Professor of Economics from Denmark.

As the policy of the ICFTU was for Industrial Democracy and Workers Participation and against the Nationalization policy, the ICFTU with its Danish Trade Union Federation started helping the MLC Workers Education Project.

The ICFTU sent another Educator in the person of Mr. Preben Karlsen a Swedish Economist, to train the Trade Union leaders of the MLC in Labour Economics - to those who might be on the Board of Directors of the Companies. (i) How to read a Balance Sheet; (ii) How to prepare a Collective Bargaining document, study the response of the Counter proposals of Employers. (iii) To understand the overall economic situation of the country. Mr Preben Karlsen remained in Mauritius for about 2 months to arm the Trade Union leaders, to understand the company Accounting Systems, who might have the opportunity to sit on the Board of Director of the company. But I should say that a number of Trade Unionists who followed the courses left the Trade Unions Movement for other positions. I was among the very few who remained, maybe because I was full time in trade unionism.

In1981, the AALC had hired Professor Charles Cambridge from Harvard University who was specialized in Labour Economics to help the Trade Unions on the African continent including Mauritius. The MLC in conjunction with the AALC had organised it first 2 week residential Seminar on the theme "Labour Economics" at Ile France Hotel – Grand Baie, which was attended by Top Trade Union leaders, I am pleased to mention that among our participants were Dan Maraye who became The Governor of the Bank of Mauritius; Dan Cunniah - Director of the Bureau for Workers' Activities of the ILO and myself Chairman of the National Remuneration Board.

Professor Cambridge held several seminars to prepare our trade unionists on Collective Bargaining.

In the late 80's the AALC sent a Permanent Representative Mr Maurice Goyette, who was the Auditor of Canadian Labour Congress for six months. During his stay he organised seminars and workshops for MLC affiliated union members. He also financed the renovation of the MLC Building and premises and provided office furniture. He left Mauritius after six months to resume his duty in Canada.

In 1981, Mr Maurice Goyette was replaced by Mr Eddy Milano a retired Vice-President of Lady International Garment Workers' Union, USA; He was very much interested in the promotion of Workers' Education. After he studied the Trade Unions situation in Mauritius, he often told me, that he was of the opinion that workers' Education could boost up MLC membership. He met the Managing Committee and suggested that an Education Officer be appointed on a Permanent Basic. After public advertisement was made Mr Dev Lutchmun was selected. He worked as MLC Education Director up to 2003. It is important to mention here the MLC was organised for the benefit of its members around 50 seminars and workshops yearly financed by the AALC & ICFTU.

In 1984, Mr Bhagirutty negotiated with AALC Director, to finance the purchase of a car for the PWU. The same year I went to follow up a high level Training Course in Washington organised under aegis of the District Colombia University together with my friend Dan Cunniah. I took this opportunity to make a request to Mr Patrick O'Farrell Executive Director of AALC to finance to purchase a car in replacement of the Old VW AT322 which was an old one and got often broke on the road, which I was using for MLC and AGWU activities. MLC purchased two New Toyota Corolla Cars one Bearing CC 156 which was used by Mr Bhagirutty and the second one CC 358 was used by me under specific conditions that the PWU and AGWU would bear the running cost, i.e. Maintenance, Insurance and Road Tax will be beard by the respective union.

I was elected President of the MLC, a post which I relinquished in 1994, in view of my decision to retire by 1997 when I would be 60. My aim was to give chance to a young leader, the first Vice-President Mr Radhakrishna Sadien, so to follow the tradition and the principle adopted by the processor since its' creation i.e. to give the leadership to one who had proved his capability to take the lead. I wanted to devote the three remaining years of my mandate to the unions, the AGWU, the TGWU, and the TEU of which I was the President and Negotiator, and also to spend some time with my granddaughter Yashvi who was living with my family, until she was 3 years old.

THE LAST CONGRESS PRESIDED BY ME

The last MLC Annual Congress presided by me was the 31st Annual Congress held on the 27th March, 1994. As President of the MLC, I said that "I felt honoured to chair the Congress, as it was my last one. As usual I welcomed the delegates and guests. The function was honoured by the presence of the Prime Minister, Sir Aneerood Jugnauth Q.C., Hon. Dharmanand G. Fokeer, Minister of Labour and Industrial Relations, Hon. Kailash Ruhee, Minister of Agriculture, Mr Robinson H. Sikatwe ICFTU Representative and several distinguished guests."

I seized this opportunity "to thank the ICFTU for their continued support to the MLC and I am pleased to announce that we have among us today Bro. Robinson, ICFTU Representative and thank him for his presence. On the other hand, ladies and gentlemen, and annual delegates meeting being a stock taking exercise and analysis of achievements, shortcoming & handicaps that an organisation might have encountered during the period under review, I would wish to start my comments on the state of Industrial relations at National level.

The most meaningful event in the field of labour management relationship was undoubtedly the holding of the 8th Regional I.L.O. Conference on the Mauritian soil early this year which I had the honour to preside. As a matter of fact and satisfaction, the MLC as a National Centre, has contributed in its humble way to the success of the conference. The Public appreciation expressed by top I.L.O. Officials and delegates present should be a matter of reference to the people of Mauritius in general. It is my earnest wish that the resolutions taken now meet the consideration of the Government as the very credibility of Mauritius is at stake.

However, as our country has been projected as a model of tripartism, its consolidation will warrant the notification of ILO Convention No. 144 and the scope of the National Tripartite Committee be enlarged to cater for major issues of national interests and not restricted to only Industrial Relations matters."

I further raised a few important issues of non ratification of the ILO Convention No. 87 on the Freedom of Association and the right to organise. The ILO Convention No 87 was rectified and the IRA was repealed and replaced by the famous employment Relations Act 32 of 2009.

During my intervention, I made an appeal to the Prime Minister "requesting your Government to find a solution to the redundant workers of the Ex-CHA. They have the right to have a secured job which is the essence of self-respect and social development, and also because their families are having a hard time. On humanitarian grounds and in the name of social justice, it is felt that Government has some moral obligation towards these workers."

It is to be noted that my plea did not fall on deaf ears, as most of the workers were afterwards redeployed in different institutions.

As a final word, I said that "we should be proud of the economic status of our country which has through a political will, warranted the commitment, involvement and support of the working class in general. What is now required is our legitimate share of the national cake which we have contributed to enlarge as the wellbeing of our own self and that of our families depends largely on our pay packet we bring home.

"I would furthermore appeal to the Government to refrain from following to the letter the prescription of the **IMF** & the **World Bank** as regards economic measures. Experience has proved that the capitalist system is always detrimental to the vulnerable strata of the society, the so-called" *"ti-dimoune"*

The MLC as a national centre has always acted in a responsible manner. However, at the same time, we would like to make an appeal to the Government that the trade union movement as a social partner be allowed to play its legitimate role in the true spirit of tripartism.

I hope that the new team which will take over will be as dynamic if not more, in sustaining workers' rights and struggle unflinchingly for the welfare of all our members. Before ending, I will make an appeal to my friends of the MLC to continue acting as responsible trade unionists and fulfil their role as economic partners in the development of our country. The old team of Bhagirutty, Allgoo, Cunniah and others has fought hard to make MLC what it is today. So dear brothers and Sisters my earnest wish is that you continue to keep our flag flying well high in the sky."

Anti-democratic practice at the MLC

Many trade unionists have struggled hard, to keep trade unionism alive in Mauritius, unfortunately, as in many other sectors in our country, there have been some "brebis galeuses" in the trade union movement too, and who have done much have to the Mauritius Labour Congress by that anti-demonstration practice. As from April 1997, just after my retirement as president of the MLC, the new Secretary General, with the help of the president, started a plan to destroy little by little the trade union democratic principles. Though it is very painful for me to relate about these things, I think it is my duty to come forward and make this "mise en garde". And prevent future mismanagement in the trade union movement.

In fact, this was done with a specific strategy to remain in power and just enjoy the fruits of their predecessors. In March 1994, the MLC had million of rupees in its fund which was accumulated during several years and the MLC had also 4 good cars. First thing they did was to invent false charges against the GSA leaders, Mr Vinod Ramdharry, the Vice-President of GSA, and Mr. Radhakrishna Sadien, the President of the Government Servants Association and equally President of State Employees Federation. They managed to manipulate a few members to get a majority of half plus one who voted to expel them. Needless to say that both GSA and SEF withdrew as members and the MLC lost around 18,000 members.

Secondly they suspended the Artisans and General Workers Union as an affiliated union, without giving them opportunity to defend themselves. The reason was the General Secretary wanted to use for his personal business the new car 1604 MY 97, which was given to the AGWU under a specific agreement.

When the General Secretary could not get the car for his personal use, he was so annoyed that he made a statement to Police Station. The Police wanted to arrest Mr. Lall Dewnath the Acting President of AGWU fortunately, I had very good relations with Mr. Dev Hurnam. Dewnath, Rajcoomar Sydamah and I went Mr. Dev Hurnam at his Residence late at night around 9.00 p.m. He on the spot called the Commissioner of Police and explained to him that the car was given to AGWU which had a written Agreement with the MLC. In fact, Mr Dewnath had never stolen or refused give the car to MLC whenever necessity arose. Thanks to the intervention of Mr. Hurman the Acting President of AGWU was not arrested.

Nevertheless, the General Secretary was not satisfied and he wanted at all costs to get the car by filing a case in Supreme Court according to a statement of Mr Lall Dewnauth to the Police and to the Supreme Court in an affidavit dated 16th December, 1997. He said the following:-

Sno. 2380/97

IN THE SUPREME COURT OF MAURITIUS
In the matter of: - Artisans & General Workers Union – Applicant -
versus
Mauritius Labour Congress & an or - Respondents
And in the matter of: - Ex Parte : - Artisans and General Workers Union - Applicant

O R D E R
Upon the application of Mr Attorney O.D. Cowreea for the applicant and after taking cognizance of the proecipe and affidavit registered in Reg A 574 Nos. 5130 & 5131 respectively and the other document filed in support of the application; I decline to make the interim order prayed for. Instead let the respondents appear before the Honourable Judge sitting at Chambers, on Wednesday the 24th day of December, 1997 at 10.00 hrs in the forenoon, to show cause why an interlocutory order in the nature of an injunction should not issue restraining forbidding and prohibiting (a) the respondents either personally or through their agents, servants and or preposes from taking any decision against the applicant in relation to the returning of any cars, equipment and/or sanctioning the applicant in as much as they are null and void to all intents and purposes in breach of section 6 (f) and 11 (c) of the Rules of Respondent No. 1 (b) Respondent No. 2, from claiming to be the General Secretary of respondent No. 1 and acting in such capacity as he is in arrears of respondent No. 1 and has therefore disqualified himself automatically from respondent No. 2. Chambers, this 17th day of December, 1997 - Certified a true Copy

JUDGE.

MLC Event after March 1994

I feel very sad for what happened after my departure as President of the MLC in 1994, to one of the prestigious Trade Union Organisations in Mauritius, well known to international Trade Unions movement, which is affiliated to the ICFTU, and was supported, by the AFL-CIO, AALC, BTUC, F.O. etc. We, (Bhagirutty, Cunniah and myself) had worked in a team to make the MLC the largest Confederation of Trade Unions in Mauritius with a membership of 68,000 and Union fund in the Bank was around several million rupees and four very good cars.

The New General Secretary Mr Jugdish Lollbeeharry and the President Mr Roy started securing their own positions by eliminating their potential challengers: for example they expelled two Executive Board members namely, Radhakrishna Sadien and Vinod Ramdhary, respectively President and Vice President of GSA, one of our strongest affiliate with more than 14,000 members. GSA and SEF left the MLC with around 18,000 members followed by other unions who voted against the expulsion. The MLC lost nearly about 50% of its membership and also lost the rights of representing the Mauritian workers at the ILO Annual Conference in Geneva.

After the departure of Lollbeeharry, this time another quarrel of leadership between Cassam Kareeman supported by Roy and Deepak Benydin led again to the loss of GTU, FSCC and others and the membership had gone down to around 6,000. It was very sad to learn that two MLC cars had been sold without the approval of the general delegates meeting and the money had not been deposited in bank on the account of the MLC. I **hope the Registrar of Associations is aware of this matter, and I feel even Police and ICAC can take up this matter.**

It is very painful for me to witness the dramatic situation of the MLC to date. I have given more that 25 years of my youth in building this organisation. At the time we took over, the MLC was running on deficit. Sometimes, the MLC did not have the necessary funds to buy typing paper for communication. It was the PWU or AGWU which were providing this facility. When overseas Trade Unions delegates were coming on mission, the MLC did not have money to give a reception or even to invite them for a lunch or dinner. As a Director of Organisation, I was finding myself in a very embarrassing situation. I was taking them to my residence for lunch or dinner and sometimes Brother Bhagirutty invited them for lunch.

Chapter 15

AGWU-PWU &
SIOA STRIKE – JULY 1979

I became President of the Artisans and General Workers' Union in 1978, at a very critical period for employees in general and sugar industry workers in particular. No sooner was I placed on the saddle than started a vast campaign of mobilization which culminated in a general 4-day strike in July 1979. The AGWU was joined in this action by two other affiliates of the Mauritius Labour Congress, viz. the Plantation Workers' Union (PWU) and the Sugar Industry Overseers Association, (SIOA).

The sugar workers were generally frustrated at an ever-eroding purchasing power as the prices of consumer goods kept sky rocketing while the NRB refused any wage increase on the pretext that the MSPA was unable to bear any additional expenditure in terms of wages or fringe benefits. The employers were unwilling even to sit at the negotiating table with the unions.

We had no other alternative but to resort to a strike action. All the branches of our three unions were duly mobilized and we went on strike on 22 July 1979. The strike ended on the 25th July after a number of benefits had been consented to the workers.

We were joined by members of other unions on certain estates, and at the very outset the union leaders, together with the workers, had taken the firm decision that the strike would not be called off until the workers obtained satisfaction.

68
A Brief History Of **Trade Unionism** In Mauritius

Government took the strike very seriously, especially as it was during the crop season, and opened negotiations with the three striking unions affiliated to the MLC on the very next day of the strike.

On the third day of the strike Cabinet met urgently to discuss the demands of the unions. An agreement was reached in the afternoon of 25th July and most of the demands were granted. The strike was then called off.

The following fringe benefits were given to sugar workers:-

(1) Housing allowance was increased for Agricultural Worker Sirdars (Overseers) from Rs 35 to Rs 85 (i) Labourers Rs 35 to Rs 45.-
(2) Every female worker who in the course of a normal day's work, is required to do trashing, relevage de paille, spreading of fertilizer, etc, shall be entitled to an allowance equivalent to not less than 15 percent of her wages for that day;
(3) Two (2) additional local leaves for labourers and artisans who during the harvest season attend work 90 percent;
(4) Maternity allowance for a labourer wife being an allowance of Rs 40 same as the artisan;
(5) Special Leave: Four (4) days leave on full pay instead of half pay for on the occasion the marriage of their children or death of a close relative;
(6) Bicycle allowance increase from 65 cents to Rs 1.25
(7) 40 Hour Week: the Government agreed to set up an Ad-Hoc Committee to review the implementation of 40 hour week in the sugar industry;

(8)   Salary Compensation: Government agreed to set up a Select Committee to fix salary compensation;

(9)   Reclassification of Trade men, Government agreed to set up an ad hoc Committee to review the reclassification.

It is worth noting that a couple of other sugar industry unions (AUSI, SILU & OUA) had attempted to sabotage the strike movement by circulating hand bills, but their efforts had remained unsuccessful.

The strike had registered only two victims: me and Alain Victoire. I was dismissed and Alain Victoire OAU Branch President, was suspended for one month.

The other workers were not unduly harassed and were allowed to go back to their jobs as one of the conditions for putting an end to the strike was that no disciplinary action was to be taken against any worker who had gone on strike.

The MLC leaders tried to intervene in my favour. They met the Prime Minister, Sir Seewoosagur Ramgoolam, with a request to obtain my re-insertion, as I reckoned 21 years' service. The Prime Minister asked his Minister of Labour and Industrial Relations to look into the matter, but the MSPA refused to reintegrate me.

The MLC declared a trade dispute on the ground of unjustified dismissal. A tripartite meeting was called with some Ministers of the Government Cabinet, (Sir Veerasamy Ringadoo, Sir Kher Jagatsingh, and Mr Yousouf Mohamed) the Representatives of the MLC and those of the MSPA. This meeting yielded no positive result as the MSPA considered the strike to be illegal.

A few weeks later, I had a very frank discussion with Mr. Robert Lagesse, General Manager of St. Antoine S.E concerning my job. The General Manager agreed to reinstate me to my former job as Shop Steward with my previous facilities, but he attached one important condition: I would have to quit my position as President of the AGWU.

I found myself confronting a very difficult situation. On the one hand I had to cater for my family, consisting of my old ailing father of 80 years, my mother, my wife, who had never worked, and four school going children; on the other hand, there were the thousands of workers who had pinned all their hope on my leadership. Was I going to betray them for selfish motives?

In fact I will never stop thanking God for leading me on the right path: I preferred to remain at the service of the working classes. And I must say that I have never ever regretted taking this bold decision.

This matter brought, in the wake of the strike, an unprecedented disagreement between the Mauritius Sugar Planters' Association and the Government. The following extract from: "Le Mauricien of 27 July, 1979 explain the situation"

De violents propos tenus au cours d'une rencontre MSPA – Gouvernement – NRB

Les nouveaux avantages consentis coûteront Rs 23 million à la MSPA, formule de sérieuses réserves –

Signe de nervosité qui caractérise les rapports gouvernement- secteur privé depuis peu ? Un violent incident a opposé, hier, a l'Hôtel du Gouvernent des dirigeants de la MSPA (Association de Usiniers de l'Industrie Sucrière) au Ministre du travail, M. Yousouf Mohamed, et à certains de ses collaborateurs, à l'issue d'une réunion tendue autour des récentes décisions du Cabinet sur des « fringes benefits » à accorder aux employés de l'industrie sucrière, décisions qui ont mis fin à la grève dans le ce secteur hier. Des propos ont été échangés de part et d'autre, et la réunion a pris fin en eau de boudin, M. Mohamed demandant à M. Staub, directeur de la MSPA, de quitter son bureau, le menaçant de le mettre lui-même dehors, à la suite de certains propos tenus. La décision du Conseil des Ministres d'accorder de nouveaux « fringe benefits » aux travailleurs de l'industrie sucrière a été mal accueillie par la MSPA- les avantages consentis coûteront en effet Rs 23 millions de plus, alors que l'industrie passe par une phase difficile, déclarant des pertes de plus de Rs 40 million annuellement. Dans ce cas précis, la MSPA fut mise au pied du mur. Le ministre du travail lui-même fut placé dans une situation délicate, n'étant pas au pays quand le Cabinet prit ces décisions. Il fut d'autant plus embarrassé que le NRB n'avait pas été consulté par le gouvernement avant l'annonce des avantages consentis et que la grève avait un caractère illégal du point de vue des techniciens ou du Ministre du Travail. »

Chapter 16

Rajpalsingh Allgoo -
A Man for the Workers

August 22, 2012. I celebrated my 75th birthday amidst friends and relatives in my home at Grand Gaube, a prospering village in the north of Mauritius. After completing three-quarters of a century, I have not retired. I am still active and kicking, full of pep and gusto, after a lifetime dedicated to the cause of the hundreds of thousands of workers of this country.

Childhood and School Days

Born at Couacaud Road, Grand Gaube, a tiny coastal village of labourers and fishermen, I can humbly say that I have been mostly a self-educated, self-made man. My father Ragoonauth was a Sirdar, (an overseer) at Mapou Sugar Estate. He had also inherited some land on which he grew sugar cane and vegetables near his house. His mother, Beerangeea Jodhun was, like most women of Indian origin of the time, a housewife.

I was fondly nicknamed Raj by my near and dear ones, and belonged to the fourth generation of coolie descendants. My father's grandfather, Dwarika Allgoo, Immigrant No 247009, had been shipped from the Port of Calcutta in India in 1859 on board the Comode 903. He passed away four years after his arrival, in the morning of 4 December 1863, as he was not able to survive the malaria epidemic raging at that time.

The house where I was born stood at the very same place where I now live. But it was then a small hut thatched with straw, consisting of two big rooms and two "godons"- two much smaller rooms appended to the house to accommodate the growing children and visitors staying for the night, a feature which was quite common in those days of scanty transport facilities.

The inhabitants of Grand Gaube, consisting mainly of descendants of Indian indentured labourers and those of African and Malagasy slaves, were a laborious class who lived from hand to mouth, taking each day as it came and whatever it brought. The descendants of the freed slaves, the Creoles, were mostly engaged in fishing activities. Many were employed as artisans on the sugar factories.

Living was a perpetual struggle in a society where the workers had no better status than the domestic animals which they reared, or the fish that they caught in the treacherous sea. Poverty was their daily diet and misery their life's companion. Labourers were earning about 50 cents for a whole day's work and a kilo of fish went for a few cents. Making ends meet in such conditions was a real act of faith and bravery.

This woeful condition was made even more wretched with the outbreak of the Second World War two years after my birth. Many thousands of Mauritians joined the Royal Pioneer Corps and were taken to foreign shores to help Great Britain in the war efforts. Ships practically stopped calling at Port-Louis, thus cutting the supply of food and other essential commodities. I was still a young boy at the time, but old enough to know that the family as well as the neighbours had to survive on home-grown corn, manioc and sweet potatoes as staple foods.

A fierce cyclone which blew disaster and devastation in 1945, when I was eight years old, made life worse for all the inhabitants of the colony.

At that time, America had been ravaged by the fiercest recession in its history. The famous American writer Sidney Sheldon recounts in his autobiography which appeared two years before his death in 2005 that "thousands of banks had failed. Businesses were folding everywhere. A million vagabonds, including 200,000 children, were roaming the country. We were in the grip of a disastrous depression. Former millionaires were committing suicide, and executives were selling apples in the streets. I had reached the depths of despair. I could see no rhyme or reason for my existence." But I, as a young boy, was blissfully unaware of what was happening in the other side of the world. Nor did I know that there was another side. The existence of a power called America was nowhere within the reach of my perception.

Like many kids of my time, I was admitted to primary school at the age of five. My parents sent me to the Roman Catholic Aided School of the village, but I stayed there for a mere six months. I recall an incident which prompted this migration from the school at Grand Gaube to another school in the nearby village of Goodlands.

It was my first year in school and I had made friends with a number of kids from the Christian community. It was at that time that I was made aware that there was a difference between Hindus and Christians.

At the start of the catechism lesson at school, our teacher would order all non-Christians to go out of the classroom by shouting "Païens dehors" – Pagans out!

My Hindu friends and I felt badly insulted. We didn't understand what the word "Païens" meant. To our innocent ears it sounded like "panier", which is the French and Creole word for "basket." Why were we being treated as baskets? We Hindus were already taken for a lower category, a class of second grade citizens, often pejoratively referred to as "Malbars" and "Coolies."

I could take it no longer and reported it to my parents. When my uncle Rampertab Allgoo heard about it, he immediately withdrew me from the RCA School in Grand Gaube and got me admitted to a non-RCA school in Goodlands. This school is today known as the Doorgacharun Hurry Government School."

Thus I went to stay in Goodlands at my uncle Rampertab place, in order to be able to attend school, going to my parents' home on weekends and during the school holidays. Rampertab proved to be a very strict disciplinarian who did not even allow me to go out and play with boys of my age. But he inculcated a strong sense of discipline in me. I was not born with a silver spoon in my mouth, but I had the blood of trade unionism flowing freely in my veins. Uncle Rampartab (known as Partab) was at that time the General Secretary of the Mauritius Labour Party. He was also an influent member of the Mauritius Engineering & Technical Workers Union, which later became the Artisans & General Workers Union by which appellation it is still known to our days.

As a member of the Rampertab household, I got to be acquainted very early with the leading figures of the Labour Party: Emmanuel Anquetil, Guy Rozemont, Philippe Rozemont, Seewoosagur Ramgoolam, Renganaden Seeneevassen, Aunauth Beejadhur, Harilall Vaghjee, Veerasamy Ringadoo, Raymond Rault and several others. I recall that every time some of them were coming home to visit my uncle, the latter would send me to Virahsawmy's shop nearby to buy drinks and refreshments for them.

While I was still at school, I was given two responsibilities. Every morning, before going to school I had to clean uncle's car, an Austin bearing registration number 2079, and check the water level in the radiator and the engine oil. This created an early interest for cars in me at a time when cars were scarce in the rural landscape.

In the afternoons, I had the charge of the office of the Mauritius Engineering & Technical Workers Union which also housed a sub office of the Mauritius Labour Party. My daily task was to open the office at 4 pm and to attend to members of the public who called. I also had to collect the monthly fees from the members of the Union and fill in their cards in lieu of a receipt. Little could the little boy that I was suspect, at that age, that destiny was in fact grooming me for a rich, lifelong career in the trade union movement!

After my primary schooling, I very much wanted to pursue my secondary education. Unfortunately, there was no college to go to in the whole region. The nearest college was situated in Port Louis, some 35 km away. Transport was another problem.

Travelling by bus, apart from the daily fare involved, meant a journey of around 3 hours per day to go to school and come back. The few students who went to college from the village had to stay at their relatives' places during the week in order to be able to do so. But my parents were not inclined on sending their son away to stay with relatives.

I thus had no other option than to take private tuition from a friend's elder brother and to prepare for my Junior Cambridge. Shortly afterwards a private secondary school, Magdaland College, was opened in Goodlands and I took further private tuition from the teachers of the college. In the meantime, I had also spent a brief spell at Neo College in Port Louis.

At about that time, when I was 15, I joined the Arya Samaj movement and became a member of the Grand Gaube branch. I devoted myself heart and soul to the teachings of Swami Dayanand, the founder of the Arya Samaj movement, and these have had a tremendous effect upon my character and behaviour.

Started Working at the Age of 17

At the age of 17, I was offered a part-time job as bread seller. My uncle, Mr. Mohit Fokeer, who owned a bakery in Goodlands, suggested that I earn some pocket money by delivering bread to shops and individuals. The job required that I should wake up daily at 4.30 am, pedal to Goodlands to collect the bread for distribution. At the end of six months I gave up the job because of bad payers.

Now a young man of 18, after being apprenticed to a tailor and after having failed as a bread seller, I had to think very seriously about a career. Like all youngsters of my age, I had a penchant for a job in the Government services. I wanted to be either a Nurse or a Police Officer. But none of these pleased my mother because both of these jobs meant postings far away from home and staying in the regions where I would be posted. I was highly discouraged from taking these two options.

I then thought of becoming a ticket examiner with a bus company. But first I had to become a bus conductor, because the post of ticket examiner was a promotional one, from the rank of bus conductor. A ticket examiner's job, I thought, was quite an easy one, with the added advantage of having to wear a uniform with tie, which made the wearer quite smart. Moreover, this would give me the opportunity of travelling the whole day, instead of being pinned to an office chair.

I applied for a conductor's job to the Northern Transport Company and was employed as a relief conductor, which meant that I would be called upon to replace, on an ad hoc basis, any permanent conductor who would be absent for the day. This required that I should report to the Company's depot in Goodlands at 5 O'clock every morning and try my chance among the dozens of relief conductors.

Caption

Caption

Caption

Caption

Caption

Caption

Caption

Caption

Caption

Caption

This employment as relief conductor came to an end after ten months as a result of an incident in which the bus driver and a stand regulator of the company were involved. I was not prepared to tell the truth because this might entail the dismissal of the driver. I decided, there and then, to give up the job.

In 1959 Raj joined the St. Antoine S.E. as an employee

I found myself once again without a job. I was once again swelling the number of unemployed, but not for long. My father, who was a Sirdar at Mapou Goodlands Sugar Estate, managed to get me a job as driver and purchasing officer with St. Antoine Sugar Estate through his contacts. My job consisted essentially in going to Port Louis to buy spare parts for the estate vehicles which were repaired at the factory's garage.

One morning, I was accosted by an elderly worker, Luchumaya, who was among a small group of factory employees. Luchmaya told me: "You work here, don't you?" I replied in the affirmative. Luchmaya continued, "I'll tell you something, but please don't be offended by what I say. I see that you are wearing a woollen suit to come to work every day." I replied that it was the only convenient dress that I possessed and so I wore it to come to work every day. Luchmaya then pointed out that the owner of the factory wore a "Tussor" suit which was of a quite inferior material.

I got the message and got myself two "Tussor" suits made which I now started wearing to go to work. But that was not the end of my botheration. I was again apostrophized on the factory premises and this time the remark was that I was wearing the same type of material as the boss. I immediately understood that there was nothing wicked or reproachful in their comment, but I could not quite grasp why they were after my personal dress code.

Later that day, I went to two garage employees, several years my senior, in fact as old as my own father, and related my morning experience to them. I wanted to know what was wrong with this way of dressing. The two elders then recounted how one Sunday morning some 20-25 years earlier, an Indian labourer residing in the factory camp had donned a white dhoti and jacket and was going on his way. He was espied by White staff who was supervising the cleaning of the factory yard. On seeing the Indian labourer so smartly accoutred, he got a shot of adrenalin mounting from his heart to his head. He called the poor labourer, although it was a Sunday and the latter was off, and ordered him to remove a few cane stalks which had fallen in the molasses pool. The labourer had no option but to obey, with the result that his costume got profusely soiled with the molasses.

This news soon became the talk of the whole of Goodlands and all the neighbouring villages. I had heard another story with the same substance in my own village. One Sunday morning a labourer from a village had donned a shining pair of black shoes with a snow-white dhoti and a coal-black woollen jacket and was going past one of the White staff's house. He had the misfortune of being seen by the lady of the house who harangued him in these terms: "Where do you think you are going wearing shoes and coat? How dare you wear a pair of shoes and a coat like my husband? Do you want to become my husband? Go back home immediately and remove your shoes and coat."

Another incident that I carried in my heart all these years is one concerning my car. Quite often, especially when I missed the bus in the morning, I would report for work driving my father's car which I parked very close to the factory. One day one of the factory workers told me: "Are you not afraid to park your car near the factory"? On being asked why I should be afraid, the man replied, "These Whites are very jealous and don't like it when they see a worker achieving some progress or improving his standard of living. I myself come to work by motorcycle from Piton every day, but I never bring it to the factory. I leave it at a friend's place and walk from his house."

These and other incidents on the site of work laid the basis of my joining the world of Trade Unionism. I could not tolerate injustice, especially towards workers. Moreover, my uncle Partab, who was both a politician and a trade union leader, provided a great inspiration. My role model was at hand. Those were the days when the Labour Party had started a relentless struggle for workers' rights and dignity in the country. My adhesion to Arya Samaj principles was also another propitious factor that prepared me for my future career.

I already possessed an inkling of union work as I collected members' subscription fees at my uncle's office in my student days. I now joined the Artisans and General Workers' Union and was made the branch representative. The check-off system was unheard of in those days and my job also consisted in collecting member's fees every month.

I still remember how people were afraid to join trade unions and those who did always beseeched the leaders to keep their membership a secret, for fear of losing their jobs if the boss came to know of it.

Raj Allgoo family life

A few years later, when I was just 23 years old, my parents decided that it was time for me to get married and found a family. I was thus married to Sunyo Devi Dusowoth, daughter of Mr. and Mrs. Shreekissoon Dusowoth, on 23rd November 1960. I was then earning a monthly salary of Rs 70, as a driver and purchasing officer at Saint Antoine Sugar Estate. Although it was by no means easy to make ends meet, I held on with great tenacity and hope, looking forward to better days.

Sunyo Devi gave me four children, all of whom have been well educated and have turned professionals. My eldest son, Dr. Vinod Kumar Dwarkasingh Allgoo MBBS, MD (Ortho), is a medical practitioner. He is also a social worker and is responsible for the organization of Art of Living in the North, married to Sita Devi Choose B.Com (H),

M.Com (H) Teacher working at Friendship College. Both are Teachers of Art of Living (AOL) and they have one son Raviraj, two and a half years old.

Dr. Kaylash Dwarkasingh Allgoo holds a Master's Degree in Business Administration and PhD. He is presently the Director of the Mauritius Qualifications Authority, married to Pirate (Kabul) Anathema BSc., and they have two sons: Rohan is doing H.S.C. and Dhanish is in Form V.

Daughter Sangeeta Devi Allgoo read a BSc degree and she is the Principal Auditor at the Ministry of Business Enterprise and Cooperatives, she is married to Ram Goolaup, who started his career in the Police force. After completing a Diploma in Civil Engineering, he pursued his studies and obtained a Master's degree in Management. He is a lecturer at the University of Mauritius. They have one daughter studying at York University Toronto-Canada and a son Ravish doing his H.S.C.

The youngest son, Ranjeet Dwarkasingh Allgoo, possesses a B.Com Degree and is the Manager of an Insurance Agency, married to Sangeeta (Cavite) Ramsooroop BSc (H), MSc (H), MA Examiner at Mauritius Examinations Syndicate, they have one son Savesh doing H.S.C. and a daughter Kamna who is in Form II.

My three sons and grandsons have been named Dwarkasingh after their great grandfather.

My daughter Sangeeta (Baby) used to help me in my Trade Union activities. During that time, she was at the University. Furthermore during the Sinotex strike, she was the only one who was keeping in touch with the workers on strike and keeping their moral up, as MLC officers were afraid to be arrested. It was unfortunate that the secretary of the AGWU was allowed only one day off per month for trade union activities. Vinod gathered a good experience in the field of industrial relations during his school days, as he was helping me in writing documents. Today despite being an Orthopaedic Surgeon, his interest for trade union activities has not diminished. He is presently the President of Government Medical Officers and Dental Association.

GOLDEN JUBILEE
WEDDING ANNIVERSARY CELEBRATION

My wife Sunyo Devi is engaged in social work and community service. She has been the Secretary of the Grand Gaube Women's Association for a number of years.

We celebrated the Golden Jubilee of our wedding on 23 October 2010. It was a great honour and privilege to celebrate our 50th wedding anniversary among hundreds of relatives and friends by a special ceremony performed by Pandit Jaychand Beeharry and Pandita Suresha Bowan.

I seize the opportunity of this book to thank my wife Sunyo Devi for her contribution in taking care of our children's bringing up growing and their education. Words alone would not be enough to thank you, for all the years of love and care you have given to our kids and me. I am grateful to you and want you to know how much I appreciate all the advice and care given to our children's needs, and attention paid to my late father and mother.

Despite the fact that you had only primary education, you helped the children in getting proper education. We are lucky to have three children out of four to be scholarship winners and professionals or Degree Holders.

You helped me in good times and bad as well and given me the extra confidence I needed for my work, study and Trade Union activities. You always tell me that everything is ok. Sunyo Devi, you have been and will always be the sunshine of my life.

SETTING UP THE ERIDEN CLUB

A few years after my marriage, in 1964, I decided to involve myself in youth and social activities in my village. No youth club existed in Grand Gaube or in nearby Roche Terre, and the young people remained idle most of the time. Together with my friends Atmanand Fokeer, Gianduth Burrun, Premchand Jogee, Vellah Sooprayen and a few others, we pulled our resources together and founded the Eriden Youth Club to organize activities for young people in Grand Gaube and the neighbouring villages. Satyawon Jogee joined slightly later, after completing his secondary studies.

Eriden Youth Club started with a membership of about 50 and was affiliated to the Northern Clubs Association. That was a time when the youth movement was flourishing in Mauritius. All the youth clubs in the island were affiliated to the youth federations catering for the region in which they were located. Mauritius was divided into five regions with one Youth Federation each: Port Louis Youth Federation, Northern Clubs Association, Moka-Flacq Youth Federation, Grand Port Savanne Youth Federation and Plaine Wilhems Black River Youth Federation.

These federations were administered by the Youth House in Belle Rose and each had two or three Youth Officers attached to it. These Youth Officers were recruited from among the primary school teachers. Each federation was run by a committee selected from among representatives of the clubs affiliated to the Federation. Courses in leadership were frequently held during workshops, seminars and conferences at the Anse La Raie Youth Training Centre. Issues of national interest were also addressed during these seminars.

At the level of Eriden Youth Club, my friends and I were very busy organising sports and literacy activities for the benefit of the members, and we won several competitions organised by the federation. We also ran private tuition classes as most students came from poor families.

The club had been honoured by the visits of several personalities including Sir John Shaw Rennie, Governor of Mauritius and Lady, Hon Aunauth Beejadhur, Minister of Education and Sir Robin Ghurburrun, famous barrister and social worker, M. Philippe Forget, Editor of L'Express daily newspaper, and others.

Eriden Youth Club was bubbling with activities and the members decided to bring their contribution at Village Council level in order to take initiatives for the development of the area. They got this golden opportunity at the Village Council elections which were held on 8th August 1968, the first after independence.

ELECTION OF GRAND GAUBE/ ROCHE TERRE VILLAGE COUNCIL

The young people of Grand Gaube-Roche Terre were not happy with the outgoing management which consisted of people who were short of ideas and remained mostly inactive. However, it must be pointed out in their defence that the village council had a scanty budget and practically nothing could be done with whatever they got.

But the youth of the region, motivated by the leaders of Eriden Youth Club, had their own ideas on how to get things done. With the help of the social group of the village, they constituted a team of candidates and selected a flower as their symbol. The candidates were all in the 20-28 age group, except me, who was now 31 years old.

We won the election with an imposing majority and set to work immediately. While everybody was expecting me to shoulder the Chairman's responsibility, I chose to pass the seat on to one Ignace Moutou, because no member of the Creole Community had ever been appointed Chairman of Grand Gaube-Roche Terre Village Council although the majority of inhabitants belonged to that community. I was elected Vice President in order to provide a strong support to the chairman.

The following year, the same consideration inhabited me at the time of the election of the Chairman. In a bid to promote fair play and to give everybody an equal chance, I proposed the name of Siven Mauree, as no Tamil had ever occupied the post of Chairman. Once again, I was appointed Vice Chairman. I officially assumed the Chairmanship of the Village Council in the last year of our mandate. I set myself to work assiduously in order to complete the programme we had put before the voters.

During our three-year tenure at the helm, we had created a special fund for the welfare of the village. The inhabitants contributed voluntarily to the fund as well as the Chairman of the Village Council, who had to chip in Rs 75 out of the monthly allowance of Rs 125 that he received.

Among the several activities undertaken during the group's administration, two events stand out most in my mind. The very first prodigious project we embarked upon was the provision of street lighting along the main road. Sure enough, the District Council gladly contributed to the materialization of the venture, but its contribution did not exceed the supply of ten fluorescent tubes for a 6-km road.

The Village Council raised the necessary funds from the villagers themselves, in a great spirit of self-help, and completed the street lighting task. There was a great festival of lights on the day of the inauguration. People residing in the back streets converged to the main road and danced the sega. An atmosphere of Divali pervaded the whole village.

Another operation which the Village Council undertook with success was the creation of a football ground. Eriden Youth Club had been organizing a number of activities for the youth of the region, but a football ground was sadly missing. There had been, in the past, a small plot of unoccupied land near the Protestant Church on which the young played football. Then, a philanthropist of the village, Mr. Baboo Bhoyroo, had erected a football ground on his own premises and opened it to the young to play football. Soon a football team, Spartak, saw the light of day.

However, after the demise of Mr. Baboo Bhoyroo, his heirs decided to use the football ground more profitably for themselves and converted it into a sugar cane field. The young of the village suddenly found themselves without a football ground, and Spartak team which had won the football championship in the North had nowhere to go.

I knew I had to do something by all means to remedy the situation and the situation could only be remedied by the creation of a new football ground for which land had to be found. The Village Council set itself to task and prepared a strategy.

With the help of the District Council, we obtained a piece of State land, which had been lying fallow for centuries, from the Ministry of Housing and Land. But the land was rocky and had to be made malleable. Only Saint Antoine Sugar Estate possessed the necessary machinery and equipment to de-rock the ground which was more of a hillock. But who would convince the Sugar Estate authorities, and why would they accept to do the work for free?

GRAND GAUBE FOOTBALL PLAY GROUND

I led a delegation to meet Father Jean Eon, the parson of Grand Gaube Catholic Church, who was on very good terms with the General Manager of Saint Antoine S.E, Mr. Robert Lagesse. After paying an attentive and sympathetic heed to our request, Father Eon agreed to convince Mr. Lagesse to help the Village Council in their endeavour, and he was successful in his mission.

Things were also made easier by the fact that I was an employee of Saint Antoine and it was easy for me to get things done promptly. It took them a couple of months to remove the little hill and to level the ground, after which the collaboration of the

Development Works Corporation was solicited for the remaining chores that were required to complete the erection of the football ground. Local volunteers extended a helping hand too, especially by maintaining the turf.

Government renovated the football ground over thirty years later, providing it with a fence and other amenities and renamed it Sir Gaëtan Duval Stadium, in memory of the former Deputy Prime Minister who lived in the vicinity.

Activist of Arya Samaj Movement

Alongside the youth and Village Council activities, I was also involved in Socio-cultural and religious movements. A staunch believer in the teachings of Swami Dayanand Saraswatee, I had joined the Arya Sabha branch of Grand Gaube at quite an early age. I was greatly imbued with Swami Dayanand's precept that all people are equal and there should no difference based on considerations of caste or community.

I was once delegated by my branch to vote for the election of the Executive Committee of the Mauritius Arya Sabha in Port Louis. I was almost unknown and practically a novice in electoral matters and was really appalled when I was approached by certain people who told me to vote only for candidates of a particular caste. Soon afterwards another group came and canvassed me to vote only for candidates belonging to another specific caste.

I felt disgusted by these underhand doings and left the premises hastily in a fit of anger, even without casting my vote. I was really upset by these caste-minded people. On the way back I kept pondering over the issue. What difference is there between the Arya Sabha and the Arya Ravived Pracharini Sabha? I asked myself. I came to the conclusion that there was none since each was trying to work for the welfare of people with specific profiles, only one was doing it surreptitiously while the other was doing the same thing overtly.

The more I thought about it, the sooner I changed my mind and agreed to join the Mauritius Arya Ravived Pracharini Sabha at the behest of my friend, the Junior Minister of Health, Hon. Ramsoordur Modun, who was also the President of the MARPS. I worked with great dedication for the Sabha together with Hon. Modun and others. I was particularly engaged in organizing the branches of the Sabha island-wide.

I also plunged headlong in the campaign for independence and worked in close collaboration with Hon Ramsoondur Modun, Hon Rameshwar Jaypal and Hon Bhickramsingh Ramlallah. I fought ardently for the cause espoused by the Labour Party.

It must be said that it was much against my own principles that I joined the MARPS and became a life member. I like to revisit, from time to time, the ten principles of Arya Samaj which are:

1. God is the efficient cause of all the knowledge and all that is known through knowledge.
2. God is existent, intelligent and blissful. He is formless, omniscient, just, merciful, unborn, endless, unchangeable, beginning-less, unequalled, the support of all, omnipresent, immanent, fearless, eternal and holy, and the maker of all. He alone is worthy of being worshipped.
3. The Vedas are the scriptures of true knowledge. It is the paramount duty of all Arya Samjists to read them, teach them, and recite them and to hear them being read.
4. One should always be ready to accept truth and to renounce untruth.
5. All acts should be performed in accordance with Dharma, that is, after deliberating what is right and what is wrong.
6. The prime object of the Arya Samaj is to do good to the world, that is, to promote the physical, spiritual and social good of everyone.
7. Our conduct towards all should be guided by love, righteousness and justice.
8. We should dispel Avidya (ignorance) and promote Vidya (knowledge).
9. No one should be content with promoting his/her good only; on the contrary, one should look for one's good in promoting the good of all.
10. One should regard oneself under restriction to follow the rules of society calculated to promote the wellbeing of all, while in following the rules of individual welfare all should be free.

I wish to have these principles to be ensconced here for the guidance of many champions of Arya Samaj, who tend to forget them and often find themselves far away from these precepts.

JOINED TRADE UNIONS MOVEMENTS

I was no longer employed as Purchasing Officer at Saint Antoine Sugar estate. My job now consisted in driving the children of the management staff of the estate to and from school in Rose Hill. I conveyed them to school in a van in the morning and stayed idle in Rose Hill the whole day waiting for afternoon to drive them back home.

It was at that time in the mid 1970s that I was invited by Hon. Alex Rima, the founder of the Organisation de l'Unité des Artisans (OUA) to join the union. I had by now acquired quite some knowledge and experience with the trade union movement after having been active with the AGWU for so many years. Moreover, I had pursued my education in the field of trade unionism by reading books which I purchased from the International Labour Organisation. I was quite conversant with Labour and Trade Union Laws and possessed adequate negotiation skills.

The OAU was founded by Hon Alex Rima on 13 June 1973. Rima was a close friend of Gaëtan Duval, and the owner of Rima Motors, a top vehicle repair garage in Grand River North West off Port Louis. He was also a member of the Legislative Assembly belonging to Duval's party, the Parti Mauricien Social Démocrate (PMSD).

At a meeting convened to appoint the office bearers of the OAU, Alex Rima made himself the leader and negotiator. He nominated his friend Auguste Follet to the post of President. The other offices went to his other friends, all members of the PMSD.

As a politician, Rima had the gift of the gab and possessed an easy power of persuasion. He was a hard-working organizer too and held daily meetings near the sugar factories across the island in a bid to recruit members for the OAU. His main rival in the sugar industry was the AGWU, which was recognized by the Mauritius Sugar Producers' Association. Alex Rima soon busied himself assiduously poaching members from the AGWU.

It was not a very difficult task for the OAU leader to convince workers to adhere to his union. He told them that he himself had been working in the sugar factories, and as such he knew all the problems faced by the artisans. Moreover, belonging to the Creole community like most of the artisans of the sugar industry, he used this factor extensively to his advantage. In a very short time, he was able to recruit over a thousand members for the OAU, while the AGWU survived with a bare 400.

Shortly afterwards, a split occurred in the Labour Party - Parti Mauricien Social Democrate Government, Duval went back to the Opposition benches. However some of his followers refused to follow him this time and chose to continue backing the Government. Alex Rima was one among them and he was given a ministerial portfolio.

This put an end to his official involvement in trade union matters, but he remained quite active covertly. That is when he turned to me and offered me the post of part-time negotiator at a salary of Rs 250 per month. I had already joined the OAU and was in charge of its Saint Antoine Branch.

It must be said that before enrolling with the OAU, I had started keeping my distance from the AGWU because I felt that nothing was being done by its leaders for the benefit of its members. On several occasions, I had made suggestions tending to improve the conditions of work of sugar employees, but they fell on deaf ears. The General Secretary, a man of nearly 70, did not command any respect. Whenever he went to a sugar factory to meet his members he would talk to them through the fences although the AGWU was a recognised union. He travelled by bus to meet the workers while Mr. Rima had an imposing Mercedes. With its 400 remaining members, the AGWU had grown very weak and became almost moribund.

My job as school bus driver gave me ample time to devote to the OAU's activities. I was quite happy with my job, but not for long. I found Alex Rima to be a nice man, but often baffling all democratic principles of trade unionism. His only aim was to compete with Paul Raymond Bérenger, the MMM leader and negotiator of the General Workers Union, in organising strikes in the sugar industry. In so doing he often took decisions unilaterally. Often too, he acted against the decisions of the Executive Committee.

One Monday morning; I was stunned to read in the papers that a number of sugar factories were not operating because the artisans had gone on strike. I rushed to the

OAU office and there I learned by the President of the Union, Mr. Auguste Follet that the decision to call a strike had been taken by Mr Rima during the weekend. On Saturday, he had driven to several factories to exhort the artisans to launch a strike on Monday.

I was highly shocked by such a decision which was clearly contrary to the rules of democracy. I reminded Mr. Follet that only a few days earlier the Executive Committee of the Union had voted against a strike in the sugar industry at that time of the crop season, and had opted for a go-slow instead. I was bewildered to find that Mr. Rima had gone against the decision of his own Executive Committee.

That was the last straw. I immediately wrote my letter of resignation. A few weeks later, I was approached by two of my ex-colleagues of the AGWU and was persuaded to reintegrate the AGWU with the mission of consolidating it and bringing it back to the forefront of the world of trade unionism.

Re-Joining the AGWU

I was reluctant to go back to the AGWU. In fact, after the bitter experience encountered at the OUA, I had felt like keeping a safe distance from trade unions at least for some time. But Moutou and Ladouceur made a very strong appeal to me, reminding me that AGWU was a historical union, being the first ever trade union founded in Mauritius by no less a person than Emmanuel Anquetil himself, the father of Mauritian trade unionism. They told me that the AGWU was in bad shape with a scanty 400 members in a sector that counted several thousand workers. The current General Secretary was nearing 70 and he was no match for people like Rima and Bérenger. Unless new blood was injected, the AGWU was certainly going to die a natural death. "Are you ready for such an eventuality?" they asked me.

This drew an immediate reaction from me. It was in May 1975 and I decided to make my comeback to the AGWU, never to leave it again, until my retirement in 1998.

The country had become independent only seven years earlier and had known great upheavals and challenges. Duval's anti-independence campaign, coupled with his "Malbar nou pa oule" and his Hindu hegemony slogan had scared many of the brightest members of the Creole community who had left the country in panic to seek more favourable havens under foreign skies. Top civil servants, teachers, nurses, high-ranking police officials had fled to Europe and Australia.

The new nation had to be consolidated by all means. In the early 70s the economy was in shambles. There was students' unrest and thousands of school leavers were jobless.

The Mouvement Militant Mauricien (MMM) which was born in 1969, soon after Duval joined Sir Seewoosagur Ramgoolam's coalition government, had come to fill the vacuum in the opposition. Its founding fathers were mostly intellectuals, fresh from European universities with leftist and communist grooming and ideals.

The new party started gathering momentum, organizing public debates and conferences on burning issues of the day. They also organized manifestations against the visits of Michel Debré, French MP from Reunion, and Princess Alexandra. Many erstwhile followers of the Labour, PMSD and CAM parties had become disillusioned and joined the new party.

The MMM also fortified its political base by dabbling in trade unionism, and its leader Paul Bérenger appointed himself negotiator of the union of workers in the harbour and docks sector.

In spite of multiple turmoil's, illegal strikes and massive criminal arsons in sugar cane fields, the country witnessed an unprecedented sugar boom in 1975. Between 1971 and 1975 the mean economic growth was 10 per cent. Yet, unemployment was raging, especially among the youth. The Free Zone and the Tourist industry had started to remedy the situation to some extent.

As soon as I came back to the AGWU fold, I found myself entrusted with the responsibility of negotiator. This was determined by the executive committee of the union at its very first meeting after my reintegration on a proposal by the Vice President of the AGWU, Mr Fils Isabelle, who was the Chief Mechanic of Ferney Sugar Estate, and seconded by Mr. Nemoure Potage, moulder at Ferney S.E. The appointment was unanimously approved.

Paul Raymond Bérenger

My responsibilities included the reorganization of the artisans of the sugar industry and the reinforcement of the AGWU, a challenge which I undertook with the help of a few members and some former colleagues of the OUA. My efforts bore their fruits as in the short lapse of six months; the membership of the AGWU had doubled.

I solicited the collaboration of my old friends, the bus drivers who were daily conveying the children of the sugar estate senior staff to colleges in Rose Hill, Quatre Bornes, Vacoas and Cure pipe. They came from all the sugar estates of the country and they carried my messages to the artisans of all sugar factories.

The union had no transport facility to provide to me in order to carry out my task. So I used my own motorcycle during the weekends to go and meet workers in the northern and eastern regions of the island. After some time, two kind and generous souls, Mr. Beerdeo Dusowoth and Mr. Bhardhowaz Jogee, helped me in my mission by putting their cars at my disposal during the weekends so that I might go to meet workers in the South and the West. Mr. Jogee often accompanied me during these trips to faraway places like Savannah, Bel Ombre, Ferney, Beau Champ and other sugar estates. We left home at Grand Gaube early in the morning and sometimes came back at 11 p.m. I fondly remember the help of friends like Fils Isabelle, Dorsamy Appendi, Rajcoomar Sydamah, Christian Nigathe, Samuel Lafontaine, Serge Caitan, Kalid Latiff Budhoo and others.

With a view to acquiring greater exposure and experience, I started establishing contacts with international organizations. This bore an immediate fruit as the Friedrich Ebert Stiffung (F.E.S) agreed to sponsor a weeklong seminar for 24 participants from the rank and file of the AGWU. The seminar was held at the Centre Misereor in Port Louis and was the precursor to workers' education.

In March 1976, I was selected to represent the AGWU on the Board of the Mauritius Labour Congress.

Chapter 17

MONITORS' TRAINING COURSE –
MONROVIA –
LIBERIA, 1976

IN 1976, as Vice-President of AGWU, I was selected to participate in a Monitors' Training Programme held in Liberia. The course was organized by the International Confederation of Free Trade Unions (ICFTU) which sponsored the programme together with the Canadian Labour Congress. The other Mauritian participants were: Louis Emmanuel Rayepa (CEB Staff Union), Khemraze (Dan) Cunniah (MTDA Employees' Union) and Periasamy SP Narrainsamy (CHA). The course was run over a 6-week period.

It would be interesting here to go to the genesis of the Monitors' Training Programme. In 1972, the ICFTU had organized a series of regional and international events in order to evaluate its educational activities with particular reference to needs, target audiences, courses, methods and contents, relevance of existing education programmes, and teaching techniques.

The Pan-African Commission on Trade Union Education Policy (Nigeria, 1972) had stressed the need for improving the quality of trade unions internationally, thus enabling them to know their obligations to the society in which they lived and worked. Moreover, the International Workshop on Ways and Means in Workers' Education, which was held in Sweden in May 1972, had identified certain target groups whose educational needs ought to be addressed by appropriately designed and carefully tailored programmes.

A Brief History Of **Trade Unionism** In Mauritius

The Monitors' Training Programme was designed in the wake of the conclusions of these two events. The aim was to give theoretical and practical training in teaching methods to a selected number of trade unionists who would be called upon to impart basic trade union education to union members, shop stewards and branch officials.

The first Monitors' Training Programme was organized in 1973 with participants from ICFTU's affiliates in Liberia, Mauritius, Nigeria, Sierra Leone and Malawi. The programme was divided into two parts. The first part involved a five-week residential course in Monrovia, Liberia. The second part consisted of a field experience of three months in the participants' home countries.

During the 5-week course in Liberia, participants were taught basic trade union matters which included organizing techniques, finance, collective bargaining, handling grievances, the role of shop stewards, branch administration, planning a trade union education programme, producing simple teaching aids, and teaching methods and techniques.

At the end of the residential course the trainees returned to their respective countries for the second part of the programme, i.e., to put into practice what they had learned in theory.

Eight hundred workers participated in the local non-residential courses. The success of the programme and its popularity with unions, employers and the governments prompted the ICFTU to organize a similar programme for French-speaking countries in 1974. In the course of 1975 the ICFTU organized a series of local non-residential courses for the benefit of all the monitors who were trained in 1973 and 1974.

For the 1976 Monitors' Training Programme which was held in Monrovia, Liberia, the ICFTU had organized a one-week workshop in order to select the four participants. The workshop was conducted by Mr. George Grace Muwonge, a former lecturer at Kampala ICFTU College.

Opening the Programme, the Liberian Minister of Labour and Industrial Relations thanked the ICFTU for organizing such an important Monitors' Course for 22 participants coming from Ghana, Kenya, Mauritius, Sierra Leone and Liberia. She also pointed out that "the course sought to fulfil the functions of the college of training trade union educators of Kampala ICFTU College."

The course started every day at 9.00 a.m. and didn't end before 11 p.m., except on Sundays when it was over by 1 p.m. It was of a relatively high level and the participants had to work very hard in order to be able to complete it by the scheduled time.

I still remember the inspiring speech delivered by the Director of ICFTU Workers' Education, Wogu Ananaba, at the closing ceremony:

"Quite often we hear politicians and Government spokespersons as well as trade union leaders themselves talking of the need for strong and effective trade unions," said Mr.

Ananaba. "Such unions cannot emerge if the law is heavily weighted against the workers and in favour of employers; they cannot develop if labour administrators are biased against trade unions and trade union leaders; they cannot exist if the union is dominated by employers, politicians, military leaders, religious or ethnic organizations, and secret societies; nor can they exist if the union itself is not a democratic organization responsive to the wishes of its members. Strength and effectiveness in the trade union movement are closely related to the general level of understanding among members of the quality of its leadership and its dedication to the common cause and the degree of popular support of its membership and their participation in the decision-making process.

The primary aim of the course we have just ended is to train a selected number of trade unionists in the skill of organizing and conducting basic trade union education among the workers on the shop floor and to do so within the financial resources of their unions or national centres. There is a general consensus among African trade union leaders and researchers in trade union problems that our unions are weak and ineffectual mainly because of the low level of understanding among workers of the aims and principles of trade unionism. We hope that through an extensive education of the rank and file, African workers would not only understand what unionism is about, but would readily accept the responsibilities and obligations of union membership.

"Let us leave this lovely city and its good and friendly people determined to build through education strong, effective and self reliant trade unions and national centres in our various countries. Let us rededicate ourselves anew to the cause of the free and democratic trade unionism in our various countries. Let us at all times uphold the gospel of international solidarity of workers, to develop sound trade unions whose leaderships derive authority to function from their members and which are responsive to the wishes of their members. Let us learn to tap that goodwill with the understanding that heaven helps those who help themselves".

BACK HOME AND TRAINING
UNDER THE SUPERVISION OF ICFTU OFFICIAL

On our way back from the Monitors' Course, the Mauritian participants halted for a few days at Nairobi in Kenya. We seized the opportunity to visit the Kenya Trade Union Congress and were highly impressed by the organization. Their headquarters was housed in a huge building and a large army of permanent staff manned the union. The imposing union building sowed the seed of a dream in my mind, the dream for the AGWU to acquire its own building.

A dream takes its own sweet time to be translated into reality. My dream was destined to materialize two decades later, with the opening of AGWU's headquarters, the Emmanuel Anquetil Labour Centre at Grand River North West, at the end of my trade union career in 1998.

Back in the country, I embarked on a mission of workers' education. With the help of Mr. George Muwonge, ICFTU Field representative, I elaborated a plan to cover the five following areas of trade unionism:

(1)   What is a trade union?
(2)   Trade Union finance;
(3)   The role of a trade union in society;
(4)   The role and responsibilities of a shop steward;
(5)   Remuneration Orders.

Through half-day seminars on Saturdays on different sugar estates and Artisans' Clubs across the country, I shared this newly acquired knowledge and experience with the workers. This movement provided me the added opportunity to recruit new members for the union. These seminars have greatly helped the artisans to understand their role and responsibilities as branch representatives, and they started defending the rights of their fellow workers on the different sugar estates.

At the return of the participants from the Monitors' Training Course in Liberia, the Mauritius Labour Congress organized a function in our honour. Several personalities were invited and the Chief Guest was Sir Seewoosagur Ramgoolam, Prime Minister. The President of MLC, Pt Sharma Jugdambi, welcomed the guests.

Among the guests was Mr. George Muwonge who said he was happy to be in Mauritius again, adding that it gave him great satisfaction to see the success of the seminars organized by the new monitors and expressed the wish of the ICFTU to form other educators for the benefit of the workers who would be better aware of their roles and responsibilities as workers and trade unionists.

AWARDED WORKERS' EDUCATOR CERTIFICATE BY THE P.M. SIR S. RAMGOOLAM

The Prime Minister, Sir Seewoosagur Ramgoolam, congratulated the MLC for its sustained effort to promote the condition of life of sugar workers since its foundation by Pandit Hurryparsad Ramnarain. He also paid tribute to Emmanuel Anquetil and Guy Rozemont. He pointed out that it was a great honour for Mauritius as Rozemont had been invited to the birth of ICFTU in London in 1949, and since its foundation the ICFTU had been helping the African Trade Unionists in their effort to promote workers' education. The Prime Minister expressed his satisfaction and gratitude to the ICFTU for organizing the local Monitors' Course for the advancement of the Trade Union movement in Mauritius.

On that occasion, Sir Seewoosagur Ramgoolam handed over certificates to me, Kerman (Dan) Cunniah, Raj Pillay and Emmanuel Rayepa, on behalf of the Secretary General of the ICFTU.

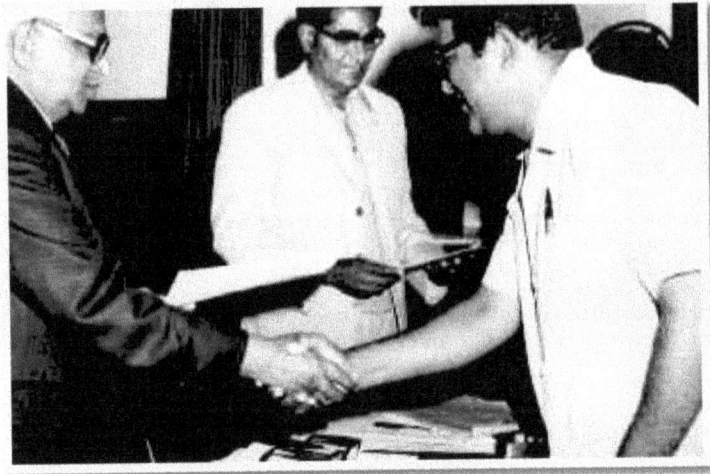

Caption

GENERAL DELEGATES MEETING AND ELECTION OF AGWU

In March 1978, on the insistence of a few influential members of the union, I accepted to stand as candidate for the post of President of the AGWU. They wanted a change of leadership because they wanted some new blood to be infused at the head of the union. Rajcoomar Sydamah stood as Secretary General and Gerard Legrand ran for Treasurer. The outgoing President, Max Kimtiah, and outgoing Secretary General Francois Roselmour Vincent wanted to be re-conducted to their posts.

On the day of the Annual General Delegates Meeting and election of office bearers, Kamtiah and Vincent discovered that a majority of those present were against them and that their chance of being re-elected was practically inexistent. So they withdrew their candidatures. Rajcoomar Sydamah and Gerard Legrand and I were respectively elected President, Secretary General and Treasurer unopposed.

It is important to remember the great work performed by Roselmour Vincent and his team in the 1960s. With the collaboration of the MLC; they were able to force the colonial government of the time to introduce the Security of Employment Act 1963. This Act stipulated that if a person had worked for a total of 80% working days during the crop season, the employer was bound to give him 6 days work per week during the intercrop period. A worker who had been present for 60% working days during the crop season was entitled to 4 days a week during intercrop time.

Prior to the Security of Employment Act 1963, even if a worker had been present for 100% working days during the crop season, he had no job entitlement during intercrop, with the result that most sugar workers remained jobless during that period. Their lives and those of their families became an unbearable ordeal during the intercrop season, as they found it almost impossible even to buy rice, flour and cooking oil. They were thus almost driven to starvation.

The introduction of the Security of Employment Act compelled the employers to keep a proper record of the sugar workers through Employment Cards. It is unfortunate that in 1994 the Mauritius Sugar Producers Association (MSPA) succeeded in getting the Trade Unions to consent to the repealing of the Security of Employment Act.

It is to be noted that Vincent, together with other union leaders, caused a legislation to be introduced whereby a sugar worker who had completed 24 consecutive months of work with the same employer had to be employed on a permanent basis.

I also salute the efforts of Vincent and his team for the following achievements in the 1960s:

1.   Grievances
      Every Trade Union member would have the right to invite officials of his union to discuss his grievances with his employer;

2.   Termination of employment
      After two weeks of service with the same employer a daily paid worker would be entitled to one clear week's advance notice of dismissal. The notice of dismissal would be forwarded without delay to the Controller of Employment.

3   Transport facilities
      Where children of the senior staff obtained transport facilities to attend school, the same facilities were to be extended to the children of the artisans to attend a secondary school. In case the facilities were no longer available the bus fare should be refunded.

4.   Food for patients in Estate hospitals
      The Ordinance Notice No 33 of 1964 provided the following on a daily basis for every patient admitted to an Estate Hospital: 10 grams of butter: 1\2 litre of milk; 300 grams of bread; 60 grams of sago; 60 grams of sugar and 5 grams of tea.

5.   Reduction of labour force
      Any employer intending to reduce his labour force, either temporally or permanently must notify the Ministry of Labour, giving the reasons for such reduction. The Minister would refer the matter to the Board constituted under

this section the Termination of Contract Service Board (TCSB). If the Board found that the reduction was justified, the employer would have to pay severance allowance to the workers who would be laid off at the rate of 15 days per year of service. If the reduction was not justified the severance allowance would be 6 times the amount calculated by 15 days per year of service.

6. **Retirement allowance**
   A retirement allowance was made payable to every worker on retirement.

7. One of the most important achievements of Vincent and his team during their tenure of office was the purchase of a building for the AGWU at 4, Guy Rozemont Square, Port Louis.

When I assumed office as President of AGWU, facilities were practically inexistent for trade union activities or workers' education. In1978, I was elected Assistant Secretary General of MLC. This permitted me to enlarge my international networking. My personal relations with the FES enabled me to procure documents on trade unionism and cooperatives. I met the Director of Afro-Asian Institute of Israel, Mr. Beniami, at an international meeting and persuaded him to allot a few scholarships to members of the AGWU in order to improve their abilities as trade unionists.

One scholarship was offered every year over a period of five years. The scholarships were of three to four months' duration, and the following AGWU members attended courses in Israel: Rajcoomar Sydamah, Christian Negathe, Samuel Lafontaine, François Alexis, Ajit Bungloll. The latter is today the Secretary General of the AGWU.

INTRODUCTION OF NATIONAL PENSION FUND IN MAURITIUS IN 1976

Since its creation in 1936, the Leaders of the Mauritius Labour Party, Dr Maurice Curé and Mr Emmanuel Anquetil had been struggling to introduce some Social Benefits to needy people in general. Prior to 1950, there was no old age pension.

"The old age pensioner has throughout the years paid taxes on commodities he has consumed as everybody else has. He has paid taxes on tea, sugar, tobacco, matches, rice, pulses, dried fish, rum, calico, and clothes etc., everything he has consumed and used to be able to live as a useful member of our society.

"One way or another he has contributed to the national budget. The Old Age Pension scheme being financed out of public funds is thus a contributory one. The Old Age Pension was paid since April 1950."

Those workers had given 40-45 years of their youth to build the Mauritian economy but after retirement they lived a very miserable life and were dependent on their children or near relatives and a very little amount from Old Age Pension.

The contributory National Pension scheme was approved by the National Assembly and assent given by the Governor General, His Excellency Sir Abdul Raman Osman in 1976.

Hon Luthmeeparsad Badry, the Minister of Social Security, had the responsibility to inform the public and the workers in particular, about the new Pension scheme. He was invited by the MBC/TV for a live interview to explain the New Pension scheme in detail. In general the interview was quite reasonable with one exception. On the quantum of Pension he wrongly said that was giving the guarantee that all members of the NPF payable would be entitled half their basic wage on retirement, which in fact was wrong according to the law.

The subsidy financed by the Fund was given to all participants who were aged 20 to 59 years in July of 1978. Workers who were older than 40 years of age in July 1978 received double the normal number of pension points for their contributions, thus a pension twice as large as they would be entitled to under normal rules.

Workers younger than 40, but at least 20 years old in July 1978 would receive sufficient bonus to qualify for the pension they would have received had they contributed at the same rate for a full 40 years. The formula for bonus points for this age group is (X-20)/(60-X), where X is age in July 1978, provided it is between 20 and 40. A worker who was 35 years old in 1978, for example, is credited with 15/25 (60%) more pension points, hence collects a 60% larger pension than would normally be payable, on retirement in the year 2003. A worker who was 21 years old when the scheme commenced received a subsidy of only 1/39, little more than a 2.5% increase in the pension that was payable beginning in the year 2117.

Example: I had contributed to the NPF since 1979 to 1997. At the date of my retirement my monthly salary was Rs 10,500. - The monthly pension was Rs 2,300. The disadvantage of this scheme that the employees and the employers contributed to a ceiling of Rs 3,600 in the year 1996, never in the lifetime of such employee will be able to receive a pension equivalent to 50% of his basic wage, because the employee and his employer have always contributed to the minimum not on full salary.

The Minister had given a wrong signal reading high aspiration in the new members of the NPF and also those who were members of the Sugar Industry Pension Fund.

The very next day a meeting was arranged with the Minister through the P.A.S. Mr Harry Ganoo to discuss about his Statement made. I had the opportunity to discuss the New Pension Scheme in detail with the P.A.S. prior to the interview of the Minister. The P.A.S. agreed with me that the quantum of Pension was not properly explained at the MBC T/V interview. It had created a lot of misunderstanding among the working class. The Minister agreed to organise a meeting with the workers at the Octave Wiehé - Auditorium, Le Réduit on a Friday. The Minister attended the meeting as scheduled, but he only made the opening speech, saying that he needed to attend an especial urgent meeting of the Parliament. Mr Harry Ganoo gave a very clear exposé in details on the NPF.

But problems did not end, as the Artisans of the sugar estates requested a detailed explanation of the difference between the NPF and SIPF. Luckily I had the opportunity to discuss the implementation of NPF with my Lecturer Mr Bert Monron from Canada, who was an expert on the issue during his Monitor course in Liberia. Furthermore, he was kind enough to give me the Complete Canadian National Pension Act. I had to organise around 25 meetings with the Artisans during lunch time with an additional one hour permission from the employer to attend the meeting. In fact there were benefits in National Pension Fund which did appear in the Sugar Industry Pension Fund and vice versa.

INTERNATIONAL AFFILIATIONS AND THEIR ADVANTAGES

Regarding affiliations, I felt that the AGWU needed to get more exposure to International Organisations by joining the International Trade Secretariat Organisations, especially to get support regarding educational materials and other assistance. I was convinced that only through Workers' education, we could build a solid trade unions organisation. In those days the International Trade Unions Movement was against the Communist Regime, one Party Systems and Military Rules. Mauritius was among the few countries, which was governed by Democratic Government. The AGWU was affiliated to the ICEF, but due to non payment of contribution its membership was cancelled. I re-applied for affiliation to the ICEF, without any difficulties and our Union was again accepted as affiliate.

Caption

Caption

Secondly, I also applied for affiliation with the International Federation Building and Wood Workers' (IFBWW). Unfortunately, the Construction and Building Workers' Union made an objection to our union affiliation. I had to write several letters, to explain our position. That the AGWU was among the few well structured Trade Unions with full time Officers and a registered Office. On the hand the union which had objected had only 25 members, the negotiator had done purposely, because he was receiving few overseas trips free of charge from the IFBWW, and he was not even a member of the Union, being a Higher Cadre of the Sugar Industry Labour Welfare Fund.

By coincidence I met Mr Chancy Kawassa of the International Federation Buildings and Wood Workers (IFBWW) of Geneva, the African Representative at a meeting of ICFTU, and after discussion he invited me to attend an African Regional Conference in Togo-Lome. The objecting union was represented by three delegates at the Central Committee Meeting in Togo-Lome. At the meeting, I discussed the matter with the General Secretary Mr Ulf Ask of IFBWW, and gave him the reason of the objection made by the CBWU. Needless to say, the AGWU got its' affiliation.

Thirdly, we applied for affiliation with the International Metal Workers' Federation, and a similar scenario was repeated. The Electrical & Mechanical Workers Union which had around 125 members objected to the affiliation of the AGWU. This time I got the support of Brother John Gould of the AALC, the African Representative, who introduced me to an Executive Board Member of the IMF, who was the General Secretary of the

International Association of Machinists & Aerospace Workers and the IMF agreed to the affiliation of AGWU. Later I also applied for affiliations with the Transport General Workers Federation, London, and the International Union of Food, Hotel, Restaurant Catering and Allied Workers' Federation (IUF) Geneva. As our union was already well known in the circle of International Trade Union Organisations, the two IT'S voluntarily accepted the affiliation of AGWU.

It is important to mention that the AGWU got trade unions solidarity during strikes, especially whenever Government wanted to introduce anti union legislations and the Trade Union Labour Relations Bill. In this connection, the IMF supported the AGWU by financing seminars and workshops for the Trade Union leaders and rank and file members locally and several members of the AGWU got the opportunities to follow courses abroad, attending Conferences. The union got a lot of educational materials and books. As a member of the ITS we were regularly invited to attend International Conferences through our five ITSs namely: IMF, IFBWW, ICEF, IUF and TGWF Air tickets, hotel accommodations and petty expenses were born by the ITSs.

Chapter 18

MY FIRST
OFFICIAL MISSION OVERSEAS

THE MLC, as an affiliate of ICFTU, entertained good relations with the American Federation of Labour – Congress of Industrial Organisation (AFL-CIO) and African American Labor Center. Hon Hurrypersad Ramnarain the first President of the MLC, had already established relations with Mr Irving Brown the President of AFL-CIO.

In 1978, after a new team took over the management of MLC, the AALC started helping the MLC in the field of "workers' education" through Mr John Gould the African Representative. In the 70s the economic situation of Mauritius was in a bad shape. Some 10 years earlier Mauritius had got its political independence from Britain on 12th March 1968, and a certain number of economic problems were inherited as well.

The attempt to solve the main acute problem of unemployment through the Import-substituting Industrialisation (ISI) strategy had not worked as expected. In fact, it was plainly disappointing. The number of jobs created through the Development Certificate Scheme was not enough to cope with the rate of growth of the labour force which was nearly 3% per annum. The direct consequence was a very high rate of unemployment lying between 15% and 20% of the labour force, in the 1960s.

The 1970s the government was very much interested to re-activate the co-operative movement to solve part of the unemployment problem through co operative organisations.

Economics Situation
in the Year 1960s and 1970s'

The growth of the Mauritian economy during the 1960s was slow and uneven; it averaged less than one per cent per annum. The sugar sector was still the dominant economic force in the economy, accounting for practically all the export earnings. At the same time, the biggest employer of labour was the government itself, with 59,030 employees. 25,528 worked for the Central Government and 2625 were employed by the local government (municipalities and district councils). The remaining 30,877 (i.e., more than 50% of government employees) were "relief workers". These were unemployed persons who were employed by the government of the day before the important general elections of August 1967, which was to decide the issue of independence. This measure was an electoral ploy used to woo the electorate and to

A Brief History Of **Trade Unionism** In Mauritius

encourage them to vote in favour of independence rather than against it. These "relief workers" worked for only four days a week on various public works projects, which were vague, ill-designed and uncoordinated...

AALC Co-operative Workshop Lesotho

To promote co-operative movement, the AALC invited a delegation of 4 Mauritian from the Ministry of Co-operative, MLC, MACOSS and GSA to attend the workshop, which was held at Holidays Inns, Maseru- Lesotho, The Ministry of Co-operative was represented Mr Chiranjivi Motee, Registrar of co-operatives; Mr Rajpalsingh Allgoo Assistant General Secretary of MLC, Mr Malleck Amode President of GSA and Mr André Fanny Director of MACOSS.

This workshop was attended by Representatives of several African countries; the courses were conducted by eminent lecturers from different universities of Africa and Europe. The subjects were Co-operative Movement in Europe and Africa; Co-operative Laws; the Organising Techniques, etc. It was a good opportunity to enrich our knowledge. We were welcomed by the Lesotho Trade Union Congress and the Officials of the Lesotho Ministry of Co-operatives. During our stay they organised several visits to Credit Co-operative Societies and Labour Department and also few site visits.

On our way back home, we had to spend three (3) nights in Johannesburg in order to get our Connecting fight to Mauritius. The Registrar of Co-operatives seized this opportunity to discuss with the South African Agent who was buying tea from Mauritian companies.

We were all new to the place; we spent the first night at the Holiday Inn, which was in the premises of the Airport. The next day Mr Motee called the South African Agent to discuss his business and also drove us to the city at Johannesburg Hotel, a three star hotel less expensive. The White Agent very politely dropped us at the Hotel under the pretext that he was going outside the City. In fact, those days South Africa was under the regime of apartheid and the white people would not be happy to see a white driving black people.

When I returned to Mauritius, I wanted to put in practice my experience at the service of the workers, but unfortunately due to lack of funds, the MLC was not in a position to implement the project, by creating the co-operative societies and even the Credit Union, because the worker's salary was not enough to make both ends meet. Fortunately later in the 1980s', the MLC had been successful in creating several Credit Unions and other Co-operative organisations in different fields, only in the year 1984.

Chapter 19

THE CREATION OF
THE NATIONAL TRANSPORT
CORPORATION

In August 1979, the General Workers' Federation/MMM had organised a general Strike in the main economic sectors such as: - Dock and Port; Bus Transport Industry; Sugar Industry; C.E.B; Sacks Factory; Tea Industry Municipalities; etc. Reason of the strike:

(i)   A General wages increase of 30 percent;
(ii)   40 hour week;
(iii)   Recognition of SILU & UASI

As a result of the GWF/MMM strikes, several companies went bankrupt, including the following:- UBS; Moka Flacq Bus Transport company Ltd.; Savanne Bus Transport Company Ltd., Northern Bus Transport Company Ltd.; Montagne Long Bus Company Ltd and Vacoas Bus Transport Company Ltd. At (VTC) alone 1,200 workers lost their jobs.

The strikes were declared illegal and as a consequence, thousands of workers with 20 years of service lost their jobs without any payment of compensation. As a result, some the workers found themselves in a very difficult financial situation and lived very miserably and did not even know, how to feed their families. It was very sad to note that when they could not bear the unfortunate misery some people even had recourse of suicide.

These strikes coupled with previous strikes since 1971 had dislocated the fragile Mauritian Economy, which was by the brink to economic collapse. And add to it the second oil shock that hit the country badly.

Despite an initial reluctance, the first IMF/WFSAP was undertaken and government had cut subsidies and devaluated the rupee by an initial 30 percent. Needless to say that Mr Veerasamy Ringadoo, Minister of Finance, became very unpopular in the country. On the other hand unemployment reached around 20 percent–affecting mainly the youths over 18 and it became an additional burden on the head of the family.

A few months after the closing down of the Vacoas Transport a delegation headed by B. Khedhun Conductor, Purmessur, Driver came to MLC Office. They met C. Bhagirutty and me, to request help. They had planned to start a small company using the redundant workers, renting Vacoas Bus Transport company busses. They suggested Government could help by setting up a new company without spending huge amount of money. The MLC leaders met the Prime Minister Sir Seewoosagur Ramgoolam and explained the plan to him. The Prime Minister understood the hardship of the workers and agreed. He said "Right now we are in a difficult financial situation. But with your help, we can overcome that."

During our meeting with Prime Minister SSR, he also exposed to us how the country had been economically affected due to the GWF/MMM strikes since 1971 up to dated in 1979.

In those days the Labour Party wanted to introduce Workers' Participation as an antidote to Nationalisation. It had taken a decision at its' 1978 Congress, to introduce Workers' Participation in our Industrial Business through a motion of Sir Seewoosagur Ramgoolam, Prime Minister and Leader of the Labour Party, to introduce workers participation in management in order to bring industrial democracy in the country. At the MLC we can proudly say that we had the first workers' Participation introduced on the National Transport Corporation. Provision was made for three Employees to represent the employees on the Board of Management.

The Vacoas Transport Company stopped its operations in August 1979; the Government took the decision to offer employment to the redundant workers of VTC and took over the assets on a hire basis and the NTC started its operation on 12 March 1980. In 1983, the MMM/PSM Government made legislative provisions for a compulsory acquisition of the assets of Vacoas Transport Company. These assets were incorporated within the NTC.

To Manage the NTC as Para-Statal Body, Government appointed Mr Saratty the Ex-Manager of DWC who had a good experience in management and few public officers were seconded for duty to the CNT Office in Vacoas. The workers and the public should be thankful to Mr Saratty for his good work and planning to make CNT a valuable company from scratch.

The MLC succeeded in introducing the Workers participation at the NTC which was an antidote to the nationalisation programme of the MMM.

The Joint Negotiation Council

In June 1980, a Management Consultative Council was set up, comprising seven representatives of management and nine elected representatives of the employees. The council was a forum where Workers' Representatives were allowed to voice their opinions, suggestions and grievances. The Transport Corporation Employees Union and the Union of Bus Industry Workers were given joint recognition by the NTC in May 1982. The Joint Negotiation Council was meeting once every month and was provided the opportunity to raise various issues regarding the methods of work, training, discipline, promotion, and leave with pay for Workers' Education and Welfare activities.

I acted as Negotiator and helped them on a voluntary basis to recruit members, set up their office, and attended all disciplinary Board and also the Joint Negotiation Council which was meeting at least once monthly, where the two recognised unions had the opportunity to discuss workers' grievances and the other general problems concerning the company. I still remember the collaboration of Mr Doolub of UBIW and this had helped us during negotiation with Management. I appreciated the stand of the UBIW. In those days they fully co-operated with the TCEU and showed the unity of Trade Unions for which I am thankful to them. After giving the trade union leaders training in Industrial Relations in including negotiation skill for nearly four years, they took over; in difficult case I did intervene.

The Employee Directors had the same status as other directors who were sitting on the Board.

To conclude I can say MLC as a Responsible Trade Union under my direction, did its utmost to help and get back the VTC workers, into the new company of the CNT and also set up the National Corporation Employees Union. But the recent events at the CNT make me very painful to see how the CNT has become nearly bankrupt, with the above safeguards?

Chapter 20

International Workshop
AIFLD-F.O.-AALC,
in Washington

In 1981, The African American Labour Centre invited la Confédération de la Force Ouvrière de France, the Mauritius Labour Congress and the Government Servants Association to attend a "Special Course" from June 1 - 12, 1981, at George Meany Centre – Washington - USA. This was the first time the George Meany College had organised such a workshop for the benefit of the French speaking countries.

The participants in the workshop were from affiliated trade unions of the Force Ouvrière, the MLC & the GSA. The following persons followed the course: Six participants from Guadeloupe; three from French Guyana; five from Martinique; One from Réunion Island; One from St. Pierre et Miquelon; One from Sénégal; two from Mauritius: Rajpalsingh Allgoo (MLC) and Alex Renold Talary (GSA); and André Frey Director of Workers Education of Confédération Force Ouvrière.

On our arrival at the Washington Airport, we were welcomed by the delegates of the Centre and AALC. Arrangements were made for the participants to stay on the campus of the Centre.

At the official opening, the leaders of the AFL-CIO, AALC addressed the participants as well as a group of 30 people who were already following a different course at the Centre; a special welcome was given by Mr André Frey. They AFL-CIO representative, welcomed us and gave an exposé regarding the creation of George Meany Centre.

Caption

The director of George Meany Centre, Professor P Joseph Campos gave details of the centre and he talked on the life and mission of William George Meany the President of AFL-CIO.:

William George Meany (August 16, 1894 – January 10, 1980) led in the United States. As an officer of the represented the AFL on the during .

Caption

Meany served as President of the (AFL) from 1052 to 1055 and as President of the AFL he proposed in 1052 and managed in 1055 its merger with the (CIO). He served as President of the combined from 1055 to 1070. Meany had a reputation for personal integrity, opposition to corruption and anti-communism. George Meany was called the "most nationally recognized labour leader in the country" for the more than two decades spanning the middle of the 20th century.

THE AFL-CIO ESTABLISHED
THE GEORGE MEANY CENTRE FOR LABOUR STUDIES

The AFL-CIO established the George Meany Centre for Labour Studies in Silver Spring – Maryland in 1074. The Centre was renamed the "National Labour Centre – George Meany Campus also housed the George Meany Memorial Archives.
The National Labour College is the only accredited higher education institution in the United States devoted exclusively to educating union members, leaders, and staff. It was established as a training centre by the in 1060 to strengthen union members' education and with the organizing skills. Etc.

Professor Compos introduced the Programme of the following two weeks, with the main subjects:

1. First lectures were given by Professor Dr. Ducarmel Boacage on the Economics situation in the region – Comparative Economic Systems – Employments – Social Structures in French-speaking Caribbean;
    - Comparative labour Movements – The Labour Movement in France and French -speaking Caribbean – (a) Development of trade Unions, (b) National labour confederations (c) Trade unions in the Society by Professor Andre Frey
    - Development on Trade Unionism around the World; the Trade Union movements and the ideologies in different Countries' East and West;
    - Role of international Trade Union Organisations including ILO - The Role of International Trade Secretariat by Professors Daniel Harowitz and James Ellenberger;

2. Democracy in Developing Countries by Professor Dr William A. Douglas;
    - Dictatorships in developing ,(a) Closed societies in developing countries, (b) Social organisation under totalitarianism; (c) Political process and social Structure By Professor: Dr Luis Aguilar

3. Labour and Political Systems: (a) Trade unions under totalitarian rule, (b) labour in economic and social development under democratic rule, (c) Trade unions in modern times; Marxism, Neo-Marxism, social democracy, populist and centrist movements by Professor Daniel Montenegro

4. Advance Collective Bargaining: 1. Introduction, (2) The National Income; (3) Supply and Demand: (4) Income Distribution; (5) Labour Economics (6) Economic Development (7) International Economics by Professors: Murchison Henry; Josef Solterer; Louis Rodriguez and William A.Douglas.

5. Labour in the Modern World: (Panel Discussion) by Professors: Andre Frey; Dr William A. Douglas and Daniel Montenegro.

The course ended on 12th June 1981.We had a break of 2 days and opportunity was given to visit the White House, the USA President's residence, the Capitol, the American House of Parliament and an Aero Spatial Museum in Washington and other places.

A Special Graduation Ceremony was organised on the 15th June, everyone got Certificates from the Heads of the AFL-CIO, Dean of the University. All the participants went on an excursion tour by Coach to New York. We got the opportunity to stay there for 4 days and visited several important places including United Nations Head Quarters; Empire Building and Statue of Liberty. On the fourth day everyone returned to their respective countries. I still keep a very good souvenir of this trip to America.

I am thankful to the AALC for having given me the opportunity to follow a very important Special Course on Labour Laws of different countries. This course combined with the Monitors' Course which I followed in Liberia with the ICFTU had helped me in my day to day Trade Union activities and especially during the time I was delivering lectures on Workers' Education.

Chapter 21

WORKERS' PARTICIPATION & LABOUR RELATIONS SYSTEM IN MAURITIUS

T HE system of labour relations in Mauritius has been conditioned by its peculiar colonial history, the structure of its plantation economy with a very heavy reliance on sugar, its oligarchic and monopolistic ownership pattern, and its autocratic and pyramidal management structure. The multi-unions system complicated legislation and its institution framework, the composition of its multi-racial, multi-religious, and multi-linguistic population. In recent years, International Monetary Institutions like the IMF and the World Bank have also been exercising strong influence on labour relations in the context of a heavily indebted import-export economy with a structural balance-of-payments deficit situation.

The agricultural heritage, however, and in particular slavery and the indentured labour system and the plantation economic framework, had heavily influenced patterns and style of management in the sense that an autocratic and paternalistic authoritarian style of administration has been transferred into industrial set-up from an agricultural one when industrialisation was undertaken. Human and labour relations had been in the traditional agricultural zone. It has been poor historically. The "inter alia" may well have contributed to a secular decrease, since 1970, in the percentage of young people engaged in agriculture. Occupational aspirations to young Mauritians are in the direction of blue-collar and white-collar jobs; labouring class is perceived as being undignified. (See e.g. the Noel Report to the Chamber of Agriculture, 1973; Ah Chum; Hossenmamode and Gujadhur 1975).

Institution Framework in Mauritius

After the great labour unrest and manslaughter of 1937 and the recommendation of Hooper Commission of Enquiry in the sugar industry, the colonial Government had tended to intervene promptly by forcing the parties to settle their problems, in labour-management disputes failing which, by referring the matter to a Conciliation and Arbitration Boards or Arbitration Board. The practice of setting up conciliation and Arbitration Boards existed since 1938 and 1944 respectively, during the colonial Government. But, it was with the Government that large institutional provisions were made for the conduct of labour relations in the island.

Labour Ordinance No 71 of 1961 empowered the Minister of Labour and Industrial Relations to set up Wages Councils to provide adequate machinery for the effective regulation of Remuneration and other conditions of employment in any trade, industry or occupation. Accordingly two Wages Councils were set up in 1963 and the Industrial Relation Act of 1973.

In addition, under the Industrial Relations Act, 1973, the following institutions were set up, the NRB, PAT, IRC and Termination of Contracts of Service Board; Government created the Pay Advisory committee and the Pay Research Bureau in 1978. The objective of the PRB was the formulation of a pay policy for the country as a whole.

Collective Bargaining

Collective bargaining started in 1938 when an agreement was reached between the Wharves and Docks Workers Industrial Association and Port and Harbour Employers' Associations. In 1945 an agreement was reached between the Chamber of Agriculture and the Engineering and Technical Workers' Union relating to overtime due to artisans of the sugar industry. In 1962 not less than ten collective agreements were reached with the help of Conciliators. Initially, wages and leave privileges constituted the exclusive subject matter of collective bargaining but gradually bargaining covered a wider spectrum of grievances which included salary, hours of work, grading of workers, overtime, Housing allowance, gratuities, recognition and so on. There seems to have been, superficially, a certain tradition of voluntary Collective bargaining and legislative instruments to support it. (IRA)

The MMM and the Trade Union Movement were against the introduction of the Industrial Relations Act of December 1973. The Trade Union Movement as a united force opposed and denounced this anti union repressive industrial law. The MMM qualified the IRA "as la loi-baillon". This legislation was introduced after the industrial unrest of early 1970s' fomented by the MMM/GWF.

Select Committee on IRA in 1983

The MMM/PSM Government, that won a landslide victory in the general elections in June 1982, was well aware of the various problems regarding the IRA. The report of the Select Committee composed of Hon Jayen Cuttaree and Hon Kader Bhayat, proposed "to restore fundamental industrial relations rights to workers in general, to ensure the smooth development of industrial relations toward a participative pattern of society and to encourage the development of a strong and responsible trade union movement". The select Committee, inter alia, recommended the revision of the substantive aspects of the operations of the NRB and the PAT, establishment of a Permanent Conciliation Units of which the two social partners, would work in complete independence of the Minister the integration of the termination of contracts Service Board in the industrial relations machinery, the establishment of a Labour Relations Commission and a National Council for Industrial Relations. The Select Committee concluded that the institutional machinery provided for by the IRA had contributed to the decline of Collective Bargaining and that " the concept of compulsory arbitration should disappear from our legislation and that arbitration should be resorted to only when the workers agree to submit themselves to an arbitration body."

The select committee also recommended that provision be made in the new legislation (Trade Union and Labour Relations Act) to sanction the following: (1) acts of anti-union discrimination; (2) refusal by employer to recognise for collective bargaining purposes the bargaining agent, (3) the refusal to meet the bargaining agent, (4) refusal to bargain in good faith, (5) refusal to disclose information which is required for collective bargaining and (6) the refusal by the employer to discuss with a trade union representative of the legal rights of an employee. Furthermore, the Select Committee felt that, with their recommendations "the social partners would be encouraged to sort out their grievances by themselves instead of having, by compulsion, to look towards third-parties for settlement. The parties should be free to conduct the settlement of their disputes in any way they think fit.

1.   By the late sixties the need to promote more systematic workers' education was felt. The Mauritius Labour Congress sought and received aid from international organisations to train educators abroad and to organise training courses for its members locally. The Federation of Civil Service Unions was then affiliated with MLC. In 1971, the Friedrick Ebert Stiftung (FES), the German foundation, sent a resident representative to Mauritius who collaborated very closely with the MLC. Apart from giving technical aid, the FES financed educational programmes for workers. Those programmes gave a new impulse to trade union education and training. The University of Mauritius also collaborated in those programmes and a few seminars were organised seminars at the School of Administration. After this pioneering step by the MLC, emulation followed, and other unions drew up and implemented some programmes on their own. Another FES representative came to Mauritius in 1974, and the main activities of the foundation shifted from trade union to co-operative education. In the following few years, other international organisations joined to sponsor workers' education activities, namely the ILO. ICFTUand AALC.

MINISTRY OF LABOUR & INDUSTRIAL RELATIONS

2. In 1968, the Ministry of Labour, with the collaboration of the Danish Government launched a Workers' education pilot project. This project was very ambitious and was conducted on a fairly large scale. According to the report some fifty courses were organised throughout the Island and 2,000 trade union members attended these courses. Two courses for trade union instructors were also conducted at the University of Mauritius. Subjects such as labour laws and Economics were taught at different levels. Organisations such as MBC, the trade unions, Government Ministries and agencies and the University showed a keen interest and participated actively in the implementation of the project.

    In the report, the Danish Expert, Mr Silliman, made the following suggestions and recommendations:
    1) A national board be established to promote workers' education;
    2) Full-time educators be employed under the control of the National Board;
    3) Individual unions could organise elementary courses, which could cover subjects such as trade union work, labour laws and civics;
    4) Further courses could be organised at a workers' Education Centre-
    5) The School of administration of the University could organise advanced courses for Top leaders after completion of the elementary courses.
        In September 1976, the Ministry of Labour and Industrial Relations set up the first Workers' Education Advisory committee. The Advisory Committee had the following terms of reference:
        (a) To identify the categories of workers, their organisations and the educational needs in each case;
        (b) To suggest methods, techniques and organisations required to develop practical programmes to meet these needs.

The Committee was made up of two Government Officials, two employers' representatives and nine representatives of workers chosen from unions and federations. One of the officials acted as chairman.

Following the report the workers Education unit was set up in September 1977. The Workers Education is staffed with a senior labour officer assisted by one labour officer. At its very inception, the unit at the Ministry faced serious problems. The situation has not changed much. It has remained more or less the same, with one additional labour Officer and it is having the following problems:
(a) A limited budget;
(b) An inadequate staff and resource persons;
(c) Absence of equipment;
(d) Absence of a proper library on Workers' Education.

Most of the various education activities were implemented at the federation level. But very few federations, with the exception of the MLC, FCSU and FSCC, were conducting workers education activities in a systematic way. The MLC had taken the challenge to set up its own Workers' Education Committee since 1970s and having resource persons with experience in the field of workers education and in 1981 with two full time permanent staff. Later in 1984 it set up a workers education centre.

The Select Committee of 1983 on the IRA had even envisaged legislation to make the work Council compulsory in enterprises employing over 100 workers. It may be true that enterprises employing 100 workers constitute a small fraction of enterprises in the economy but it would be interesting to observe the trends and the various issues connected with Work Council in Mauritius.

The MLC was considering workers education as one of its main objectives. Consequently it has set up a Workers' Education Department with a permanent staff and Director of Education since 1981, responsible to prepare education materials to conduct seminars and workshops. It has been a pleasure for me to work with the team. The MLC had to face difficulties in its effort to implement the workers education programmes. The main problems were to negotiate the release of the participants with pay i.e. without any cut in wages and entitlements. If they did not wish to release the workers, Employers usually refused on ground of the exigencies of the service. The MLC had on several occasions requested the Government to rectify the ILO convention 140 on paid Education Leave but unfortunately it has not done so yet.

Negotiations took place between GSA officials and the university. A Two- year non-award course was launched for some GSA leaders at the University. These Courses were due to the stringent and rigid academic entry-requirements. After GSA, another similar course was mounted for the FSCC. A stumbling block in the organisation was faced at the University. Several trade union leaders despite having considerable experience in the field of industrial relations failed to qualify for admission because they did not possess the minimum academic requirements.

The select committee on IRA made mention of the urgent need for a comprehensive workers' education programme. The committee had taken note of the existence of a workers' Education Unit within the Ministry of Labour and Industrial Relations, but felt that the whole system should be reviewed so as to better equip workers to contribute to the social and economic development of the country. This involved a formation programme for the Trade Unionists as well as training courses in specialised subjects.

The committee recommended that legislation should, for the purpose of setting up a permanent workers' education programme, provide for the establishment of a *Workers' Education Council composed of members representing various social, cultural and economic interests.*

The Council's main function would be to organise and supervise the work of the workers' Education Unit as well as advise the Minister on all matters of policy relating to workers education. It also recommended that new legislation should provide for the establishment of a workers' education fund.

WORKERS PARTICIPATION PROJECT
IN MAURITIUS

The MMM-PSM alliance won a land slede victory without opposition in 1982 there even the Prime Minister Sir Seewoosagur Ramgoolam who led the country since 1948, who struggle for the Independence and succeeded in pulling the Union Jack down and replaced it by our quaricolor, lost his seat.

Unfortunately the new Government could not survive for more than nine months due to difference between the Prime Minister Hon Anerood Jugnauth and Hon Paul Raymond Bérenger Minister of Finance and the Government was dissolved.

Mr Anerood Jugnauth resigned as President and member of the MMM and set up a new political party, the Mouvement Socialiste Miliant. With the help of SSR and the Labour Party, he came to power once again in 1983. He changed his previous political strategy of *Nationalisation* of the Sugar Industry, Dock, Bank, Insurance companies, etc. As an anti-dote to Nationalisation, he proposed to introduced the Industrial Democracy by introducing the Workers Participation and amended the Company Law. In this line he requested the Mauritius Sugar Authority to send a delegation to study Workers' Participation in Germany and Sweden for a period of two weeks. The delegation was composed: Mr. Ramdaja the Secretary of MSA; Mr. Rajpalsingh Allgoo – AGWU; Mr. Jean Claude de Fontenay – SISEA; Mr. Priadursun Appadoo – PWU and Mr. Bidianand Jhurry – SILU. The delegation had the opportunity to visit and discuss with Trade Union Federations, the Employers Federations, different institutions dealing with Workers Participation in Germany as well in Sweden and the Government Officials. Back to Mauritius the delegation prepared a comprehensive Report to the Government, but as usual the Report remained the drawer of different Ministries.

It was only when the Government decided to withdraw levy on sugar, then the Prime Minister had made a deal with the Mauritius Sugar Producers' Association. Then the Government introduced the Workers' Participation in the Sugar Factories. This concerned the Sugar Workers and Small Planters to the tune of 20%.

Chapter 22

INDUSTRIAL DEMOCRACY
IN MAURITIUS

MODERN industrial economies had adopted several aspects of industrial democracy to improve productivity and as reformist measures against industrial disputes. Often referred to as "team working", this form of industrial democracy had been practiced in Scandinavia, Germany, The Netherlands and the UK, as well as in several Japanese companies including Toyota, as an effective alternative to Taylorism.

The term is often used synonymously with workplace democracy, in which the traditional master-servant model of employment gives way to a participative, power-sharing model.

INDUSTRIAL DEMOCRACY THROUGH
LITRA WORKSHOP

In Mauritius, the Industrial Workplace democracy was introduced by Mr Jack Bizlall at a time when Mauritius was facing economic crisis and severe unemployment problems in 1983, with a view to prevent redundancy at Cassis Ltd.

The Cassis Limited was one of our oldest workshops specialized in the production of heavy machinery for the sugar industry which started its operation in 1945. This company was owned by Genève Langlois and was taken over by Ireland Blyth Limited in 1973.

However, Cassis Limited started facing financial problems as from 1981 and accumulated losses of about Rs 3 million per annum in 1981 and 1982. As far back as 1978, workers had pulled the alarm on the deteriorating finance situation of the enterprise, blaming management of mismanagement, fraud and corruption. In the meantime, cost of production was going up dramatically, and various petitions were sent by workers representatives to Management. Relationship between Management and workers was strained and the latter resorted to demonstrations, sit-in and work stoppages to protest against what was considered gross mismanagement due to the incompetence of the management team.

In 1981, 54 employees, including 12 staff members were found to be redundant. In 1982 management informed the Cassis Limited Workers' Union, the official trade union of the enterprise's workshop workers that two alternatives existed as far as the fate of the enterprise was concerned?

(1)   Closedown of the enterprise; or
(2)   a "mini" Cassis Limited.

The Trade Union came up with a third proposal - takeover of the workshop by the workers.

However, it was soon found out that with the Rs 800,000. - of compensation; for 72 workers it would be practically impossible to take over the assets of Cassis Limited.

At the request of the Trade Union, Government appointed a Commission of Enquiry presided by Mr Daureeawoo to look into allegations of fraud, corruption and mismanagement. Management however refused to depose before the Commission and instead insisted that the matter be referred to the Termination of Contract Service Board (TCSB). The T.C.S.B. finally recommended that Rs 2.3 million in compensation be paid to workers, calculated on the basis of 5 weeks of compensation for each year of service and 4 ½ months of salary compensation.

Faced with the possibility of losing their jobs, employees of the enterprise decided to pool their efforts and takeover the enterprise from Ireland Blyth Limited. It was not an easy task to get all the 72 workers to agree on the proposal of takeover, but finally it was decided that the Rs 2.3 m of compensation could be invested in the enterprise.

NEGOTIATION
FOR THE TAKEOVER

According to Mr Roland Felix, the then President of the Cassis Limited Workers' Union and later Chairman of the Cassis Limited Workers' Union and Chairman of the Board of management of LITRA Workers' Union, "negotiations were held in a very cordial atmosphere in ensuring that negotiations were successful.

Management finally accepted responsibility for mismanaging the enterprise and the principle of takeover by workers was accepted too. However, Management imposed a date limit for the completion of negotiation: 31st March 1983.

Considering the delay too short, a strategy had to be worked out by trade union to get management to prolong discussions. The workers decided to occupy the premises of the Cassis Limited, a trade union action unknown in Mauritius till then. Starting on Monday 28th March 1983, the public and Police became aware of the trade union's action.

The occupation was illegal and warrants were issued to each individual worker by the Supreme Court. Workers were requested to appear before a disciplinary committee but they categorically refused to do so. After discussions, it was finally agreed that further negotiations would be held concerning modalities for the takeover.

This was a milestone in the history of workers emancipation and also insofar as a new tool in the hands of the workers in making their voice heard; workers occupied the premises for 45 days, spending day and night there.

It should be noted that during the period January to May 1983, work continued normally in the workshop, during which time, negotiations were being held.

GOVERNMENT CONTRIBUTED TO TAKEOVER

When workers proposed to take over the enterprise, Government ordered a Feasibility study to be carried out by Messrs Manraj of the Ministry of Finance and Rivaltz Chevreau de Montelu. The main finding of the Committee was that annual turnover should be around Rs 3.8 million to by break-even and this was possible according to studies made by trade union officials.

Government decided, consequently, to buy shares for the amount of Rs 750,000.-. Besides, Government provided the services of Mr Manraj as Financial controller to the newly born LITRA abbreviation for "Lalit Travayer".

MANAGEMENT OF
LITRA

LITRA was managed by a Board of Directors comprising 12 representatives of Workers, duly elected by the latter and 2 trade union officials who had no right to vote. Besides, Mr Jack Brizlall former negotiator of the trade union also attended the Board in his capacity as Secretary of LITRA but had no right to vote.

Unfortunately, this dream situation for a worker came to an end. And Litra closed its doors forever. But for many youngsters who do not know Mr Jack Brizlall, he is the trade unionist who made this dream come true. And for this, his great contribution in the history of trade union movement needs to be remembered.

Chapter 23

COMMISSION OF INQUIRY
ON THE SUGAR INDUSTRY, 1983

THE senior staffs of the sugar industry consisting almost exclusively of Whites have always been regarded with animosity and rancour by the workers. This feeling of ill-will was shared by Trade Unionists, politicians, small planters and the public in general, and it came to a peak towards the end of the 70s and early 80s. There was widespread suspicion and a perception of mismanagement in the sugar industry.

There was an outcry against the Whites of the industry who enjoyed fat salaries and fringe benefits like princely houses situated on land varying from 4 to 10 arpents depending on their status, cooks, maids, gardeners, drivers and several other perks. The vast army of workers consisting of labourers, artisans and small planters felt that they were being robbed of their fair share of benefits in order to finance the high life of the Whites.

A movement of protest was set afoot since long and a Commission of Inquiry was being pressed for in order to throw some light on the sugar industry and to put a stop to the shameful exploitation of the workers. The several conventions of the United Nations and the International Labour Organisation and the provisions of the Constitution of Mauritius were being regularly baffled.

After a long, relentless struggle that went on for years, the newly elected MMM-PSM Government under Prime Minister Anerood Jugnauth agreed to set up a Commission of Inquiry in 1982. On 24 December of the same year, His Excellency Sir Dayendranath

123

A Brief History Of **Trade Unionism** In Mauritius

Burrenchobay, Governor General of Mauritius, appointed a commission of Inquiry with the following members:

Dr Dragoslav Avramovic, Senior Adviser to UNCTAD, Chairman
Prof. Jagadish Manrakhan, Vice-Chancellor, University of Mauritius
Mr. Ramsamy Chedumbarrum Pillay, Director of Audit (later replaced by Mr. Rama Sithanen)

The object of the Commission was to inquire into all aspects of the sugar industry in Mauritius and everything relating thereto, with special regard to the following:

1. The organization and structure of the industry;
2. The ownership, control and organization of growing, processing and making units;
3. The relations between all categories of cane growers and the miller planters;
4. The finances and general economics of the industry;
5. The production of sugar and all related processes;
6. The by-products of the industry;
7. The local and international operations for the marketing of sugar, molasses and other by-products;
8. Employment and industrial relations in the industry including;
    i. The availability, training and utilization of manpower;
    ii. The productivity of labour;
    iii. The implications of mechanization;
    iv. The methods of recruitment at all levels;
    v. The terms and conditions of employment;
    vi. The remuneration of manpower at all levels taking into account fringe benefits;
    vii. Job contracting;
    viii. Health hazards and safety measures;
    ix. Amenities and facilities provided at site of work and housing estates;
    x. Measures to increase the socio-cultural welfare of all employees and workers;
9. Diversification in the industry;
10. Utilisation of the limited land resources and water resources of the country in relation to the industry.
11. Investment by the industry in non-sugar activities locally and abroad;
12. The legislation regulating the activities of the industry;
13. The need for a Sugar Authority;
14. Increased public sector participation in the industry;
15. The role of the industry in the Mauritian economy.

The Commission started its hearings as from 2 March 1983. More than 110 individuals and organizations deposed before the Commission of Inquiry, among whom:
    Mauritius Chamber of Agriculture – Jacques Koenig, Peter White
    Mauritius Sugar Producers' Association – Herve Koenig
    Mauritius Cane Growers Association
    Lalit – Mrs Lindsey Collen, Bernard Moutialoo, Bidianand Jhurry.

Organisation of Artisans' Unity –Souresh Moorba, Babet, Roy Ramchurn;
Mauritius Cooperative Agricultural Federation – N. Dookhony, Sidambarum
Sir Gaetan Duval
Artisans and General Workers' Union – Rajpalsingh Allgoo
Sugar Planters' Mechanical Pool – S. Issur
Plantation Workers Union – C.Bhagirutty, Baguant

I deposed on behalf of the Artisans and General Workers' Union on the following issues as per the memorandum submitted by the Union:
1.   The huge disparity in salaries and fringe benefits between the senior staff (etat-major) and the artisans and labourers;
2.   The forty-hour week;
3.   The deplorable state of sugar camps houses and other amenities;
4.   Social problems and social amenities;
5.   Health and sanitation;
6.   Human factors.

I deposed on 13th and 14th July 1983, and spoke lengthily on the points submitted to the Commission in the memorandum. I spoke about the unbelievable discrepancy that existed between the salaries of the senior staff and those at other levels of employment. I pointed out that the wages paid to the workers in general were hardly sufficient to enable them to lead a decent life with their families. The senior staffs, on the other hand, were drawing princely salaries together with untold fringe benefits and perks.

Regarding the 40-hour week for sugar industry workers I pointed to the stark injustice meted out to them. I argued that workers in the public sector observed 40-hour weeks since 1978, whereas those in the sugar sector were made to work much longer hours. That was most unfair, I told the Commission, that social justice, was baffled especially as the sugar workers were the ones who had been producing the wealth of the country. The MSPA always came with the same argumentation during negotiations, namely that they didn't have the money to afford a reasonable wage increase or to implement the 40-hour week. I provided facts and figures to prove that the introduction of the 40-hour week in the sugar industry was, after all, not such a burden as the MSPA was claiming.

I also made a clear exposé on the situation as regards the houses in the sugar camps. I explained that the employees of the sugar industry had been surviving in utterly depressing conditions all trough their existence. In1978, after pressures from the government and the unions, the straw huts had been replaced by more appropriate buildings, but the same insalubrious conditions of living were still being endured by the workers and their families. In many cases the new buildings were badly constructed and slabs from the ceiling were falling on the dwellers. Ventilation was poor or almost inexistent, the doors and windows were too small, the roofs were low and there was scanty lighting. The kitchens were tiny; there was hardly any privacy in the bathroom. In certain places, the inhabitants had to walk a distance of some 150 metres in order to go to the common toilet, without any lighting facilities at night. The premises were not tarred. I invited the Commission to visit some of the camps and see for themselves.

The Chairman and the members of the Commission subsequently visited a couple of these housing estates and were flabbergasted to notice the highly deplorable state of the housing units. They were simply shocked by the dirty goat pens and pig sties that were adjacent to the dwellings. I made a strong plea for the construction of new, proper dwellings for the workers. In the meantime, the existing houses should be urgently repaired and rendered more inhabitable. I also called for improvement works to be effected on the camp roads which were all untarred, muddy, deprived of drains and lighting.

Some of the other recommendations that I made were included:
- Sports and Leisure facilities. I advocated the construction of recreation centres with indoor games, sewing classes, a library, and other facilities.
- The provision of kindergartens and adequate facilities for infants as well as nurseries where working mothers could leave their babies while they were at work.
- An adequate system of drainage for the evacuation of water from bathrooms and kitchens.
- The existing communal latrines should be scrapped and replaced by more proper lavatories.
- Bins should be provided to each household and refuse collection should become a regular feature.

CONTRADICTORY REPORTS

In October 1983, two contradictory reports emanating from the Commission of Enquiry on the Sugar Industry landed on the table of Sir Dayendranath Burrenchobay, Governor-General of Mauritius. One report was submitted by the chairman of the Commission Dr, Dragoslav Abramovic, and a dissenting report came from the two members, Prof. Jagadish Manrakhan and Mr. Rama Sithanen.

This sent a chill down the spines of all those who had pinned large hopes on the findings of the Commission. The small planters, their trade union representatives and politicians were utterly disappointed.

ABRAMOVIC'S REPORT – SALIENT POINTS

1. The Mauritius sugar economy is in trouble. After three unprofitable years, 1980-1982, it is likely that the sugar estates with factories have experienced a major loss on their sugar activities in1983. Sugar is being produced under a severe financial strain. Fixed investment has virtually collapsed. Failure to maintain irrigation canals, coupled with sharply rising electricity and water charges has severely affected the crops. Activities in the engineering industry, producing and repairing sugar mill machinery and equipment, have been reduced sharply,

causing large layoffs and attempted closures of smaller plants. Several sugar estates have been selling land and their non-sugar investments; this has included distress sales to non-Mauritian interests.

2.   The deterioration in the performance of the sugar industry is due to rising costs of production resulting from low average sugar cane outputs, rising financial costs, and depressed prices at which about 15% of the output is sold. Its tax system is bringing adverse results. No account is taken in levying the tax of cost increase and falling profit margins, and this has led to a perverse result that the tax has been raising as income has been shrinking. Furthermore, as the export tax is levied at graduated rates inversely related to the size of output, with total exception for small holders, it induces parcellisation of land leading to a loss of fiscal revenue and entailing less productive uses of land in crop yield and in real estates.

3.   The present tax system is also inappropriate for the periods of high sugar prices as it fails to capture for the nation as a whole most of the resulting windfall gains.

4.   Urgent action is needed to enable and encourage the resumption of investment in fixed assets; raise the ability of planters to pay for water and other inputs; facilitate recovery of real wages; and generally assist the financially pressed sugar sector. Other issues to be addressed include: better organization and management, stabilization of costs, rehabilitation of existing waterworks and construction of new reservoirs, promotion of growth and diversification, expansion of exports of sugar-mill machinery and equipment, etc.

5.   The tax system needs to be overhauled and a systematic planning and policy for the industry should be instituted. The export tax should be abolished and replaced by the excess profits tax on windfall gains at high rates.

6.   The government revenue loss resulting from the abolition of the export tax would in part be recouped through higher receipts of the company income tax. Substitute sources of revenue, or reduction of expenditures, would have to be found.

7.   The establishment of a Sugar Authority is recommended in order to ensure systematic planning and policy, to coordinate the activities of the different government departments and private organizations dealing with the sugar industry, to regularly review the industry's economic and financial performance, problems and prospects, and to provide guidelines for future development.

8.   These recommendations are based on the assumption that the ownership of the estates, which is almost entirely private, changes gradually through the acquisition of shares and other properties by a workers' managed investment fund. Should it be concluded that the abolition of the export tax is not acceptable to the population at large unless it is accompanied by a swifter ownership change, an immediate nationalization of all sugar estates with factories and of large individual planters' properties should be considered.

9. The third alternative is to do nothing across the board and instead to try to solve the individual company or planters' groups' problems as they arise, hoping that a succession of good years and a price boom may improve the situation. A favourable turn of events is possible, although views will differ as to its timing. If it fails in the near future and the existing mechanisms remain in force, it would be difficult to manage the situation. While emergency financing is inevitable at present in order to carry on with work and maintain employment in a number of plants, it is essential that a comprehensive plan covering the next three years period be prepared as soon as possible. It is interesting that the government is now preparing such a plan.

10. A factor of growing importance in the crisis of the sugar economy and the general difficulties which Mauritius is experiencing is the high rate of interest domestically. Borrowers other than Government now pay close to 10% per year in real terms. The Government has already reduced the domestic rates somewhat, but it is suggested that it proceeds with further reductions to the extent possible, and that it joins other countries in efforts to explore urgently the international measures that may be taken to cut down the rate to a level which would permit the debtors to survive, expand productions, service the debts, and contribute to economic recovery.

DISSENTING REPORT

The two other members of the Commission of Inquiry into the Sugar Industry, Prof Jagadish Manrakhan and Mr. Ramakrishna Sithanen subsequently submitted a dissenting report to the Governor General, entitled "The Human Factor, the Sugar Industry of Mauritius: A vision for the future."

In the introduction they wrote, inter alia: "It was in the evening of Friday 30 September 1983 that we received, well behind schedule, the draft Commission Report (with attached draft staff papers which had largely ignored our views) from the Chairman... We worked flat out during that weekend discovering, even after Chapter 1 of the draft Commission Report, just how wide was the gulf between us and the Chairman on fundamental matters concerning the sugar industry. We went on to list all the points of difference, major and minor. On Monday 3rd October 1983, we called for a Commission meeting during the course of which we tried to bridge the wide gulf between our stand and that of the draft report by questioning the basic assumptions underlying the latter. We succeeded in getting nowhere fast on that track. Nor were we anymore successful in discussing other items we had listed and where disagreement existed. The Chairman insisted that we should give reasons for not accepting the draft recommendations that we should spell out in detail our own views and the reasoning to support the latter. We pointed out that we would indeed do so...We believe it is only fair to state, here and now, that from all the evidence we heard and examined in the context of the present Commission of Inquiry, we are firmly convinced that the fundamental problem in the Sugar Industry is one of human relationships. The latter have constituted the starting point in our analysis, paving the way to our subsequent recommendations.

Salient Features

The two Commissioners anticipated very difficult days for the Sugar Industry over the next 30 months and strongly suggested that Government "should prepare itself to inject state financial aid." They thus recommended that, starting from January 1984, the following measures should be implemented.

1. Transform the proposed Sugar Authority into functional reality.

2. Render the export duty more flexible, less blunt and more sensitive to changing circumstances.

3. Prepare and conduct an Independent Audit of all millers and miller-planters.

4. Prepare a feasible and viable centralization and rehabilitation plan for the sugar-milling sector, integrated within an industry-wide plan for large-scale electricity generation from bagasse.

5. Examine how best to improve the performance, and hence the well-being, of small planters.

6. Work out how best to cope with the 'human factor' in the sugar industry.

The Dissenting Report contained a great number of observations among which:

*   the corporate section of the industry operates with high efficiency in field and factory operations;
*   when it comes to the overall planning of the industry there are clear-cut signs of deficiency, if not reluctance, on the part of those who might reasonably have been expected to perform such tasks.
*   the industry generally is poor in handling the human factor;
*   the financial position of the industry, while precarious for the moment, is not the main fundamental problem it faces;

There's a long list of recommendations, among which we have picked up the following:

-   The setting up of a Sugar Authority

-   State aid should be channelled through the Sugar Authority wherever applicable.

-   The principle of meritocracy should be observed in formulating salary structures and fringe benefits and in promotions. There should be no aid to firms engaging in colour or racial prejudice.

- Small shareholders in the sugar industry should not be unduly penalized.

The Dissenting Report further recommends that the Sugar Authority should take over the overall planning of employment and industrial relations, including:

I.   Availability, utilization and productivity of manpower;
II. Recruitment and training; equality of opportunity, avoidance of discrimination;
III. Implications of mechanization;
IV. Providing advice on terms and conditions of service, including remuneration, fringe benefits and retirement benefits, at all levels of the sugar industry;
V.   Employee welfare generally, and public relations of the industry; and
VI. The special problems facing youth and women.

Another recommendation is for the Sugar Authority to examine, soon after its setting up, the following outstanding issues:

I.   he production costs of all categories of cane and sugar producers;
II. The method and rate of depreciation;
III. The valuation of assets;
IV. The transfer of assets from sugar to non-sugar activities and the determination of the extent, if any, of asset-stripping, past and present.
V.   The determination of a fair rate of return on capital employed in growing and milling;
VI. Inadequate expenditure.

The Sugar Authority must also be called upon to establish:

1.   A Special Fund by which the State would come to the assistance of individual milling firms which face financial problems in exchange of shares;

2.   A Second Special Fund for small planters.
     The two dissenting members of the Commission write: "We are against the abolition of the export duty and recommend accordingly. However, we are of the view that certain modifications should be brought about in the export duty in order to render it more flexible, more dependent on prevailing circumstances, to act as an incentive to increased yield among planters at the margin, as well as to stabilize government revenue possibly through insurance mechanisms. We draw attention to what we thought was detected to be a feeling that the export duty is some kind of legalized daylight robbery and of dangers to society of such thinking."

On the issue of appointments, the Dissenting Report recommends that

I. All permanent and pensionable posts in the sugar industry be filled on the basis of public or industry-wide advertisements or through recruitment via the Employment Exchange;

II. No one should hold any permanent and pensionable post in the industry beyond the age of 60; there is no objection to persons beyond that age being employed on a part-time or full-time contract basis, provided such employment does not constitute barriers to promotions for those on permanent and pensionable establishments;

III. The industry must rationalize its recruitment and promotion policy to give equal opportunity to all those talents who deserve it, regardless of ethnic belonging and colour;

IV. To avoid recurrence of reported cases of discrimination, abuse of authority and sexual exploitation, the various trade unions in the sugar industry, the MSPA and the Mauritius Employers' Federation should collaborate to produce a Code of Conduct for all Sugar Industry employees.

Concerning the marketing of sugar and its by-products, the two members of the Commission recommend that all local marketing of sugar and the local and overseas marketing of molasses be taken over by the Mauritius Sugar Syndicate with an obligation on the latter to dispose of all molasses at the most remunerative prices possible. The totality of molasses deemed to have been produced from the planters' canes should accrue to the planters.

On the issue of the 40-hour week raised by Mr. Allgoo before the Commission, the two commissioners write:

"It is our understanding that the Government has taken, or is taking, a decision on the question of the 40-hour week in the Sugar Industry. In case our understanding is incorrect, we recommend that the National Remuneration Board be urged to expedite matters towards a conclusion one way or the other of this important matter."

The two reports were received with mixed feelings, in the hope that the recommendations that were favourable to the workers in general would be implemented as soon as possible by all those concerned.

Chapter 1

LABOUR STUDY TOURS
IN THE
UNITED KINGDOM

IN January 1983 the New Government MMM/PSM awarded a study tours to U.K., to four Trade Unionists namely: Mr Rajpalsingh Allgoo Director, Organisation of the MLC, Mr Krishnadeo Totayswar Dinnaram Treasurer of SILU, Mr Serge Claude Archimede Frichot, Assistant Secretary of FSSC and Mr Showkutally Soodhun President of FTU. We left Mauritius on 28th January 1983. On our arrival at Heathrow Airport the next day by 6.20 a.m. we were welcomed by Mrs Philippa Urmston of the Central Office of Information, who accompanied us to official appointments in the London area and then continued to St. Ermine Hotel, Caxton Street, London SW1. On Sunday 30th January we were free for sightseeing. I knew London from my previous visit, so I guided my friends to important places such as Buckingham Palace, Big Ben, Parliament, etc.

On 31st January at 10.00 am, we met Mr Dennis Smith, Director of Overseas Visitors and Information Studies Division of the Central Office of Information. There Mr Tim Lewis discussed the programme. Afterwards we met Mr David Moat, African Group Head, Visit Section who was newly appointed to represent the Foreign and Commonwealth Office.

At 11.00 a.m., we arrived at the Foreign and Commonwealth Office, King Charles St. SW1. We were received by Mr R.J. Barkley, Deputy Overseas Labour Adviser and he gave an exposé of the activities of his Organisation. I made an introduction on the MLC, and informed them that the union entertained good relations with his Organisation since a long time. Mr D. H. Doble, Assistant Head of East African Department, of the Foreign and Commonwealth Office, met us at the Kundun Restaurant, 3, Horse Ferry

A Brief History Of **Trade Unionism** In Mauritius

Caption

Road, SW1. We arrived at the Advisory Conciliation and Arbitration Services, where we were received by Mr Dennis Boyd, Chief Conciliation Officer for discussion on the role of ACAS. I can say it was a very enriching experience for me and I had requested on other meeting to discuss in detail our Industrial Relations Commission (IRC). ACAS is a very well established Independent Institution:

THE ADVISORY, CONCILIATION AND ARBITRATION SERVICE

The Advisory, Conciliation and Arbitration Service (ACAS) is a Crown of the . Its purpose is to improve organisations and working life through the promotion and facilitation of strong practice. It may do this through a number of mediums such as or , although the service is perhaps best known for its collective function - that is resolving disputes between groups of employees or workers, often represented by a , and their employers. ACAS is an independent and impartial organisation that does not side with a particular party, but rather will help the parties to reach suitable resolutions in a dispute. Harmonious workplace relationships are essential to get optimum business efficiency. Even minor problems can develop into grievances or disputes if they're not dealt with quickly and effectively. This is true of issues involving individuals or groups (including trade unions or other representatives).

Acas Helpline Online: This new automated system learns from your questions and, as more people use it, will get better at providing the most relevant answer to your query. We will be tracking any un-answered questions and, in each case, considering whether to add them to the system to help it fit your needs as closely as possible.

On 1st February we left the hotel by car and arrived at the British Trade Union Congress, 23-28 Great Russell St. WC1, where we were welcomed by Mr Barry Bennett, International Department, and Carl Wright, Commonwealth Trade Union Council. They gave us a brief exposé of their organizations and they requested us to introduce our Unions and their activities. I again gave a brief of MLC, as a National Trade Union organization representing around 20,000 workers. However, it was fun to listen Mr Soodhun saying that FTU do have 20,000 members while Mr Dinnaram said that the GWF had 35,000 members, and by courtesy I kept quiet. As the MLC had good working relations with the BTUC since they belong to the same International Confederation the ICFTU, Mr Wright invited me alone to discuss the industrial Relations in Mauritius. Afterwards, I met him and we had a lengthy discussion and provided a lot of materials and had lunch together.

At 14.30, we went to the Industrial Society, at Robert Hyde House, 48 Bryanston Square, W1, we were received by Mr David Crowley, Director of International Services, for discussions on the work of the Society.

NEWCASTLE-UPON TYNE

On the next day we left our hotel by car with our luggage, for King Cross Station and left London by 10.00 hours, (reserved seat) and had lunch on the train and arrived at Newcastle Central Station, we were met by Mrs Anna Gay of the Central Office of Information, North Eastern Region, and continue by car to the Park Hotel, Tynemouth, Tyne and Wear, where accommodation was reserved for five days. We arrived at the Regional Trade Union Congress Headquarters at 31, Mosley St., Newcastle, where we were received by Bob Howard, Regional Secretary for discussions with Mr Howard and other members of the staff, regarding trade union situation in the countryside.

On 3rd February, 9.30 hours we visited the Office of ACAS, at Westgate House Road. We had a group discussion with Mr Alan Carr, Manager together with Mr Ken Chambers and Mr Alan Hogan Senior Industrial Relations Officer, on the role of the regional functions of ACAS, and on Collective Conciliation. It was a very fruitful discussion where I learnt the method of British conciliation with Employers and sometimes between different Trade Unions Leaders. Our Commission for Conciliation and

Meditation (CCM) operates slightly on the lines of ACAS, I am of opinion that the CCM will be fully independent and be provided with necessary staff and "encadrement" with required documentation, with a special Department with professionals to train the Trade Unionist on proper Collective Bargaining Technic and industrial Relations Legislations in line with ACAS. I am confident that the Industrial Relations between employees, employers and Government will be much better.

At 11.00 hours we were received by Mr Edwin Grieves, the Headmaster of Langley Avenue First School and we were introduced to the Staff members and pupils. It was a great opportunity for my friend Frichot as teacher to study the method and principle, we discussed with students within one hour in different classes, and we were invited for lunch with the Teaching Staff. I personally got the opportunity to learn quite a bit on the English way of negotiating. Then we moved to the Newcastle College of Art and Technology at Maple Terrace, Newcastle, and Mr Ken Harrington, Head of School explained the education programme and we had interesting discussions when we were touring the classes. Mr Harrington introduced us to the Lecturer and students on Health and Safety at work.

On 4th February we visited the Social Services, Pen Dower Special School for the mentally Handicapped and Home for the Elderly. We met Mr Frank Graham, Deputy Director of Social Services, for discussions on the work of his department. We returned to Civil Centre for further discussions. On the 5th sightseeing tours were organized by car to the North Shields Fish Quay, Bamburgh Castle, and Holy Island, Seas houses, Alwick and Northumberland countryside. In the Evening we visited the local working Men's club.

On the 6[th,] we visited the historic University and the City of Durham and in the afternoon we went to watch a Football match between Newcastle and Nottingham. On 7th February at 8.00 hours we left the Park Hotel for Newcastle Central Station by train and reached London, King Cross Station by 12.00 hours and were met by Mrs Urmston and preceded to St. Ermin Hotel. After lunch we went to the Africa Centre at 38, King Street. WC 2. There we were received by Dr Alastair Niven, the Director General for a tour of the Centre Dr Niven gave a description of its work.

On 8th February we went to meet the Health and Safety Executive (HSE) at Baynards House, 1 Chepstow Place, and W2. We were welcomed by Mr Chris Raymond, the Head of International Section, for discussions on the work of HSE.

In the afternoon at 14, 30 hours, I went to meet a few friends at The British Trade Union Congress, where I was welcomed by Mr Barry Bennett and his Staff and also met people from Agricultural & Allied Workers Union –I got the opportunity to discuss their Collective Agreements. Mr Bennett recalled the group meeting we had few a days earlier regarding the memberships and strength of different unions in Mauritius. He knew very well that "the FTU said that it represented 30,000 and GWF 60,000 and had said that the MLC had 22,000. He gave the last MLC figure which was 20,000. Furthermore he promised to help the MLC regarding Workers Education through the Commonwealth Trade Union Congress.

In the Evening we were invited by Mrs Phillippa Urmston to the Picture House to watch the film "Gandhi" in English version.

On 9th February we went to visit the Cambridge University Campus and the Facilities available. We met the student's adviser of the Ruskin College and we got the opportunity to visit the campus by car – We were impressed by the different departments, the size of the campus looking like a large village with all facilities. It was a real pleasure to visit the different Departments of the Cambridge University which was rich in history. We also visited the University Museum's collections, consisting of many treasures which give an exciting insight into of the scholarly activities – both past and present of the university academics.

The University of Cambridge is one of the world's oldest of Universities and leading academic Centres. The Guide gave us a brief, how the University and Colleges work with more than 18,000 students from all walks of life and all corners of the world 9,000 staff 31 Colleges and 150 Departments, faculties, school and other Institutions.

I also got the chance to discuss with the Students Adviser about the future Scholarships for the MLC Affiliated Unions members. For the general information, I would like to say, that the MLC had been awarded several Scholarships by Ruskin College to follow courses in Trade Unionism, Collective Bargaining, Labour Laws, Human Resource Management, etc. The course duration was normally 6 months and there were several other courses of different durations. Unfortunately in late 80's for unknown reasons the scholarship was ceased. According to unofficial information, it seems that the participant of the MLC might have not done well by not attending regularly the courses. It seems that the university was not happy. Similarly the same scenario had produced at the level of the Afro-Asian Institute of Israel whose courses durations were 3 to 6 months, I still remember Mr Beniami the Director of the Institution told me that the participant representing the MLC was not attending courses regularly!

On 10th February we visited a primary School at the request of our friend Frichot. The Head Teacher presented us to his teaching staff and we had the opportunity to discuss with the students and later we had a working lunch with the teachers. It was an interesting discussion and my friend Frichot was the happiest person. In the same region we watched a dogsrace. It was amusing for us because it was the first time that we were watching such an event.

On 11th February, a visit was organized at Tate & Lyle Ltd. at Thames Refinery, Silver Town. There we met Mr W. D. Nelson, Refinery Manager and Mr A.G. Briggs, the Personnel Manager. They accompanied us on a guided tour of the refinery. Two Trade Unionists, Mr John Wheatley of Boilermakers and Allied Trade Union at Thames Refinery and Mr Teddy Hardy of Amalgamated Union of Engineering Workers joined us at buffet lunch. I discussed the safety issues with them comparing our local working conditions in the sugar factories.

Later after lunch, a meeting was organized with the Action Committees to discuss in detail the working conditions and other benefits they were entitled to. We left Silvertown at 16.30 hour and we went back to our Hotel quite late.

On 12th we were free for sightseeing and shopping from 9.00 to 14.00 hours and Sunday 13th was a free day. I spent the day with my relatives in London area and returned late in the evening.

On Monday 14th at 9.15 hours an interview was organized with BBC TV regarding our visits and experiences. We visited the Transport & General Workers' Union at Transport House, Smith Square, SW 1. We were received by Mr Regan Scott, the Research and Education Officer for discussions on the role of the Union.

On 15th morning we were free and I paid a courtesy visit to our Mauritian High Commissioner in London and 15.00 hours we left our Hotel for Heathrow Airport and were back to Mauritius by Air Mauritius flight and reached SSR Airport on the morning of the 16th February.

CONCLUSION

The tour enabled the participants to get acquainted with:

(a)   The British system of industrial relations and its related institutions like the Industrial Relations Commission (IRC) and the Acts;

(b)   The British trade union movement through visits to the British trade Union Congress and interactions with its officials;

(c)   Adult education facilities and activities with visits and discussion mainly with officials of Cambridge University and Ruskin College in Oxford.

(d)   Health and safety issues in the UK;

(e)   The trade union situation in the Commonwealth Countries through a visit to the London based Commonwealth Trade Union Council and discussion with its Director-General Mr Patrick Queen.

In a nutshell, the tour was very informative to the participants (us) and useful as a benchmark of reference to their day to day trade union work back in Mauritius.

Chapter 25

THE 40TH
AGWU ANNIVERSARY

IT was a great pleasure and honour for me as President of the union to organise the 40th Anniversary of the foundation of the Mauritius Engineering and Technical workers' Union (AGWU) founded by the father of Trade Union Movement in Mauritius and in remembrance of the struggle and sacrifice endured by the pioneers of the union during the colonial days. In fact the Mauritius Engineering Workers Union was created under the ordinance No 7 of 1938. Colony of Mauritius Certified that the application dated 7th November 1944, made J. E. Anquetil President; Secretary Grass, B. Herbu Treasurer. The Certificate bore number 1 and the official certificate was delivered on the 4th January 1945.

The function started by a Mass celebrated at the Immaculée Conception Church at Saint Georges Street, Port Louis. In his sermon, Father Souchon laid stress on the hard work and sacrifice made by Emmanuel Anquetil, Pandit Sahadeo and Guy Rozemont.

The Louis L'Echelle Hall – Poudrière Street Port Louis was decorated for this occasion.

Programme of the 40th Anniversary Celebration

9.15 - 9.30	Arrivals of Participants and Guests at the Mass - Immaculée Conception
9.30 - 10.20	MASS Ceremonies

Caption

The function started with a prayer and songs by Siven Chinien and Group. After the arrival of the Deputy Prime Minister, Sir Gaetan Duval Q.C. the National Anthem was played and a welcome speech was made by Mr Rajcoomar Sydamah the General Secretary of the Union. As President, I welcomed the Guests present and gave a short exposé of the union's success and failure. I said that this event has a great importance and certain nostalgia for me, as in my young days I had the opportunity to meet the Leaders of METWU, renamed by Guy Rozemont in 1056. "It is a great honour for me to be the President of this Union and celebrate its 40th Anniversary. I had the chance to associate my name with the union through my uncle Partab Allgoo, who was the General Secretary of Mauritius Labour Party and an official of METWU."

I read the messages sent by the Prime Minister Hon Anerood Jugnauth, Mr Patrick J. O'Farrell, Executive Director of AALC, John Vanderveken General Secretary of ICFTU, etc.

Mr Hurrypersad Ramnarain gave a long speech, emanating the struggles he took together with Dr Maurice Curé, Emmanuel Anquetil, Pandit Sahadeo and others.

Mr Chandrasen Bhagirutty President of MLC, said in his speech, that he knew very well the struggle started from 1036 to December 1046. He added that the late Emmanuel Anquetil was one of the pioneers of the Trade Union movement. In this colonial period, talking about Trade Union Movement was taboo. He was a courageous and genuine trade unionist who felt for the oppressed, served them and paid a heavy price. His name has gone down in the history of this country forever. The president of MLC also talked on late Guy Rozemont and several other able friends. He continued by wishing happy Birthday to AGWU, saying that "This union is one of the oldest unions affiliated to the MLC". It has left no stone unturned to improve the conditions of employment of the manual workers and it has always operated within the framework of the established rules and regulations in order to enhance harmonious Industrial Relations which are so essential for industrial and economic development. I hope that my friend Raj Allgoo who is leading the Union since some years will tribe inspiration from his predecessors to continue to serve the workers on the same line with more fighting morale. May I here pay tribute to all those pioneers whom I consider the embodiment of sacrifice for the upliftment of the downtrodden."

Chapter 26

Centenary Anniversary Celebration of Emmanuel Anquetil

THE Mauritian Trade Union Movements and the Working Class were highly honoured by the MSM/Labour Government by organising the Centenary Anniversary of Emmanuel Anquetil "the Father of the Trade Union Movements in Mauritius" on a National scale, on the 18th of August, 1985.

The main architect behind this project was the Governor General, Sir Seewoosagur Ramgoolam GCMG, LRCP, MRCS. This was his personal wish to organise this great event at the State House, Le Réduit. Apart from all manifestations, the first thing SSR had in mind was to invite Emmanuel Anquetil son, John Anquetil and his family, to the Centenary Anniversary and furthermore to stay at the State House as a special Guest. The reason behind it was to show to the British, that it was from Le Réduit that the Governor Sir Bede Edward Hugh Clifford had ordered to send Emmanuel Anquetil in exile into Rodrigues and his son John had accompanied him.

In a speech on the occasion of the Birth Anniversary Celebration of Emmanuel Anquetil, the actual Prime Minister Dr the Hon Navinchandra Ramgoolam GCSK, FRCP while expressing his gratitude to the Father of the Trade Union Movement, said: "I did not know Emmanuel Anquetil personally. However what he stood for, and the tribulations and sufferings he went through were brought home to me when his son, John Anquetil came to Mauritius with his family for his centenary celebrations. My father, Sir Seewoosagur Ramgoolam, was then the Governor-General. He wanted John and his family to stay at le Chateau du Réduit. I thought they would be better off staying at the seaside at one of the five star hotels. So one day when I saw SSR getting cross

Raj Aligoo, B. Ramlallah, SAJ, SSR, John Anquetil and others – 18 August 1985
Unveiling Emmanuel Anquetil Bust

because everything was not ready to welcome John and his wife, I asked him why he wanted them to stay at le Réduit. His answer was very revealing: "It was here", he explained, and "that the Governor of Mauritius took the decision to banish Anquetil to Rodrigues. Now I want Emmanuel's son to be my guest at this very Chateau du Réduit! It's my revenge on history for Emmanuel Anquetil", he said to me.

UNVEILING EMMANUEL ANQUETIL BUST

On the occasion of the Centenary Birthday Anniversary, the Government had erected a monument of Emmanuel Anquetil, which was put in Front of the Government House in remembrance of his work done for the uplift of the labouring class. It was Sir Seewoosagur Ramgoolam, the Governor General who had the honour to unveil the Bust of Emmanuel Anquetil, just in front of statue of Queen Victoria at the Government House in the presence of the Prime Minister, Hon Aneerood Jugnauth Q.C., Leader of Opposition, Hon Paul Raymond Bérenger, Members of Parliament, and the Foreign Diplomats. It was with great pride that I was one of the successors of Emmanuel Anquetil, who continued to keep the torch lighted, through the Trade Union founded by him, the Mauritius Engineering and Technical Workers' Union, which was later renamed by Guy Rozemont as the Artisans and General Workers Union.

Mr. and Mrs John Anquetil, son of Emmanuel Anquetil

SIR VEERASAMY RINGADOO
GOVERNOR GENERAL'S SPEECH

On the occasion of the Centenary Birthday Anniversary the Government had prepared a well organised the event. A number of activities were held to mark the Birth Centenary of Emmanuel Anquetil. One of the first events was to name the Registrar General Building – "Emmanuel Anquetil Building". The Governor-General, Sir Seewoosagur Ramgoolam, who had the honour to unveil the commemorative plate to name it "Emmanuel Anquetil Building" in the presence of the Prime Minister Hon Anerood Jugnauth Q.C. and Sir Veerasamy Ringadoo Minister of Finance.

142

A Brief History Of **Trade Unionism** In Mauritius

Sir Veerasamy Ringadoo said the following during his exposé on the Life and Mission of the Father of the Trade Unionism in Mauritius:

"The workers had started to understand the message of solidarity and they tried to make employers respect their dignity. He started to prove that workers were aroused. The Dock workers went on strike because one of their fellow workers was dismissed unfairly because he was the Ring Leader and they refused to re-instate the dismissed worker. At the same time, they asked for a wage increase and reduction of working hours.

The Governor Bede Clifford strongly suspected that the Labour Party had engineered the strike and they were the trouble makers.

By the end of August 1938 – the Labour Party lampooned the Government with vitriolic criticism - the Governor Bede Clifford was apparently alarmed on going through the police report of a meeting which was held a few days earlier in Mahébourg. His Excellency the Governor, invited Dr Maurice Curé the Leader of the Labour Party, to Chateau, Le Réduit and requested him to use moderation in his language and tone and of his men at public meetings and he also tried to convince him and wanted to reach an agreement with Dr Curé to the effect that, if the Labour Party showed its collaboration with the Government, he was prepared to adopt a more flexible policy towards the Société de Bienfaisance de l'Ile Maurice, which the Government was bent to crush.

Finally, before Dr Cure left the Chateau du Réduit Sir Bede Clifford made a promise to offer him a seat as a nominee in the Council.

On the other hand Mr Oswell, Director of Labour offered a good job to Anquetil, but this did not attract Anquetil although he was facing financial problems. Anquetil had his agenda. He was busy forming Trade Unionism on a sound footing and The Industrial Associations according to the Industrial Association Ordinance recently passed.

The Governor was very disturbed as it was evident that the Island would plunged in turmoil by the labour unrest which threatened might occur similar to Union Flacq. So Bede Clifford was of the opinion that he did not have other alternative than declaring a State of Emergency.

Anquetil Residence in Rose Hill was raided by police on the 7th September 1938. He was aroused from his sleep by Colonel Deane, and arrested in virtue of the State of emergency decreed by the Governor Bede Clifford. As the unrest in the island triggered off by labour grievance gathered momentum, Dr Curé and Pandit Sahadeo were placed under house arrest by a "Restriction Order" issued by the Governor.

Having spent the rest of the night in a cell at the Line Barracks, Anquetil was on 8 September at 13.50 led under heavy police escort to the office of Lt. Colonel Deane who informed him of the Government's decision of deporting him to Rodrigues and his son John was allowed to accompany his father.

At 16.15 hours, a van with armed Police called at Anquetil detention cell, The Deputy Commissioner of Police invited Emmanuel Anquetil, and his son John to enter the van, after which the vehicle went very fast in the direction of the Port, where the ship "Bontekoe" was waiting to sail off to Rodrigues with the Secretary of the Labour Party and John. On the same ship was Magistrate Le Gras, who was going to Rodrigues on an Assignment. Anquetil was all along escorted by two police officers.

On his return, he was welcomed by a team of the Labour Party supporters who took him on their shoulders. They shouted slogans and passed over Labour Party Office situated on the Chaussée Street, Port Louis. In a short speech Anquetil said that the deportation would not deter him from carrying out his work for the welfare and working conditions of the workers – He was "thankful to the Magistrate of Rodrigues and to the inhabitants of Rodrigues for having treated him as A King."

Speech of the Prime Minister
Hon Anerood Jugnauth

The Prime Minister Hon Anerood Jugnauth, in his speech, stated that it is appropriate, that the name of a great patriot is to be written in large letters on one of the largest administrative buildings in Port Louis. He said if certain officers could achieve high echelons it was thanks to the efforts of Emmanuel Anquetil.

Mr. Jugnauth continued by saying that "the name of Emmanuel Anquetil written on this building allowed present and future generations to recall what they had learned from that illustrious son of the soil, who never abandoned fighting for the cause of the oppressed and made for a better Mauritius."

The Municipality of Beau Bassin/Rose Hill held a three days of activities to mark the Centenary Birthday of one of its illustrious citizens of Emmanuel Anquetil, who was living at Ambrose Street up to 30th December 1946.

Beau Bassin / Rose Hill made Emmanuel Anquetil an honorary citizen posthumously in the presence of the Governor General, several Ministers, and members of the Opposition. John Anquetil and his family and several other personalities were present at the ceremony. Emmanuel Anquetil was made honorary citizen of the City. Miss Villa Seenyen Mayor of the City proposed an amendment that was read by the secretary of the City M Edmond, that the citizenship honour be conferred posthumously to Emmanuel Anquetil.

Talk at the Municipality of Beau Bassin/Rose Hill

Several other activities were organized to mark the event. For instance a Football match between Municipal Workers and Members of the Front Syndicat National was organised at Rose Hill stadium and a talk was organized on the life and mission of Emmanuel Anquetil. There were three main speakers: Hon Paul Raymond Bérenger Leader of MMM, Hon Dr James Burty David the President of Labour Party, and Kumarasawmy Venkatasamy, President of FSN.

Seminar on the Struggle of Emmanuel Anquetil & Launching of Book

On the other hand the Mauritius Engineering and Technical Workers Union (Artisans and General Workers Union) under my Leadership, to mark the Centenary Birthday Anniversary, organized a Seminar on Trade Unionism with particular reference to the life and Mission of Anquetil. A reception was organized in a Hotel in Flic en Flac in the honour of the Son of the Father of the Trade Union Movement in Mauritius, Mr John Anquetil and his wife. On that occasion I launched my book on Trade Unions Movement in Mauritius entitled "Le Movement syndical A L'Ile Maurice".

Set up of EPZ Labour Welfare Fund

During the usual Tripartite Committee meeting in April 1986, presided by the Minister of Finance, attended by the Minister of Labour and Industrial Relations, Minister of Agriculture and Minister of Planning & Economics, I was representing Mauritius Labour Congress, in the capacity of Director of Organisation. I presented a motion on Tripartite Committee to the effect that there is an urgent need to create an Export Processing Zone Labour Welfare Fund for the benefit of about 90,000 workers employed in the sector. There is a pressing need to set up an Export Processing Zone Labour Welfare Fund as it already exists for the Sugar & Docks Workers and the " Sugar Industry Labour Welfare Fund ". After enumerating the advantage the Sugar & Docks were already benefitting. I presented a formal motion for the creation of an EPZ Labour Welfare and motion was seconded by Mr. S. Soodhun representing FTU and it was unanimously accepted.

EXPORT PROCESSING ZONE LABOUR WELFARE FUND came into existence by an act of Parliament: The Export Processing Zone Labour Welfare Fund (EPZLWF) was established following the promulgation of the EPZLWF Act No. 5 in November 1987. It operates under the aegis of the Ministry of Labour, Industrial Relations and Employment.

Caption

It aims at promoting the advancement of the welfare of the EPZ workers and their families.

The Minister of Labour and Industrial Relations Mrs Hon Sheilabye Bappoo set up the EPZ Labour welfare Board Committee;

The Committee
(1)   The Funds shall be managed and administered by a Committee which shall consist of-
    (a)   two representatives of the Ministry of Labour and Industrial Relations, Women's Rights and Family Welfare;
    (b)   a representative of the Ministry of Finance;
    (c)   a representative of the Ministry of Industry;
    (d)   four representatives of workers appointed by the Minister after consultation with such trade unions catering for workers as he may deem fit;
    (e)   four representatives of employers appointed by the Minister after consultation with such organisations of employers as he may deem fit.

(2)   The Chairman shall be appointed by the Minister from amongst the members. Mr Motalib Toofany, the Permanent Secretary acted as Chairman
Board members:
Rajpalsingh Allgoo; Yusof Sookdall; Sharah Toofanny; representing the Textile and Garment Workers; and others

To start the fund activities some staffs from the Ministry were seconded for duty at the EPZLWF.

I was nominated and associated on the Staff and Scholarship committee, responsible for recruitment of employees of the EPZLWF. We recruited employees including the General Manager and the Accountant, etc.

Benefits were given by the EPZLWF to EPZ Workers such as:
(i)   To improve the quality of life of the EPZ workers; in 1990 the fund started giving Loans for:
(ii)   House hold appliances (Refrigerator; Washing Machine; rice cooker; micro-ovens etc. Zero interest;
(iii)   Housing enhancement Loan and marriage loan
(iv)   Social Aid, in case of flood; fire & cyclone
(v)   Leaisure management programme
(vi)   Day care Centres

Its objectives, among others, are to improve the quality of life of workers by providing educational support and training; creating awareness on welfare matters at place of work and at home; and promote family socialisation and personal dynamics through increased engagement in leisure and sports activities.

On reaching my retirement age, I decided to resign as Board member of the EPZLWF. The Management organised a farewell party at the Centre and thanked me for my contribution by offering me as souvenir a Video Recorder, which in turn I donated to the AGWU Workers Education Centre.

Board in the year 1990

Representatives of Government
Mr M Toofany (Chairman)
Mrs L Dubois
Miss A Maulloo
Mr D Chintaram

Representatives of Employers
Mr P Chan Kin C.B.E.
Mr D Hunma
Mr A Currimjee
Mrs D Wong

Representatives of Workers
Mr R Allgoo M.B.E.
Mr Y Sooklall
Miss S Toofany

Chapter 27

SINOTEX (MAURITIUS) LTD SAGA

GENESIS

In the year 1988, there was a Prime Minister and his name was Anerood Jugnauth, later to be known as Sir Anerood Jugnauth Q.C. or SAJ. On the 11th of July there was a strike at Sinotex (Mtius Ltd) at Terre Rouge and Pamplemousses Textile Factories, initiated by the Workers Delegates themselves, to the utter ignorance of their Union leaders.

SAJ used this Sinotex strike to send me to prison unjustly, wilfully and unlawfully, due to a personal grudge against Mr Chandra sensing Bhagiruthy, the President of the Mauritius Labour Congress for his statement at an ILO Conference in June 1988, regarding the wages and conditions of work which were described as "inhuman" the daily wages being below one Pound sterling. SAJ was extremely annoyed by this statement and wanted to use me (Allgoo) as scapegoat to instil fear in the minds of other Trade Union leaders.

This strike caused a terrible disagreement in the Alliance Government of MSM-Labour-PMSD. Sir Gaetan Duval the PMSD leader and his party left the Government.

Why SAJ might have been angry against me? Giving the IMF had written to Queen Elizabeth II, about the treatment given to me in the following terms 'The international trade unions sympathised with Mr. Allgoo and other persons who were jailed. But what was more important was that they were very active and demonstrated their spirit of solidarity with the Mauritius Textile & Garment Workers Union". The following steps were taken to get the release of the Trade Unionists:

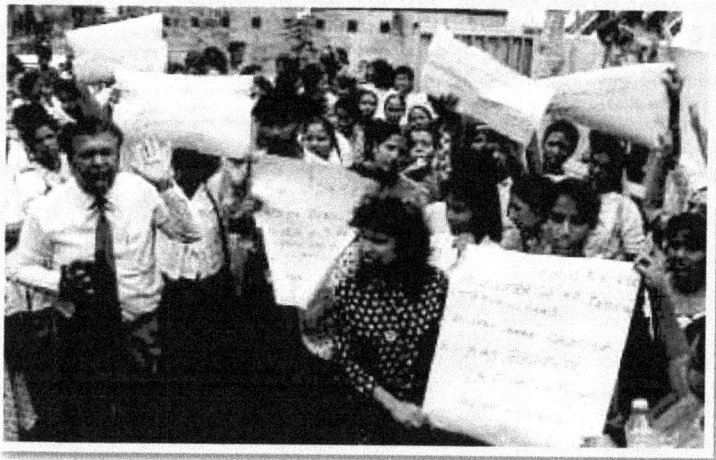

Caption

1. *The International Metalworkers' Federation (IMF) which groups trade unions of 70 countries and 14 million members, asked the Commonwealth Secretary to protect and, if necessary to take action following the arrest of Rajpalsingh Allgoo, leader of the trade union movement Mauritius. It had also "informed Queen Elizabeth of England about the arrest of Mr. Allgoo who is well known in the Commonwealth circle as a trade unionist and who was awarded the M.B.E., last year (1987) by the Queen. It expected that the Queen, as the Sovereign of Mauritius intervenes behind the scenes to ensure that such behaviour against a world Respected Trade Unionist was at once corrected" The Geneva based IMF had "launched a worldwide protest".*

To have a better understanding of the origin of the Sinotex strike, it has to be linked with the labour Act of 1975, the Industrial relations Act of 1974, and the Export Processing Zone Act (EPZ Act) which governs the industrial relations in the private sector in Mauritius. The Labour Act is applicable in industrial relations in the EPZ sector only in the case of unjustified dismissals. Otherwise it is not valid in the Free Zone. Similarly the EPZ Act is without force in areas not connected with EPZ. The IRA lays down principles to regulate trade disputes, strikes, lockouts, and the procedures of trade unions administration.

It is to be noted that the EPZ Act was promulgated in 1970, with a view to attracting foreign investors in Mauritius. According to the government, this was the only way to solve the acute unemployment problem that prevailed in Mauritius in the 70's.

Awareness of the workers of such discrepancies and the feelings that they were being exploited caused them to be discontented in their work. The rigidity of the EPZ Act, its inflexible nature, the refusal of the government to amend it in accordance with evolution in society and in all sectors of the lives and activities of workers also led workers and their representatives to be very unhappy.

Secondly, there was a clash of personality, temperament, philosophy of life and attitude wages increase towards workers. Supervisors and managers of Hong Kong origin who were in Mauritius for a short time only were not well-versed in the custom, practices and the way of life in general prevailing here. Difference in perception resulted in communication blockage and therefore engineering conflicts.

Thirdly, other causes of the strike:
1. The workers wanted management to continue giving the workers the same privilege regarding overtime as computed sometime back. Overtime should be paid after 8 hours work daily and on Saturdays after 5 hours work.

2. Request was made to the management to increase the daily wages from Rs 28. - To Rs 45. – one the following ground:
    (i)   Small enterprises were operating in Mauritius were already paying that Rs 45.- daily and yet they were making profits;
    (ii) The labour turnover was high and hence by increasing wages there could be stability.

3. The rate at which performance was measured was same throughout the day. Hence as man is not machine to speed up at the same rate, normally the rate of production should be less during the afternoon.

4. Request was made to management in case of breakdown the workers should be guaranteed their daily basic wage according to Remuneration Order and when new production design is made, due to lack of adaptability workers should be paid the basic wages.

5. The unskilled workers were requesting a bonus too because the workers were helping to reach the production target.

6. Supervisors press upon workers to do overtime though they have already performed ten hours of overtime according to law. They should not mistreat them, if they refuse to do overtime over and above 10 hours. The supervisors should not demote them and make them an unskilled worker. Etc.etc.

Observations

1. There was formerly a practice at Sinotex before February 1988 of computing overtime on a day to day basis after hours of work as stipulated in the Labour Act but not in the EPZ Act. When management with a view to reducing cost, changed this practice, started paying overtime according to the EPZ Act, employees were dissatisfied.

Chronology of Events Before the Strike

The union had submitted a memorandum previously. A meeting was arranged to meet Mr. Eddy Leung, the former manager of Sinotex, to discuss the following points for a first meeting on the 30th March 1988:

(1) Improvement of the unhealthy sanitary conditions existing at Sinotex. Separate toilets for males and females. The existing ones were meant for ladies only.
(2) Improvement of human relationship and understanding between supervisors and employees.
(3) Excess of overtime.
(4) Computation of overtime on a daily rather than a weekly basis.
(5) Wage increase at par with other factories.

At first Mr. Leung did not attach much importance to the remarks of the leader of the MTGWU. But later, after mature reflection, he realised that if the above short comings could be set right, it would be to the management's advantage too. Negotiations started and were likely to become positive. But unfortunate events at the factory necessitated the departure of Mr. Leung from Mauritius. He was replaced by a new manager, Mr. Eric Mogk.

The MTGWU had a meeting with Mr. Eric Mogk. This gentleman advised the union leader to consult Mr. Kam who would soon replace him in Mauritius.

Naturally these involuntary and abrupt changes at management level at a time when workers were growing more and more impatient did much to aggravate shirking of responsibilities. Relationship between management and workers continued to deteriorate for the existing problems had to be resolved within a time limit. Frustration was consequently reaching a culminating point.

2. When the new manager took office, I, accompanied by my regional organiser, Mr. Mario Darga, went to meet him. As the union leader, in addition to the points mentioned in the preceding section, I raised the question of sick leaves and annual leaves which were often refused to employees when they needed them. The factory manager heard the grievances but as he was newly appointed

in Mauritius, he said that he did not have the Document file relating to procedural agreement signed by his predecessor. He demanded sometime before taking a decision. He asked the representatives of employees to be patient.

On the 4th July, there was another meeting between the union leader and two personnel managers. The same grievances were discussed, in the end, the two personnel managers assured the union leader that they would send minutes of proceeding of this meeting and decision of management after consultation with the General Manager by the 8th July 1988.

But unfortunately, there were rumours that management had a meeting with Workers' Council representatives. Discussion was centred on wage increase. A proposal would be made on the 7th July that is one day before the date on which the personnel managers would inform the decisions of the General Manager on the grievances of the union. Meanwhile the psychological climate had deteriorated a lot; workers had exhausted all patience because they considered that the employer was playing a dirty game against their Trade Union.

The meeting scheduled for the 8th of July was postponed to the 11th of the same month. It seems that in the meantime (on the 8 or 9th of July) there was a works council meeting. Attention was focused on salary increase. The Personnel manager proposed an increase of 3% of wages which meant an increase of 84 cents per employee per day. In a country which talks of economic boom and where the prices of foodstuff were escalating day after day, 84 cents in wages seemed to be absurd, the more so because the workers were expecting Rs 48.- per day . This was the last straw that broke the camel's back. The workers, losing confidence in management, chose to go on strike on their own on the 11th July 1988.

Our Deduction

1. The wild cat strike meant disaster to all the major parties. The workers had to stay at home for more than a month. They were therefore bound to be penniless for some time, and this entailed misery in their lives. The Union leaders were arrested and jailed for more than a week. Management suffered drastic losses.Government grew unpopular.

    Had there been any sound industrial relations policies, more particularly a good grievance handling procedure, this unfortunate event could have been prevented.

2. Was management trying to by-pass the trade union of workers by attempting to negotiate wage increase with Works Council? I remarked that, earlier, management had signed an agreement with the union when it was stated that salary increase and conditions of service should be discussed with Mauritius Textile & Garment Workers' Union. On the other hand, the general Manager observed that he was not aware of such a procedure.

SINOTEX STRIKE

The workers of Sinotex Textile Factory of Pamplemousses and Terre Rouge were members of the Mauritius Textile & Garment Workers' Union (MTGWU) and some 80% of the 3,000 workers of Sinotex were members of the union.

I have been accused by the Prime Minister, Sir Anerood Jugnauth and Mrs Hon. Sheilabhai Bappoo, Minister of Labour & I.R., that I was a trouble maker in the sense that I had compelled workers to go on strike. In fact, I was not even aware of it at the moment it was made. I was in his office discussing with two foreign delegates, Mr. Raphael Nedzynski and Miss Annick Zuliani of the **"Force Ouvrière of France"**, and at the same time waiting for the time to negotiate with management, when I received a phone call from Mario Darga, informing me about the strike.

The delegates were very annoyed against the decision of the Management to negotiate Wages increase. The management had proposed an increase of 3%. The delegation understood the trick the Management wanted to play against the trade Union.

Mr. Vijay Ramanaik, the Branch President, took the decision to go on strike with the Union delegates and requested the workers of Sinotex Terre Rouge factory to stop work and later informed the Pamplemousses factory to stop work as their colleagues of Terre Rouge were already on strike. The size of number of workers on strike had an impact on management and government as well. The fact that the workers of Pamplemousses factory also ceased work immediately was very significant. There was a will in them to fight ills long repressed. The strike was an opportunity for them to materialise their aims, to redress grievances which were pending since long.

But since Mr. Vijay Ramanaik was a Representative of the union, he should have known that the strike was against the law. But we should agree with the words of Shakespeare: "Anger knows no bound". As an employee like his workmates, he forgot his primary role as a representative of the union.

TACTICS OF THE TRADE UNION AND MANAGEMENT

This unexpected stoppage of work put the major actors, the trade union, management and government, in a delicate position.

What should the trade union do in a situation where a strike has been made without its consent – and a completely illegal strike? Should it intervene or leave its members to their own destiny? Should it consider only those people who were its members and neglect non-members? Shock was my first reaction as leader of the MTGWU. But as a well recognised Representative of the workers, I was morally bound to intervene at Sinotex to inquire about the causes and circumstances of the strike. It was then that I learnt about the particulars of this industrial incident. I, who inwardly disapproved of the stoppage of work, was seen as a moral support by employees, especially those who were not unionised, and therefore powerless before management.

The discussion that took place between me and the General Manager was centred mainly on the way the question of wage increase was dealt with. I observed that management had signed an agreement with the union where by all salary increase and conditions of service were to be discussed with the MTGWU. Why then had management accepted to negotiate with the Work Council the question of salary increase? The General Manager declared that he was in good faith not aware of such a procedural agreement signed between management of Sinotex and the Union. This was why the proper channel for discussing on wage increase was not used. But the cost of this mishap, whether deliberate or not, was very high.

Despite this bone of contention, the union was willing to open negotiation with the General Manager in the presence of his legal adviser, Mr. Edwin Venchard Q.C., in order to normalise the situation. The General Manager, on the other hand, was not agreeable to this proposal. He could not take a decision before 14th July 1988. A Director from Hong Kong was expected in Mauritius on or before that date. He would have to discuss the matter with him. But the latter would no doubt need a little more time to study the case.

The Government and General Manager requested the Work Council and the Union delegates to persuade the strikers to resume work. Negotiation was expected to start on the forthcoming Thursday the 14th July 1988. The Union could not accept this suggestion and so the strike continued.

Two facts appear crucial here:
(1)   Failure to use the proper mechanism to deal with salary increase;
(2)   Inability of the management to take decisions at a moment which demanded THEM URGENTLY.

The problem of salary increase is really a thorny one. In general, wages and conditions of work in the EPZ sector were determined by the National Remuneration Board (NRB).Wage increase depends on inflations; it was decided by the Tripartite Committee as a government policy. Most of the times when Trade Unions ask a Company to grant a wage increase; the employers' reply is that the salary was fixed by the Government. In those days there were several medium standard Textile companies paying much better salary than the Sinotex. The Employers very often said "how can a company grant a wage increase when government has decided not to do so"? And the policy of the company would not be in accordance with that of the government. But in principle, we should agree that the company, at its discretion, can raise the salaries of workers to be in line with other companies. Then the questions arise how the medium standard companies were able to pay better salaries? The state of things was such that the workers needed a wage increase to make both ends meet, and this feeling among workers had much to do with their bitterness.

The failure to take rapid decisions and the desire to postpone negotiations added insult to injury. This helped the situation to deteriorate.

Anyway, the union had strong reasons not to ask the workers to resume duty. Their bargaining power would weaken and their problems would most probably remain unsolved, especially because the strike started on the instigation of the union delegates. Moreover, experience taught the union that once work started, before negotiations, the strike would end in disfavour of the workers and the latter would be at the mercy of the management and government.

In this dramatic situation, the Minister of Labour and Industrial Relations could have intervened to redress the grievances. But she did not do so on the ground that her ministry acted on principle and according to law. She said that she would not intervene as long as the strike continued. (We shall consider her role later in detail) Negotiations between the union and the Minister had a negative result. On the 13th July 1988, the Minister of Labour & Industrial Relations declared that if the strike would go on, she would request the management to take necessary action, which meant dismissal of the workers on strike.

Management on its part tried its level best to have the workers back at work. It was in vain. It circulated the following tract:

> "To our fellow workers victims of a small number of people – Work Council request workers to   resume work – contacted Minister advised to resume work – cool down – consider livelihood of all – management accepts contractual workers dismissal"

On 14th of July 1988, the workers still on strike were dismissed for breach of contract. (According Labour Act No. 50 of 1975 - Part VI –section 30. (4) An agreement shall be broken -

(a)   by the worker, where he is absent from work, exclusive of any day on which the employer is not bound to provide work, without good and sufficient cause for more than 2 consecutive working days

Attempts made to recruit new workers

This final decision of management made the situation become more explosive. Disappointed, the workers wanted to march towards Port Louis with the intention of manifesting in front of the Government House. But this course was discouraged by the union leader. A manifestation could entail some unplanned reaction. Besides, certain political parties could take advantage of the situation, and this could lead to disorders and attacks from police force.

On the same day, the union wrote to the Minister of Labour & Industrial Relations, requesting her immediate intervention and the setting up of a tripartite meeting to discuss the causes which had led to the strike and to try to find solutions. Unfortunately no response was obtained; no action was taken.

On Friday 15ᵗʰ July, the workers felt that they were sacked. Feeling depressed as negotiation was at a standstill workers had resolved to march towards Port Louis. This is a typical characteristic of workers on strike in Mauritius. I could not allow this event to occur. The first person to be arrested would thus be me, and subsequently negotiation would never take place. Activities of the workers, their patience, and their courage would have been fruitless. Besides I was fully aware of the stand of the Prime Minister SAJ, in such circumstances and his proverbial repeated phrase: "Leda pouf al sate". P.M. had warned to have recourse to the Public Order Act which was considered as a repressive law. So I could only entreat the workers not to move towards Port Louis.

But the workers, in the fury of their despair, attempted to discard the reigns of the union and even the government. They did not move towards Port Louis but they had their secret plan. They had the intention of gathering at the Pamplemousses Village Council Building. The decision was communicated to me afterwards. I informed Mr. Bhagirutty, the President of MLC, accordingly.

The strikers were fed up of waiting near the factories. The premises were beyond control, they wanted action. What could I do then?

The only solution for me was to address a solidarity message to a mass of 3,000 workers to cool down their bellicose enthusiasm. This needed a megaphone, police authority, and the help of legal advisers. It is during the course of activities leading to the fulfilment of these needs that crucial things happened that gave industrial relations a new dimension.

In Port Louis, in my search for a megaphone, I met Mr. Tulsiraj Benydin, the President of the FSSC. The latter gladly accepted to lend his megaphone, and expressed his desire to support me. He would like to join me at Pamplemousses and talk to the crowd of strikers. A few minutes later I reached his office, still at Port Louis. There he met the President of the MLC, Mr. Bhagirutty. This gentleman informed him, that a High Officer of the Police had warned him (Mr. Bhagirutty) in the following terms:

"Do not poke your nose in this affair! You are a learned man. You can guess the Consequences"

This warning had influenced Mr. Bhagirutty, the leader of the MLC – to which the MTGWU was affiliated not to proceed to thru gathering at Pamplemousses. On the other hand insured by my sense of duty and solidarity with the workers, made my way to the Pamplemousses mass meeting.

At the level of the MLC it was only Dan Cunniah who was helping by liaising with International organisations, the Minister of Labour & Industrial Relations and the

National Trade Union Council and the Local Press. Later I learned the reason of his absence as the General Secretary of MLC at Pamplemousses Village Council meeting where 3,000 strikers were assembled because Police had already warned him not to address the strikers; otherwise he would be arrested too.

The arrival of Mr. Benydin just before the end of my speech was a further encouragement to me. Mr. Benydin conveyed a message of solidarity of the Government employees to the workers on strike. This meeting showed the unity between the leaders of two completely different trade unions- the FSSC which groups civil servants and the MTGWU which groups workers of the private sector. And it marked the foundation of a new trend in trade unionism in Mauritius.

When the situation was without issue, the union tried to make use of its other weapon: the press. By this means, it tried to arouse public opinion on the fate of the 3,000 workers and the stand of government and management.

On the same day, the 15th of July, a Free Zone Unions meeting was held at Marie Reine de La Paix centre at Port Louis, in relation with Sinotex Strike. I attended the meeting, though late. The following points were discussed:
(i)   The EPZ Act;
(ii)   Computation of overtime on a daily basis;
(iii)   The double cut system;
(iv)   Severance allowance.

It is there that attempts were made by Police to arrest me. Instantly I reflected over these facts:
(1)   Once arrested, I would be detained in legal custody unnecessarily during the whole week-end on the pretext that police enquiry was not yet completed.
(2)   Magistrate could be available on Monday the 18th July only (for my release on bail)
(3)   There would be nobody to give assistance, instructions and guidance to the delegates.

Prudence advised me to escape despite the presence of more than twenty Police in uniforms and civil, by moving through the back gate of the social centre of Immaculée church. I took the advantage of a moment's inattention of the CID Officers by leaving my personal belongings and my jacket at the residence of Father Souchon.

My car bearing No CC358 was consequently seized and directed to the Line Barrack Police Head Quarters, Port Louis.

On Saturday 16th July, Mr C. Bhagirutty, before leaving Mauritius, advised me to surrender to police on Monday 18th. On Friday 15th Mr Mario Darga, the regional Organiser of MTGWU and Mr Vijay Ramanaik, Branch President of the union, were both arrested in the evening.

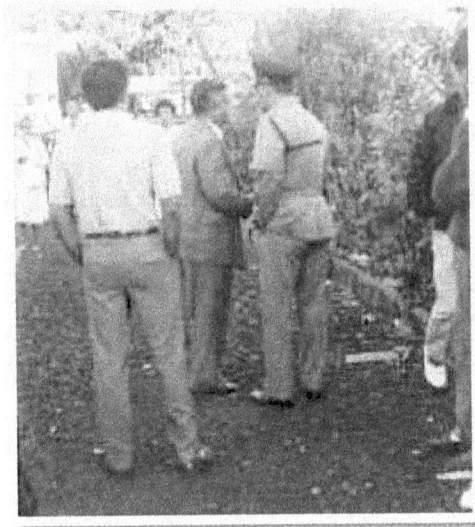

Caption

It was very important for me to escape from Police custody; otherwise there would be no one to comfort the moral of the strikers. Every night, as from Friday to Sunday, I was meeting the delegates at their residences till late at night, thus keeping the strikers active.

My house was surrounded by a group of Police and CID Officers. Needless to say, I was not residing at my place. From 15 to 18[July 1988] I was staying at an unknown place.

On Monday 18th, I called at the Sinotex Factory of Pamplemousses. There I was approached by about 10 police officers who requested me to call at the Line Barracks Police Head quarters, to give a statement in relation with the strike. I asked them to give me a few minutes so that I might meet the management of Sinotex. One of the managers declared that Sinotex was still willing to negotiate with the union. This gentleman offered to go to the Line Barracks where I could finish the statement. He would then return to Sinotex of Terre Rouge for negotiations.

But unfortunately, I was arrested and jailed on a false charge under section 102 (1) (a) of the Industrial Relations Act No 67 of 1973, which read: Any person who in connection with any strike or lock-out which is unlawful –

(a)   Calls, instigates, organises, carries on, procures or incites other persons to take part in, the strike or-

(b)   takes part in or assists in the strike or lock-out, shall commit an offence and-

     (i)   *in the case of an offence under paragraph (a) shall, on conviction, be liable to a fine which shall not be less than five hundred rupees nor more than one thousand rupees or to imprisonment not exceeding twelve (12) months;*

     (ii)   *in the case of an offence under paragraph (b) shall, on conviction, be liable to a fine not exceeding five hundred rupees and to imprisonment not exceeding three months.*

From the events of Sinotex strike, two conclusions can be drawn. In the first instance, the workers of Sinotex have displayed a new characteristic which was unseen in Mauritius in the past.

All the strikes that took place in the past in Mauritius were instigated either by a Trade Union Leader or agents of a political party. Workers' activities and movements were influenced by these persons. In the case of the workers of Sinotex, decision to go on strike was taken by the workers themselves. In previous cases, the leaders who were responsible to organise for stoppage of work could not plead ignorance of the industrial laws even though the workers were unaware of them. In the actual case, the workers were in fact not well versed in the laws regulating strikes or any other similar activity. Yet they went on strike with determination. What is also striking is that they were ready to bypass management and government as they were so frustrated. We have seen that when I had advised them not to march towards Port Louis, they had another plan in mind: to meet at Pamplemousses Village Council premises. They were ready to act with certain autonomy from their main Trade Union Office, Police and the government as well. This aspect of workers' nature was something new in industrial relations in Mauritius. It was the symptom of a new class of workers of a new industrial society.

Another important aspect in the Sinotex strike, the coming together of Mr. Benydin, leader of the FSSC, and me, as leader of the MTGWU and the meeting of the trade union leaders of textile and garment trade unions were highly significant.

Though at the time of these meetings, there were ideological differences between the different unions; there was also a latent desire to unite. But this had not materialised. The Sinotex episode played a tremendous role in this field.

One of the outstanding features of the late seventies and eighties in Mauritius is the absence of strikes of dramatic nature. Trade union leaders believed that this was due to the IRA and POA which limit the freedom of action of trade unions. But this does not mean that the trade union were not active. They were busy and attempted to solve industrial problems by the process of collective bargaining or direct negotiation between management and themselves. In addition, the incorporate attitude and inflexible nature of the Prime Minister limited the scope of trade unions' activities.

Moreover, the weakness of the trade unions was the lack of unity that could have transformed them into a cohesive group. Each one operated in isolation as best as it

l'express

APRÈS UNE SEMAINE DE DÉTENTION

Les syndicalistes Algoo, Darga et Ramanaick libérés sur parole

● Ils comparaîtront demain devant le tribunal de Pamplemousses

LE POINT DE VUE SYNDICAL

M. C. Bhageerutty (président du MLC):

"Zotte fine gratte lédos lion"

Le Socialiste

affaire SINOTEX

e "forcing" de Duval arrasse le groupe Jug

Les syndicalistes traités d'«irresponsables» par Jugnau qualifiés comme des gens «intell

Plusieurs fonctionnaires en com délibé afin de ne pas travaillé avec

Zone Franche

Au rendez-vous des syndicats

La MEPZA inquiète de la situation actuelle dans la Z

Twin

could. Their bargaining power was limited and so, they could easily be overthrown or manipulated by government or employers' associations. Besides, inter union conflicts linked to the character differences of leaders and their ideologies prevented them from joining together under a common banner. Some were pro-government, some were in favour of the opposition parties; others were neutral or aspired to be so to keep their identity and autonomy.

My arrest and that of Mr. Mario Darga and Mr. Vijay Ramanaik and our stay in miserable conditions in jail for more than a week, and government's intransigent attitude towards unions, led the union leaders to think about their own lot. It is always the miseries of others that make one think of one's human conditions. Consequently, the desire to unite which was latent materialised spontaneously on the 18th of July 1988, the day on which I was arrested.

The meeting at Marie Reine de la Paix and the attitude of government towards unions kindled this desire to unite. The "Fron Sindika Travayer Zone Frans" was constituted. This new union conveyed the following message to the MTGWU and workers on strike. Fron Sindika Travayer Zone Frans appeal to workers of Sinotex branch of Terre Rouge & Pamplemousses.

"Friends,

Fron Sindika Travayer Zone Frans which groups seven trade unions are fighting for the amelioration of the conditions of work in the Free Zone. These unions have met on Monday evening (18.07.88) to study the evolution of the situation at Sinotex.

The 'Fron" is informing you that the seven trade unions support your struggle at Sinotex. We condemn the imprisonment of the three trade union leaders. We consider that the struggle must continue until your demands are met. Government must undertake its responsibility and arrange for a tripartite meeting the soonest possible. The Fron is also mobilising the workers in the neighbourhood of Sinotex. We also let you know that International Trade Unions have been informed of your struggle and they are expressing their solidarity. In unity, we shall succeed.
1.   Export Enterprises union (FTU)
2.   Mauritius Free zone and Secondary industry Employees Union (FTU)
3.   Mauritius Textile & Garment Workers Union (MLC)
4.   Union of workers of alliance spinners (FPU)
5.   Diamond cutting factory Workers Union (FPU)
6.   Private Enterprise Union (FPU)
7.   Textile, Clothes and Other Manufacturing workers Union (GWF)

This letter was written in Creole for specific reasons: to be close to workers by adopting their medium of communication, and to facilitate understanding between the unions and employees. However, the letter reveals the following facts:

1.   A spirit of solidarity had germinated in the minds of trade unionists. A desire to revolt which was long restrained suddenly found an outlet. This new body of

trade unions not only decided to watch the evolution of the state of affairs at Sinotex, but also took steps to mobilise the workers of the textile industry of the vicinity of Terre Rouge & Pamplemousses with a view to making government change its attitude towards the workers and the trade unionists.

2. The new trade unions Front were imbued with a sense of power from the International Trade Unions, which were kept informed of this struggle of workers. They were expressing their solidarity with them. This explains why the new group of trade unions said to the workers:
"The struggle continues! Don't retreat! No retreat no surrender. In unity we shall succeed"

3. Trade unions unanimously condemned the arrest of Mr. Allgoo, Mr. Mario Darga and Mr. Vijay Ramanaik. They blamed government and requested to take its responsibility and arrange for a tripartite as soon as possible.

4. They are fighting for an amelioration of the conditions of work in the EPZ and an amendment of the EPZ Act.

CREATION OF
NATIONAL TRADE UNIONS COUNCIL (NTUC)

But the events did not stop there. The constant criticism of government that the illegal strike was triggered by "irresponsible" trade union leaders who acted impulsively without reflecting on the consequences of their actions led the union leaders, on the 20th of July to take three decisions:

1. To give the Sinotex affair a national dimension;
2. To meet at the seat of the MLC at Port Louis on the 25th July at 6.00 p.m.;
3. To hold public meetings at Pamplemousses, Terre Rouge, Triolet and Rivière du Rempart, to rouse public opinion;
   (i) Against the stand of government during the strike;
   (ii) Against management which had sacked some 3,000 workers.

On the 25th of July, all the unions of Mauritius united under a common banner: there were (in addition to the above mentioned seven unions):
1. The Mauritius Labour Congress (MLC)
2. The Fédération des Syndicats du Service Civil (FSSC)
3. The Fédération des Syndicats des Corps Paraétatiques (FSCC)
4. The General Workers Federation (GWF)
5. The Front des Travailleurs Unis (FTU)
6. The Federation Progressives Union (FPU)

The National Trade Union Council (NTUC) thus took birth. Definitely the bargaining power of this muscular body of trade unions had increased considerably; it could challenge the government. Trade unions were no longer vulnerable to attacks by government or management.

Impact of Union strike and the arrest of Mr. Allgoo on the International Trade Unions

Before the strike at Sinotex, workers and even government and management were unaware of the strength and power of the Trade Unions because of a period of lull in the field of industrial relations during the late seventies and eighties No major industrial dispute characterised this period. The 11th July 1988, appears as a crucial day in the history of industrial relations in Mauritius. Workers, government and management became conscious of the strength, power and deadly weapons of the trade unions.

The Mauritius Textile & Garment Workers Union & The Artisans & General Workers' Union of Mr. Allgoo are not only affiliated to the Mauritius Labour Congress but also to several International Trade Union Federations(International Trade Secretariat):

1. The MTGWU was affiliated to International Textile, Garment & Leather Workers Federation (Brussels)

2. The AGWU was affiliated to the following International Trade Unions Federations:
    (i)   International Metalworkers' Federation (Geneva- Switzerland)
    (ii)   International Federation of Building & Wood Workers (Geneva)
    (iii) International Transport Workers' federation (London U.K.)
    (iv)   International Federation of Food, Restaurants & Allied Workers' (Geneva)
    (v)   International Energy, Chemical & General Workers' Federation (Geneva)
    (vi)   and International Confederation of Free Trade Unions (ICFTU) Brussels, and had several friendly organisations
           (a)   La Confédération Ouvrière of France (F.O)
           (b)   British Trade Union Congress (BTUC) U.K.
           (c)   Japan Trade Union Confederation (Tokyo –Japan)

African American Labour Centre (AALC) is an emanation AFL-CIO of U.S.A; in addition it has links with trade unions in many other countries like Kenya, South Africa, Zimbabwe, Hong Kong etc.

The refusal of government to intervene so as to settle the dispute, the sacking of the 3,000 employees, the arrest of the trade union representatives, the ill-treatment received in jail and the seizure of the car of the MLC were reported to these international and national trade unions.

The International trade unions sympathised with me and the other persons who were jailed. But what was more important was that they were very active and demonstrated their spirit of solidarity with the MTGWU. They took the following steps:

1. The International Metal Workers' Federation (IMF) which groups trade unions of 70 countries and has 14 million members asked the Commonwealth Secretary to protest and, if necessary to take action following the arrest of Rajpalsingh Allgoo, leader of the trade Union Movement in Mauritius. It had also "informed Queen Elizabeth of England about the arrest of Mr. Allgoo who is well known in the Commonwealth circles as a trade Unionist and who was awarded the M.B.E. last year (1987)". It expected that the Queen, "as the Sovereign of Mauritius will intervene behind the scenes to ensure that such behaviour against a World Respected Trade Unionist was at once corrected".

THE GENEVA BASED IMF HAD "LAUNCHED A WORLDWIDE PROTEST"

2. The IMF had also contacted "relevant unions in Britain, The United States, in Europe and in countries which have economic relations with Mauritius so that further actions could be taken" if Mr. Allgoo was not released from jail.

3. The International textile, Garment & Leather Workers Union declared that "it was ready to do anything which could help Mr. Allgoo or clarify the situation" The ITGLWU based at Bradford had this to say to Mr. Allgoo:

    "It may be useful, if you could ascertain information related to customers of company's products especially if they are situated in the United Kingdom. If this is the case this would allow us to exert some pressure on the company through their customers."

    "If there is any other way which you feel we can help, please do not hesitate to let (us) know".

4. The ITGLW Federation based at Brielle's circulated a letter where it is stated that: "As the company wants to humiliate the workers who have now gone two weeks without pay and it appears that the government wants to use the situation as deterrent to future action, any financial assistance affiliates can give would be appreciated. Solidarity assistance may be transferred to our accountant in the General de Banquet....."

    A similar step was taken by the IMF; it had sent financial support to the MTGWU to enable it to pay lawyers for the release of the leader who was in jail.

Protest Telefax to P.M., Employer and Queen Elizabeth II

5.   Without exception all the national and international unions, were filled with compassion for the fate of the leader of the MTGWU. They all exerted pressure on the management of Sinotex, the Minister of Labour and Industrial Relations and the Prime Minister Sir Anerood Jugnauth Q.C. by phone and by telefaxes. To cite but two examples out of many, we can consider these two letters sent to the manager of Sinotex and the Prime Minister on the 20.07,1988 by the IMF.

(1)   Mr. Kam
     Managing Director
     Sinotex (Mtuis) Ltd.
     Terre Rouge
     Mauritius

     On behalf of 14 million metal workers I urge you to see to immediate release of Mr. Rajpalsingh Allgoo plus reinstatement of 3,000 workers, followed by fair negotiations recognising workers' reasonable demands. I have alerted key union's worldwide, commonwealth and British throne to this treatment of a most distinguished popular Commonwealth leader – anti-union action is more reminiscent of South Africa than Free Mauritius.

     Herman Rebhan
     General Secretary IMF
     Geneva.

(2)   Mr Anerood Jugnauth
     Prime Minister
     New Government Centre
     Port Louis – Mauritius.

     On behalf of 14 million metal workers I demand the immediate release of Rajpalsingh Allgoo, President of Artisans and General Workers' Union. Allgoo is known and respected as a sensible trade union leader worldwide and we are shocked at his arrest, as if he was in South Africa, and the behaviour of Sinotex in firing 3,000 workers. I urgently suggest you order his release and conciliate Sinotex dispute before this becomes an international issue affecting commonwealth, Queen Elizabeth II, and industrial unions worldwide.
     Herman Rebhan
     General Secretary
     IMF - Geneva.

In these two telefaxes, we notice there is a change in style and tone of language. The IMF is particularly harsh towards management of Sinotex and a bit moderate in its attitude towards the Prime Minister who possesses the key to the solution of the dispute. This reflects the general attitude of the international trade unions towards management of Sinotex and the government, namely the Prime Minister.

This is implicit in the words of the ITGLWF:

"We are extremely disturbed that help for you (Allgoo) had to come from Minister of Justice, Sir Satcam Boolell. He had to intervene with the commissioner of Police, while the Prime Minister and Minister of Labour have been silent.

We are appalled at the circumstances surrounding this dispute and the way in which your members and officials have been treated not just by the company but also your government."

Thus, the Sinotex strike which was illegal, gave industrial relations first a National dimension, and then and International one. It strengthened the dying bonds between the local trade unions. Similarly the links between these unions and international unions were consolidated. Their bargaining power was no doubt enhanced. A cooperative spirit emerged between both national and international unions. Such an occurrence was not seen in Mauritius in the past. This emphasises the unique nature of Trade Unions in Mauritius.

ROLE OF THE NTUC

The release of the jailed trade unionists and the promise to reintegrate the dismissed strikers cooled down the spirit of the workers and the trade union. Pressure from International trade Unions subsided. But the NTUC became active more than ever. It could stand and say boldly that:

(i)   Trade unionists are not "irresponsible" persons. They are people who think about the welfare of workers and are always conscious of the consequences of their actions. They are not against the development of the Free Zone which provides employment to thousands of persons. They are aware that a certain rhythm of productivity is necessary so that Mauritian products remain competitive in the international market. But the wages and conditions of work of people labouring in this sector should be bettered.

(ii)   Trade Unions, far from being an obstacle on the government, help in the construction of the country. Since sometime they have been raising their voices against the malpractices of certain employers thereby indirectly or directly affecting government, they should not be judged as undesirables. Trade unions cannot be silent and accept everything that management or government does. Otherwise they will not have their "raison d'être".

The second step was that a meeting of the executive members of the NTUC was held on 20th August at Port Louis Theatre where the following points were discussed:

(1)   Wage and salary increase;
(2)   Amendment on the IRA;
(3)   Amelioration of the conditions work in the Free Zone;
(4)   Introduction of the 40 hour week in the Sugar Industry and Hotel Industry;
(5)   Protest against all rise of prices of goods;
(6)   Privatisation;
(7)   Amendment to the EPZ Act and the POA;
(8)   Price control
(9)   Reintegration of dismissed workers of Sinotex;

Protest against the decision of government to increase contribution to the National Pension Fund by 1%;

(10)   Publication of Chesworth Report;
(11)   Creation of a solidarity fund for workers.

Thirdly, the NTUC tried to activate the workers' Education Unit to make workers conscious of their rights as workers and role as delegates of their respective unions.

Fourthly, the NTUC appealed to the "conscience" of the Ministers and people's representatives no matter to which political parties they belonged. A petition was addressed to the four major political parties of Mauritius, namely the PMSD, the PTr. the MSM and the MMM on or about the 1st August 1988.The NTUC addressed a copy of the petition letter to each cabinet member, especially to those who, prior to the general election of 1987, vehemently denounced the bad conditions of work in the EPZ sector; to those persons who were trade unionists before their actual job as MLA.

Still no response was obtained. The NTUC was dismayed but kept on its struggle.

ROLE OF THE GOVERNMENT OF MAURITIUS

The existence of the labour Act, the Industrial Relations Act, (IRA) the Export processing Zone Act (EPZ) and institutions like Industrial Relations Commission IRC), The Permanent Arbitrations Tribunal (PAT), the Industrial Court, the National Remuneration Board and the Termination of Contracts Service Board (TCSB) clearly indicates that the state plays a vital role in the field of industrial relations in Mauritius. The aim of the government by forcing these acts and establishing these institutions is to promote industrial peace which is a pre-requisite for investments (by foreigners) and economic growth in the country.

Secondly, the importance that is given to the Ministry of Labour and Industrial Relations which investigates and handles industrial problems, the Labour Inspectors and Labour Officers highlights the state's concern for better relations between employees and employers, both of whom are equally important to the country. Both enhance the standard of living in the country and eradicate poverty and unemployment.

ROLE OF MRS HON S. BAPPOO, MINISTER OF LABOUR & I.R. & SINOTEX STRIKE

The strike at Sinotex provoked a confusing situation, subject to diverging/conflicting interpretations. The strike, as has been shown, was unexpected on 11th July 1988 and was decided solely by the workers themselves.

In the past, more precisely from the 70's of 20th century, all strikes and industrial actions directed against the interest of the capital owners were instigated by a strong union leader or a competent politician. Sometimes, workers were manipulated and made to act for a common and just cause. - Higher wages and better conditions of work and better treatment- under the leadership of somebody. By contrast, the workers of Sinotex went on strike on their own initiative; they were neither backed by their trade union leader nor any politician when they took their resolution to decide by themselves their own fate at work. A similar phenomenon was observed a few months back at Stylex Garments, a factory situated at Plaine Lauzun. The new educated generation, exasperated by meagre wages and unhealthy working conditions and the industrial laws which tend to muzzle workers and their representatives, in attempts to shake off their heavy shackles to claim their due: a decent wage.

Now let us come back to the Minister Mrs. Bappoo, a close friend and colleague of the Hon. Prime Minister, Sir Anerood Jugnauth. On having wind of the strike, declared that it was illegal and was instigated by "irresponsible" and reckless trade union leaders who did not take at heart the progress and economic development of the country. As proper machinery for the settlement of dispute opposing workers and management was not utilised, she publicly avowed her intention not to intervene to arbitrate the matter. She also stressed that she was a woman who acted in accordance with principles and always stayed within bounds of the law.

Trade union officials believe that Mrs. S. Bappoo should have been moderate in her approach to industrial relations; that would have saved the situation from further deteriorating. A tripartite meeting round a table of the three actors- the trade union leaders, management representatives and the Minister where everyone would have had the opportunity to voice their grievances and feelings might have definitely helped to locate the origin and causes of the strike. A remedial step could have been taken on the spot. Then there would have been no need for the intervention of Justice Balgobin and spilling of much ink on the daily papers of the country. Nor would she have been taxed as incompetent or siding with the employer.

On the 12th July 1988 at 3.30 p.m., The Minister of labour and I.R chose to phone to Mr. Rajpalsingh Allgoo, Director of Organisation of MTGWU, requesting him to ask the strikers to stop the strike and resume work. She would intervene afterwards to find a solution to the crisis. This is a traditional tactics whereby one has "to comply and complain". I made a negative reply for reasons which we have mentioned earlier.

However, on 13th July 1988, I and some delegates met the Minister with a view to asking her to intervene so as to settle the dispute. The latter was firm on her decision. She would not intervene as long as the strike was on going. As a last resort she would have no alternative than to request management to take the necessary actions prescribed by law. (To sack 3,000 workers) There was a deadlock.

In such a thorny situation characterised by a tense climate and suspense, the principal actors were at a loss. Suddenly after some hesitation, the strikers were sacked by management on the 15th July 1988 and police were on the quest of Mr. Allgoo, V. Ramanaik and Mario Darga for inciting people to go on strike" wilfully and unlawfully". Mr. V. Ramnaik and Mario Darga were arrested and remanded to jail on 16.07.88 whereas I was lucky enough to have had a narrow escape, but for a short time only. I surrendered myself to police on 18.07.88.

I was arrested in front of the Gate of Sinotex Pamplemousses and was escorted by CCID Officers to the Line Barracks in Port Louis. There I gave my statement in presence of my two lawyers Mr. Dev Hurnam & Mr. Razack Peeroo. In my statement I explained that I was not aware of the strike, until I reached my office accompanied by two International Delegates.

This event leads us to reflect on Industrial democracy, the extent to which Trade Union leaders are free to carry out their activities, and the fate that was reserved to them. In fact, as the Judge Harris Balgobin pointed out, I was innocent.

First, on 18th July, 1988, the CCID Officers drove him to Piton Police Head Quarters to lock him there but the cells were full and then to Trou aux Biches Police station where Mr. Allgoo spent one night in the cell. The next day the CCID Officers transferred him to Line Barracks Police Station, which was meant for criminals and Drug smuggle, the condition of the Cell was extremely deplorable, even we treat animals in much better conditions than the line Barracks prison:

(1) The W.C. Flushing system was broken since a long time;
(2) No beds facilities – sleeping on floor (Cell 7 x 4) + No ventilation
(3) the Cell was infected with bugs.

When I inquired about the reason why I was being transferred to Line Barracks, I was told that they have been instructed to do so by High authority. (According to another source the transfer was linked to security, 3000 workers wanted to march to protest in front of the Trou aux Biches Police Station to ask the release of their Trade Union Leader).

With pressure of the newly created National Trade Unions Council, the government was forced to set up "Fact Finding Committee" under Judge Harris Balgobin. In fact, as the judge *Harris Balgobin pointed out in his fact finding, that Mr. Allgoo was innocent; he did in no way urge the workers to go on strike.* So he wondered who gave the directives and based on which criteria the commissioner of Police ordered his arrest.

SIR GAËTAN DUVAL AS ACTING PRIME MINISTER AND HIS CONTRIBUTIONS TO INDUSTRIAL RELATIONS DURING THE STRIKE

Sir Gaëtan Duval, Minister of Tourism & External Affairs and Vice-Prime Minister, stepped onto the Chair of the Prime Minister when the latter left for England on the 23rd July 1988, for a period of two weeks to receive his Knighthood from Queen Elizabeth II. Hence these two weeks are memorable in the history of Mauritius, especially in the sphere of industrial relations.

We have already seen that the Prime Minister and the Minister of Labour and Industrial Relations had chosen a harsh approach towards trade unions. They saw them as a hindrance to the flourishing of the economy of Mauritius, as groups were acting "savagely" for personal motives and not for the interest of the national economy. The appearance of Sir Gaetan Duval gave a new dimension to Industrial Relations. In total contradiction with the principles and approach towards Industrial Relations of his Leader SAJ and Minister of Labour & Industrial Relations, Sir Gaëtan Duval chose the soft way of dealing with industrial relations. He listened to the representatives of management in his office. He equally heard the representatives of the employees on the strike with a sympathetic ear. After meeting me and Mr. Bhagirutty and hearing our complaints, Mr. Duval declared in the Press that he had discovered a new and bright generation of trade unionists who are endowed with a keen sense of responsibility. He even apologised on behalf of the Prime Minister and the Government. The laudable terms Sir Gaetan Duval used while talking to the trade unionists and workers and his courtesy had no doubt had their impact on these people. Whatever were the motives of Duval in adopting the soft approach, he used his tact to calm the spirits of the strikers, and he was successful. Had the Minister of Labour and I.R. and the Prime Minister not intervened afterwards, the strike would have reached its end, and the situation normalised.

SIR ANEROOD JUGNAUTH CRITICISING SIR G. DUVAL "MANGE BANANA DANS 2 BOUT"

Judge Harris Balgobin had completed his enquiry and had submitted his report to the Minister of Labour and Industrial Relations on 8th August 1988, date on which the

Prime Minister returned from London with his Knight. It was clear in the report that the strike was affected on the workers' own initiative, and that trade union leaders were not to be blamed for that. Both the Prime Minister and the Minister of labour were aware of this fact.

But what was striking during the intervention of SAJ & Mrs Bappoo at Sinotex, and their subsequent discourses, was that they still laid the blame for the strike on the back of the trade unionists, especially Mr. Chand Bhagirutty who did not even attend any meeting with the workers. The latter was taxed "as a disguised wolf whose industrial actions were motivated by personal interests and not those of workers." (SAJ)

This disparity between the content of the Judge Balgobin Report and what the Prime Minister of a government said gives us food for reflection. Was the findings of Judge Balgobin ignored or misinterpreted – especially the part that spoke of those persons who were responsible for the strike? Or were those two persons namely: the Prime Minister and Minister of Labour & I.R. in question deliberately feign not to know about it so as to discredit the trade union leaders in the eyes of the workers of Sinotex, to discourage the latter from being members of "irresponsible" trade unions? We have no precise and relevant answers to these questions.

Anyway, the intervention of Mr. Jugnauth and Mrs. Bappoo at Sinotex on the 9th August 1988 is a memorable episode in the history of a Government. A battle was against on two fronts simultaneously. The virulent attacks of Mr. Jugnauth to: (1) Mr. C. Bhagirutty and (2) Sir Gaetan Duval. The following points were raised:

(1) Mr. Jugnauth is the leader of a government which shoulders its responsibility in times of hardship as well as prosperity. At no time has it failed its duty.

(2) While others were arousing workers to strike, government had done its best to save the country from bankruptcy.

(3) The aim of government is to see to it that everybody has a job security and fair standard of living. For this reason it has laboured hard to attract foreign industrialists who now offer employment to more than 90,000 workers.

(4) Government has at heart the future of the country. It wants it to be prosperous for the population that had voted for it. It will not beg for votes as others do.

(5) Mr. A. Jugnauth once belonged to the "Hindu Congress" but this does not mean that he practises the policy of racial discrimination. He believes in God and fights for social justice. His past life is not stained with blood.

(6) If precautions are not taken in the economic field, if the mass of money that is in circulation in the public is not controlled or channelled, competition in the market will be difficult.

The future of the Free Zone is threatened; industrialists can choose to go and invest in Madagascar where labour is much cheaper than in Mauritius. Mauritians should prevent this from happening, otherwise they will be ruined.

(7)   There are two categories of trade unionists. The first category is sincere and fights for the interest of the workers in a civilised manner. The second category uses workers to achieve their personal objectives. The leader of the MLC is cited as an example (according to Mr. A. Jugnauth)

(8)   Mr Duval is a "Jouisseur". He likes to *"passe sirop, essaye passe pou bon dimoune"*

(9)   Mr. G. Duval is a man who uses a language with a double meaning. At one time he was of opinion like the other members of the government that wages should not be increased. Now he is fighting for a general increase in salary/wages.

(10)   Law should be obeyed and strikes avoided for the interest of the country, to avoid social problems- suicide for instance – as those that cropped up during the strike at Vacoas transport.

(11)   The Government believed that Sinotex had acted legally during the strike; it could not be blamed. But the Trade unionistes desserve a « *sévère remonstrance* ».Sir Anerood Jugnauth also says: *"Je ne peux aussi condamner des employeurs qui agissent correctement, ziste pour faire plaisir travailleurs"* ...... *Les syndicalistes irresponsables ne devraient pas se plaindre ensuite des traitements qu'ils reçoivent en retour de leurs actes irréfléchis".*

When, on 15th July management sacked some 3,000 employees, the Minister of Labour declared that "it was regrettable" but nothing could be done to avoid this event; the strike was illegal and was likely to imperil a fragile economic sector. On the other hand, the Prime Minister openly declared on 9th July on the premises of Sinotex that management of Sinotex had acted according to law. So it could not be blamed. But he also added that both employees and management were responsible for the strike, but for this reason the MLC was the more responsible for it, and so it (MLC) deserved a harsher treatment. For this reason government was taxed with acting in collusion with the "Patronat" the capitalists, to the detriment of the labouring class.

In fact, this criticism appeared on the front page of all local newspapers. The trade unions also formulated similar criticisms addressed to government.

What was also significant was that the strike like all dramatic events unveiled the true face of the various key members of the alliance government. There was a difference in their attitude and approach towards industrial relations. Mr. Jugnauth had had Mr. Rajpalsingh Allgoo, leader of the MTGWU, Mr. Mario Darga and Mr. Vijay Ramanaik arrested, handcuffed and jailed. The leader of the union Mr. Allgoo had had the unpleasant experience of lying sick on a hospital bed with handcuff in his hand " as though he were a criminal", thanks to the good office of Mr Bhickramsingh Ramlallah, who visited me though there was restriction to meet me? When Mr Ramlallah daily visited me, he was very annoyed to witness that I was handcuffed like a criminal. He arranged a meeting with Sir Satcam Boolell the leader of the Labour Party and Minister of Justice Accompanied by Mr B. Ramlallah, Mrs Raj Allgoo met Hon. Sir Satcam Boolell explained the deplorable conditions of her husband. Hon. Minister of Justice & External Affairs ordered the Commissioner of Police, on 23th July, to remove the handcuffs immediately.

Here we should note that Sir Satcam Boolell Minister of Justice and External Affairs was not in Mauritius at the time of the strike and arrest of trade unionists; he had just returned from mission abroad. How the situation would have been if he were in Mauritius? Mr. Duval, leader of the PMSD, affirmed that he had his own "style" of dealing with industrial relations and people; he wanted to save a situation which was degenerating day by day. He asserts his stand in humorous and mocking style which aims at denigrating the Prime Minster and the Minister of labour:

> "Pendant ki Rambo pa la, syndicats menace pou boycotter,
> ou coire mo bizin dire zotte attane, mo mari pas la,
> quand li vini nou a guette"
>
> (Le Socialiste 15.08.88)

He also believed:
(1)   that trade unionists should not be treated as criminals:
(2)   that workers should be given a salary increase

This divergence of attitude and opinion on industrial relations matters indicate that conflict was imminent in the alliance government.

The Intervention of Judge Balgobin

Judge Harris Balgobin is a man who has "long experience in industrial matters" His appearance on the industrial scene helped to unlock many situations. The emergence of the Judge in that chaotic period gave industrial relations a new facet. In a deadlock situation, there is still place for voluntarism. Such a phenomenon was unseen in Mauritius in the past. However, since the judge was an employee of the government since long, there was a feeling among some people that he might be a man of the government and so likely to distort the reality of facts. This called for utmost caution on both sides: Each of them tried to depose before the Judge in the company of a lawyer. The General Manager of Sinotex Mr. T. Kam was accompanied by Mr. Edwin Venchard Q.C. the MTGWU by Mr. R. Peeroo, barrister-at-law and assisted by Mr. Dan Callikan, technical adviser.

Fortunately, the Judge did his job objectively and was able to determine the facts that had led to the strike. The report satisfied all the parties concerned. He showed that he was neither biased nor in favour of the trade union nor in the favour of management.

The Reports of the Judge Harris Balgobin.

1. **The works Council.** Workers believed that the "Works Council is a rival to a trade union and merely serves the interest of management". Some believed that the bonus which was given at the end of the year to the members of the works council was in fact bribes. Further, they complained that the workers did not represent them as they were not selected by them. Their grievance about the bribe does not seem a genuine one but I am satisfied that they genuinely felt that the election was not properly conducted.

    Judge Balgobin also adds that "attention must be drawn to the possible confusion, although this is not obvious at Sinotex, with transforming works councils into parallel unions, i.e. negotiating wage increase.....

2. **Supervisors.** Some supervisors treat the factory workers in a "high-handed" and "vulgar manner". They "appear to confuse the factory room with an army barrack". This grievance, although it is exaggerated, explains the unsatisfactory atmosphere at Sinotex.

3. The report brought light to a sombre and hazy situation where workers were despondent; union leaders were jailed; management had resorted to the dismissal of its employees; the facts that triggered the strike were exposed, and the responsibility of each party to the dispute was highlighted.etc...

Sir Gaëtan Duval Intervention & Resignation

God had willed that Sir A. Jugnauth should be absent from the country for a fortnight as from the 23rd July 1988. The result was that Sir Gaëtan Duval stepped in his shoes as Acting Prime Minster. The role he played – in contradiction with the principles laid down by his government- eclipsed that of the Minister of Labour, and even made her blush and feel belittled in the eyes of the workers, trade unions and the general public.

The outcome was however drastic. When the Prime Minister returned to Mauritius on 8th August 1988; he decided to intervene at Sinotex to redress the situation on the 9th of August 1988 What he proffered had negative effects on Mr. Duval and his Party members. Sir Gaëtan Duval resigned from his post of Vice-Prime minister. The reasons for his resignation are clearly stated in his letter which reads as follows:

207

12 August 1988
The Hon, Sir A. Jugnauth, Q.C., KCMG
Prime Minister
Government House
Port Louis.

Dear Sir A. Jugnauth,

Please find enclosed a copy of a letter of resignation of Sir Gaetan Duval Deputy Prime Minister which was sent to his Excellency the Governor General. It speaks for itself:

Regards
Sir Gaetan Duval Q.C. –
Cabinet de Vice Premier Ministre - Ile Maurice

Ce 12 aout 1988.

Son Excellence
Sir Veerasamy Ringadoo GCMG, Q.C.
Governor General
Le Réduit.

A la réunion du conseil des ministres hier, tous les membres du gouvernement, sauf mon frère Hervé, ont approuvé la politique du Premier Ministre dans l'affaire SINOTEX, y compris la réaction brutale envers les syndicalistes et les travailleurs. Ils ont dans le même souffle, désapprouvé la politique de dialogue suivie par moi pendant intérimat. Ils ont de plus refusé de discuter même le principe d'une compensation salariale. La question n'est donc pas de forme ou de manière, mais une question de style et de fond. Nous allons donc, selon notre analyse, devant une confrontation qui va détruire la paix sociale, qu'est la base même de notre progrès économique.

Si le Parti travailliste, reniant son passé, est disposé à participer avec le MSM dans une telle aventure, le PMSD ne peut que s'y opposer de la façon la plus catégorique. C'est pourquoi mon frère Hervé, le Dr Brizloll et moi-même, nous avons l'honneur de vous soumettre notre démission de nos postes respectifs.

Nous tenons à vous remercier de toute l'aide que vous nous avez apportée, de vos précieux conseils durant notre mandat, et vous prions d'accepter l'expression de notre haute considération.

Sir G. Duval, Hon. Herve Duval, Hon. Dr. P. Brizloll

Indeed, when he passed away, Sir Gaëtan was mourned by all Mauritians. And I can say today that I wept when I learned about his demise. This man was a "bénédiction" for this country. He was not a politician who lived for communal purposes. He was not a man who calculated his moves, like a chess-player. Sir Gaëtan was a humanist in himself. And I am particularly proud that we both lived in Grand Gaube village. What he did in my favour and for the workers of Sinotex, I will always cherish his action. May his great soul rest in peace!

I will always be indebted to Mr Dev Hurnam who had spared no effort to get me and my two colleagues released. Furthermore, to get me admitted to hospital after I fell ill in the Line Barracks Police Station Cell, the Doctors refused to admit me to the Civil Hospital as they were afraid of Rambo. The very day around 9.00 p.m. Mr Dev Hurnam came to visit me and he managed through the intervention of the Commissioner of Police, to send me to hospital and I was admitted to "La Salle 15" after being examined by a panel of Doctors and I was discharged after 10 days.

Chapter 28

SEMINAR ON
LABOUR LEGISLATIONS

I am pleased to say that due to the affiliation with different International Trade Union Federations, such as: International Metalworkers Federation – Geneva; ICEM – Brussels; IFBWW – Geneva; IUF- Geneva; International Transports Federation – London & MLC, the AGWU has been able to organise a large number of seminars and Workshops regularly for the benefits of the Leaders and the Rank and file members on different subjects, such as Grievance Handling, Collective Bargaining, Remuneration Orders, Occupational Safe, Health and Welfare and Labour Legislations, etc

The AGWU might be the unique union in Mauritius to organise a workshop on a high level on the amendment to be brought of Trade Union Relations Bill and Occupation safety, Health and welfare. Some of these seminars & Workshops were residential held in Hotels for the duration between one to three weeks conducted by eminent persons, Lawyers and Dr Ben .O Alli ILO Consultant .

RESIDENTIAL WORKSHOP ON O.S.H & WELFARE

The ICEM was very much involved in promoting Occupational Safely, Health and Welfare of Workers in their programme for its affiliates. In this connection the ICEM had sponsored a high level residential workshop on Occupational Safety, Health and Welfare in 1002, for 25 participants to be trained as Trainers, under able Dr Benjamin O. Alli, the Ex-ILO Consultant, who was at that time employed with the ICEM. The

Caption

Residential workshop was held at the Island View Club Hotel – Grand Gaube for duration of Two weeks. The aims of the workshop were to train the participants on the OSH&W promotion and maintenance of the highest degree of physical, mental and social well being of the workers in all occupations; the prevention amongst workers of departures from health caused by their working conditions, the protection of workers in their employment from risks resulting from factors adverse to health; the placing and maintenance of the worker in an occupational environment adapted to his physiological and psychological capabilities; and to summarise: the adaptation of the work to man and each man to his job. Always taking into consideration of the Mauritian labour legislations, O.S.H Act 1988 and they studied other countries occupational Health, Safety & Welfare Regulations. This workshop made several suggestions to the Government to amend the existing O.S.H Act to be in line with the ILO conventions.

A further workshop was organised at the same place for one week to evaluate and access the participants, under an able Lecturer from South Africa.

The official opening ceremony was performed by the Hon Dharma and G. Fokeer, Minister of Labour and Industrial Relations in the presence of Dr Ben O. Alli and other eminent personalities and the Closing Ceremony was done by His Excellency Robin Ghuburrun the Vice –President of the Republic of Mauritius.

White Paper on Draft Trade Union & Labour Relations Bill

In May 1994 the Government introduced a White Paper "Draft Trade Union and Labour Relations Bill" on the amendment of the Industrial Relations Act of 1973, with Brief Explanatory notes together with the Special Law Review Committee Report on the Industrial Relations Act.

Since the inception of the IRA the Trade Unions Movement have made several protests & representations to the Government but unfortunately no serious attempt has been made by several successive Government including the MMM Government, whose unions had suffered a lot due to this anti-union legislation and on several occasions promised to bring changes to this piece of legislation which they used to call "La loi-baillon".

The Trade unions Leaders had manifested in Front of the Parliament in protest against "the new Draft Bill of the Trade Unions and Labour Relations with Brief Explanatory Notes, to gather with "The special Law Review Committee report on the Industrial Relations Act" to show their disapproval and disagreement. This was considered as a repressive and anti-democratic legislation which impedes the scope of action of the trade union in many areas and during demonstration the Trade Unions Leaders in sign of disapproval burned the Draft Bill, but unfortunately they did not presented a counter proposal to the Bill. Contrary to the AGWU, MLC and GSA as responsible trade unions despite disapproving the Bill but had considered it important to make counter proposal point by point, on section they disagreed and which were not in favour of the workers. The then Minster of Labour and Industrial Relations Hon Clarel Malherbe and later Hon Dharam Fokeer, were both invited to our unions to discuss our counter proposal. Prior to presentation of our Counter proposal, I had asked the advice and collaboration with the IMF, BTUC and ICFTU. On my way back from the IMF conference in Germany, I went to Brussels to discuss the amendment to be brought to the above Bill with Mr Bill Jordan the General Secretary of ICFTU and his Staffs and also the General Secretary of the BTUC. It was a mere coincidence; the Minister Fokeer went also to discuss the issue with the BTUC a few minutes before me. Needless to let you know that MLC Leader got lot of information.

With the above background, accompanied by Executive members, we held at least twelve working sessions with the Minister of Labour & I.R and his Officials. The proposed amendment was discussed and explained in detail and all the points which were not in favour of peaceful industrial relations were noted.

Contrary to other Trade Unions the AGWU, GSA and the MLC made a counter proposal point by points with proposed amendments. The AGWU had around 10 to 12 meetings to discuss in details their proposed amendments with the Minister of Labour assisted by his Technician. All this was possible because I got the support of the IMF, ICFTU, British Trade Unions Congress; every one of them had sent their written counter proposals.

Since its inception of the IRA, the Trade Unions Movement have made several representations to the Government but unfortunately no serious attempt was made by several successive Governments. The GWF and MMM had suffered a lot due to this anti-union legislation.

The AGWU raised the issue again with the newly elected Government 1995, In January 22-26, 1996. The IMF sponsored a very high level workshop for the AGWU, which was held at Gold Crest Hotel for one week. The IMF had sent two of the Lawyers specialised in Labour Legislations, Mr Sunil Narain Senior Lawyer of the NUMSA and Mr Edwin Maepe of IMF from South Africa.

WORKSHOP WAS CONDUCTED BY EMINENT LAWYERS

The Lecturers were invited from the University of Mauritius; Professors were from the School of Management Namely: Mr Dharam Gokhool Senior Lecturer; Mr Rajen Narsinghen Law Lecturer; Mrs V. Bhadain Law Lecturer; Mrs Priya Baguant and others. The Seminar was officially open by the Hon A. Razack Peeroo, Minister of Labour and Industrial Relations as a newly appointed Minister, He promised to bring amendment in line with the ILO Conventions and he even promised to codify the Labour Laws but till today nothing has been done.

In my welcome address, I recalled that Mr Peeroo was the legal adviser of the AGWU for a long time. In his professional capacity as an eminent lawyer he was engaged most of his time in defending workers at the Industrial Court or Industrial Relations Commission and Permanent Arbitration Tribunal. So we feel that we don't need to elaborate more as he is well aware of the issue and after the Seminar we will forward him a complete report, expecting that the new government will do the needful.

The industrial relations system, characterised by a heavy inter-relation of the three forces namely Government, Labour and Capital, the partners are condemned to work together to produce the best results through a consensus within the frame work of Tripatitism which was advocated and given impetus under the new regime.

The economic situation of today warranted a consensus for:
- *Convergence of the conflicting interests of labour and capital as opposed to the philosophy of class;*
- *An Industrial peace and harmony, a sine-qua-non condition for the socio-economic development;*
- *the promotion of social justice through fulfilment of workers' needs and aspiration from work;*
- *with the new philosophy, the trade union had to refine its strategy and move from an adversarial role to a more employees'*

Chapter 29

THE CENTRALISATION AND MECHANISATION OF THE SUGAR INDUSTRY

THE Centralisation and the Modernisation of the sugar industry in Mauritius, especially the case of the closing down of the Saint Antoine sugar factory, started in a total confusion, doubt, suspicion and mistrust. The question was asked by the workers and Small Planters, "was it necessary to close down an efficient sugar factory"?

According to Hon Madan Dulloo, Minister of Agriculture through press conferences and public meetings, there was no need to close down the St. Antoine sugar factory, the reason put forward the factory was an efficient one – it had sugar canes of small planters coming from a large region of the North. The Planters will face hardship in organising to send their sugar canes to the Mon Loisirs sugar factory. Furthermore this closing down will paralyze the commercial activities in the region and will create a number of unemployment. According to Hon Madan Dulloo that's why he refused to sign the document of the closing down the sugar factory of St. Antoine.

Despite the above argument the Prime Minister, Hon Sir Aneerood Jugnauth was adamant in the closing down of the sugar factory of St. Antoine. He waited until the departure of Hon Dulloo to an overseas mission and ordered Hon Jugdish Goburdhun, Acting Minister of Agriculture, to sign the relative document concerning the closing down of the St. Antoine sugar factory.

It was a fatal blow particularly to the artisans of the St. Antoine sugar factory and the small planters and people having businesses in the surrounding villages of the factory suffered a lot. The effect of the disagreement between and Prime Minister and Minister of Agriculture, Mr Madan Dulloo cost him a very heavy price. He was sacked as Minister of Agriculture by the Prime Minister Sir Aneerood Jugnauth.

Once Hon Madan Dulloo was out of the Government, he launched a vast campaign against SAJ and this created doubt in the mind of the people, why the document papers concerning the closing down was done in a hurry, for such an important issue in absence of the Minister of Agriculture Hon Madan Dulloo? This became national issue, and people started questioning as to who had interests in the closing down of the St. Antoine Sugar Factory. Later Mr Madan Dulloo created his own political party, the MMSM.

NEGOTIATION OF CLOSING DOWN SUGAR FACTORY

Once the owners of St. Antoine sugar factory got the green light to close down the sugar factory, the management invited the recognised trade unions to discuss the conditions of payment of severance allowances and other relative benefits. A few meetings with the management were held together with (AGWU/OUA) regarding the compensation and other benefits and related conditions on which the Artisans would have been declared redundant. The AGWU had made sure that all the workers shall be entitled 3 months wage per year of Service and a plot of land 8 to 15 perches, plus 2/3 of wage as pension up to the age of normal retirement.

On 30th June 1993, the Mon Loisirs Sugar Estate sent a letter to all workers (factory which will crush the sugar canes St. Antoine Sugar Factory Area). It informed the Workers by stating "that you are aware, Société Sincere de St. Antoine will apply for official permission to close down St. Antoine Sugar Factory. Should the application succeed and should the Termination of Contracts of Service Board approve the termination of the contracts of employment St. Antoine has with its employees and should you wish to be redeployed following such closure, we are pleased to offer you employment, in our company on terms not less favourable than your present terms of employment, with effect from the date you will be released by St. Antoine Sugar estate". The Mon Loisirs S.E. sent letters to St. Antoine sugar factory workers. It stressed that re-employment is subject to the following conditions:

- Pursuant to section 24 of the Cane Planters and Millers Arbitration and Control Board Act1973, St. Antoine must obtain from the Minister of Agriculture permission to close its factory on or before 15 November 1993;

- Pursuant to section 39 of the labour Act 1975, St. Antoine must obtain from the Termination Contract Service Board permission to terminate the employment of its workers on or before 15 December 1993;

- The further conditions set out in Annexure II must be satisfied whether you are opting for comparable employment or for a compensation.

We finally wish to stress that this offer and alternative offer of compensation by St. Antoine are inextricably linked. The failure to satisfy any condition of either offer shall render both offers null and void.

The lettre signe: General Manager, Société de Rivière du Rempart.

The AGWU was surprised to receive a request by Mr Alain Victoire OUA representative and equally an employee of St. Antoine S.E. stating that the OUA represent a large majority of the Artisans in the factory and have decided that the condition of closing down St. Antoine sugar factory and informed that a committee has been set up among workers to negotiate the condition of closing down compensation or other benefits.

Finally we learned that the workers have agreed that the St. Antoine S.E. will pay 1.3 months wage per year of service, 7 to 10 perches of land depending on the number of year of service and few minor benefits and they accepted to sign an agreement with Management.

What really happened during the negotiation, it is still difficult to understand, and on other hand the employees were not satisfied with deal. But one thing is clear: the language of the letter seems that the employer was imposing their conditions. Afterward the AGWU learned that the committee under the chairmanship of Mr Alain Victoire have already signed historical agreement. A few workers came to the AGWU office and complained that they were not satisfied with the deal, but unfortunately nothing could have been done.

CLOSING DOWN OF THE MOUNT SUGAR FACTORY

Just the following year of the closing down of the St. Antoine Sugar factory, the Managing Director Mr J. M. Antoine Harel, decided to close down The Mount Sugar factory and invited the recognised trade unions sometime in August 1994 to discuss the quantum of Severance Allowance to be paid and other related conditions. The first was just an informative meeting. The second meeting was held Thursday 8th September 1994 14.30 hours at the Club House in attendance: Management side: Messer's. Antoine Harel, J. Pilot. P. De Rosnay and J. Poonith.

Members Workers committee; Messrs E. Appigadoo, Ragudu, E. Moussa, K. Bassant, A. Contran, J. Souresth, V. Panchgoolam, C. Legrend, G. Lebrasse, H. Thomas et V. Narainen.

Trade Unions: Messrs R. Allgoo (AGWU); A. Victoire (OUA); Y. B. Mooteealoo (UASI)

Mr J. Poonith read the last minute of proceeding and it was approved.

Mr Harel proposed as compensation the double legal (the Normal Severance Allowance normal rate). It seemed this proposal do not satisfy the employees. He made another proposal and said that he is of opinion the generous packet of St. Antoine S.E. will surely interest the workers. He informed the Delegates and the Trade Union Representative that he would prefer to wait the Action Plan of Centralisation of the MSPA.

Employees Demands

Mr. E. Appigadu spokesman of the Workers Committee;

(i) a list of jobs available for those who do not opt for cash compensation;
(ii) a compensation of severance allowance six (6) months per year of service;
(iii) a month pension to the order of 2/3 wage until the date of normal retirement;
(iv) a plot of land for Construction of 8to 15 perches depending of years of service and their grade;
(v) a time limit to leave the Houses occupied by the Artisans.

For those who did not agree with the above proposals where to be given a job at Beau Plan S.E. and Belle Vue Harel S.E. The delegates made a complaint to the Managing Director, stating that relations at Belle Vue Harel were too rigid. The workers said that the 5 perches of land will not suffice to build a house.

During meeting the delegates of the Artisans and Trade Unions representatives argued that we could compare the St. Antoine sugar factory with The Mount sugar factory because The Mount sugar factory was among efficient and profitable factory.

After a few meetings the AGWU stopped sending its representative to the meeting, during which it seemed that the *"Porte Parole"* were not happy to see the trade unions representatives. Thus the AGWU and UASI ceased standing representatives to the negotiation.

A last meeting was held on 30 December 1994 in Port Louis. Present: employers Representatives: Mess. J. M. Antoine Harel, Jacques Pilot, Jodhun Poonith, Dominique Piat: Workers Representatives: Kader Bhayat, E. Appigadu, L.Ragudu, K. Bussunt, V. Panchgoolam, C. Legrand, G. Lebrasse, H. Thomas, V. Narainen, J. Souresth; and Mr A.Victoire, Representative of Trade Unions. (according to the minute of proceeding) At the request of some AGWU members, Allgoo decided to send Mr Kader Bhayat it legal Advisor to the above meeting.

Mr Antoine Harel welcomed the delegates of Artisans and the Legal Advisor Mr. Kader Bhayat.

Mr Harel on behalf of the company informed the delegates that he would appreciate if a reply of the Artisans could be communicated to him before the end of year holiday the 31 December 1994.

The representative of Workers wanted to raise the question of quantum of compensation, Mr. Harel replied that this question has been lengthily discussed, but we would like to repeat what has been discussed for the information of Mr Kader Bhayat. The aim was to follow the guideline of St. Antoine rate of payment which was adopted previously. St. Antoine had offered an average of 1, 3 per months of service. But the Mount had already accepted to offer 2 months wage per year of service, to a limit of 64 months for 32 years of service and plus, refuse to increase quantum.

The spokesman of delegates made a few suggestions to confirm that the return bus fare of the children would be refunded up to one year after the closing down of the sugar factory and the compensation be paid on the total earning.

Mr Harel replied that the offer of compensation was an ex-gratia that the company agreed on the request of the workers, based on the concept St. Antoine adopted on the basic wage.

Mr Bhayat requested for a list of workers be submitted to him and Trade unions representatives, so as they could verify the amount of compensation be allocated to them.

Mr Harel agreed to give copy to Mr. K. Bhayat for his information as it was a confidential document.

The order of the day was over and the meeting ended.

In the mid of January 1995, a group of the AGWU members accompanied by other non members came to meet Mr Allgoo, made complaint that they were not satisfied with the agreement signed by the Workers Delegates. The President of AGWU found himself in very embarrassing situation. Nevertheless he could not let the workers down and tried to do whatever possible, despite the AGWU was not happy with the negotiation which took placed between Workers delegates and the Management.

INTERVENTION OF
MR G. RAJPATTI DIRECTOR OF THE MSA

First thing came to the mind of Mr Allgoo was to write a protest letter to the Director of the Mauritius Sugar Authority (MSA), with copy to the Management of the Compagnie Usinière The Mount Ltd. Mr G. Rajpatti was very sympathy to the issues and acted positively by inviting the parties for discussions, several meetings were organised under the aegis of the Executive Director of the Mauritius Sugar Authority. Furthermore Allgoo used his influence and lobby was made to the Ministers. Thanks to the good office of Mr Rajpatti the Director of the MSA, the workers of the Mount Sugar Factory succeeded in getting additional benefits such as: half month of wage per year of service and 1 to 2 perches of land compensation. Finally an agreement was signed between the management and the workers which were follows:-

Main components:
- The package was made up of two main components, first Compensation in the form of cash and land and secondly minor forms of compensation;
- Workers and Staff Two and half months per full year of service plus a proposition for any uncompleted year;
- The land compensation was made up of a basic component was linked to the length of service and an additional component which made allowance for the level of the basic salary:-
- Basic land compensation for workers and staff:

Tables

(i)

Length of Service years		Basic land compensation (perches)
From	To	
0.01	2.99	8
3.00	10.99	9
11.00	20.99	10
21.00	30.99	11
31.00	and over	12

(ii)   Additional land compensation in relation to monthly basic salary: workers

Basic Salary (Rs) as at 14.4,95 Additional land compensation

From	To	(perches)
0.0	4,175.50	2
4,175.51	4,537.50	3
4,537.51	and over	4

(iii)   Additional land compensation in relation to the monthly basic salary

Basic salary (Rs) on 31.12. 94   Additional land compensation

From	To	(perches)
5,300	15.900	2
15.90.01	21,200	3
21,200.01	31.800	4

WHY - VRS I - II & ERS

Mauritius had to face with the triple challenge of coping with a high budget deficit; adapting to the erosion of preferences in respect of sugar and textiles in a situation where the balance of trade was negative; and to facilitate the emergence of new poles of development.

These challenges had to be viewed against the background of the triple shock facing Mauritius, namely the 36% reduction of the sugar price brought by the reform of the EU Sugar Regime; the continually rising oil prices; and the dismantling of the Multifibre Agreement and the WTO negotiations on Non Agricultural Market Access which would adversely impact on the Textile and Clothing and Fisheries sectors.

The Sugar Industry Efficiency (SIE) Act amended early this year also makes provision for Early Retirement Scheme (ERS) for employees of sugar factories which will not be closed and which will establish sub-clusters. More importantly, it provides for the introduction of training/re-skilling schemes for VRS and ERS employees. The VRS , ERS and Blue Print workers will also be entitled to earlier receipt of the Actuarially Reduced Contributory Retirement Pension, as from age 45 for female workers and age 50 for male workers.

The **Voluntary retirement scheme (VRS)** is one of the main components of the Sugar Sector Strategic Plan 2001-2005. Its aim was to reduce the operation cost of production of sugar in Mauritius, according to MSPA the labour cost represented 56 per cent in 2001. Its objective is therefore to right size the labour of the industry, reducing it by at least 30 per cent in the first instance, in order to reach a level that is more in line with its actual requirements and economic realities.

To that effect, the Sugar Industry Efficiency (SIE) Act, which is the legal framework governing sugar activities in Mauritius, as well as relevant labour and pension laws, were amended to cater for the implementation of the VRS.

In 2001, this principle of compensation was extended to the growing activities of the sugar industry and the VRS was introduced. Two categories of workers were defined, those having more than a certain age and the rest. The offer was compulsorily made to those having more than a certain age. For the other employees, the employer has the liberty to choose to whom he makes an offer of a VRS but the decision to accept or reject the offer rests solely with the employee.

VOLUNTARY RETIREMENT SCHEME I

The following package was given to those who retired on the Voluntary Retirement Scheme I as from 2001:-

- Agricultural workers Male of 55 years or more — 2.0 months wage per year of service
- Agricultural workers Female of 50 years or more — 2.0 months wage per year of service
- Land compensation — 7 perches

All other cases including Staff no age limit:-

First five	1.5 months
Next ten years	1.25 months
Next ten years	1.00 month
Next ten years or more	.75 month

Total number of employees retiring was 8,317

Total land distributed to employees was 814 arpents.

The financing of the scheme, of the order of Rs 3 billion (100 million Euro), was effected through loan from local banks. About Rs 1 billion is destined for infrastructure works to be undertaken by sugar companies on the land sites allocated to VRS leavers and the remaining Rs 2 billion for the cash compensation. The financing will be recouped through the sale of agricultural lands as per the parameters set down in the SIE Act 2001.

VOLUNTARY RETIREMENT SCHEME II - 2007

- Agricultural Workers Male of 50 years and Female 45 years — 2.00 months wage per year of service
- Agricultural workers less than 50 yr for men & 45 yrs female — 1.50 per month
- Land compensation — 7 perches
- Staff no age limit — 1.50 per months wage per year of service

Early retirement Scheme (ERS)

Number of Employees retired on the Early Retirement Scheme applied by the following sugar factories Belle Vue Mauricia; Medine; Omicane and FUEL including Artisans and Staff were 209 and the cost of implementation was Rs 122 million.

The AGWU is pleased to say that thank to agreement reached between the Artisans of The Mount Sugar Factory and Mr Antoine Harel the Managing Director of The Compagnie Usiniere The Mount Ltd., the conditions of payment of compensation and other benefits on which the Closing down of The Mount Sugar factory, was followed by the preparation of the Blue Print of the Sugar Industry by the Government.

Chapter 30

IMF CONGRESS
SAN FRANCISCO - USA

THE model code below was debated within the IMF Congress in San Francisco, in May, 1997. IMF. I was pleased to be one of the delegates to endorse an Action Programme which introduced the objective of negotiating corporate codes of conduct for the purpose of making workers' rights part of national labour-management dialogue. It was clear from the outset that such codes were to be negotiated and would become agreements between the IMF and transnational corporations (TNCs). That was the last IMF Congress I attended.

The codes would be based on existing instruments such as the International Labour Organisation (ILO) Tripartite Declaration of Principles and the Organisation for Economic Co-operation and Development (OECD) Guidelines for Multinational Enterprises. The original intention was that the IMF Executive Committee should decide which TNCs to target.

Following the Congress, a working group was set up to make recommendations for codes of conduct and decided to focus its work on drafting a model code of conduct. The IMF Model Code of Conduct was subsequently adopted at the Executive Committee meeting in December 1998. The IMF model was based on that of the International Confederation of Free Trade Unions (ICFTU). Similar models were used by other Global Union Federations (GUFs).

The 2001-2005 Action Programme adopted at the Sydney Congress committed the IMF to continuing to campaign for the adoption of the Model Code of Conduct in all corporations where affiliates have members. The aim was to negotiate at least one such agreement in each of the major metal sectors during the Congress period.

Ten IFAs were signed during this period in five sectors. In reporting to the 2005 Congress, IMF General Secretary Marcello Malentacchi pointed out the problematic aspect to this success, namely that all of the agreements were with Europe-based TNCs, and called for efforts to approach companies outside Europe, particularly in North America and Asia.

By 2002 the term International Framework Agreement (IFA) had been adopted as a means of clearly distinguishing the negotiated agreements being pursued by IMF and its affiliates from the type of voluntary codes of conduct that corporations were increasingly adopting unilaterally to ostensibly demonstrate their commitment to corporate social responsibility.

There are 3 key components to the Model IFA:

1. The ILO Core Labour Standards — referenced as such.
2. The requirement for contractors and suppliers to observe the standards of the IFA.
3. Union participation in implementation.

THE ILO CORE LABOUR STANDARDS

In 1998 the International Labour Conference adopted a 'Declaration on Fundamental Principles and Rights at Work', considered to be an expression of commitment by governments, employers' and workers' organisations to uphold basic human values. The Declaration commits ILO Member States to respect and promote principles and rights in four categories, whether or not they have ratified the relevant Conventions. The Declaration makes it clear that these rights are universal, and that they apply to all people in all States.

The three categories are:
- Freedom of association and the right to collective bargaining (ILO Conventions 87, 98, 135 and Recommendation 143)
- The elimination of forced and compulsory labour (ILO Conventions 29 and 105)
- The abolition of child labour (ILO Conventions 138 and 182).

Chapter 31

INAUGURATION OF
EMMANUEL ANQUETIL LABOUR
CENTRE BUILDING

RAJPALSINGH ALLGOO'S ADDRESS

Hon. Prime Minister, Dr Navinchandra Ramgoolam, Hon. A. R. Peeroo, Minister of Labour & Industrial Relations, Dr The Hon James Burty David, Minister of Local Government, High Commissioners, Brother Ekkie Essau, IMF African Representative and Distinguished guests, as the outgoing President of the AGWU, it is a matter of pride and privilege for me to associate myself with to-day's event. As all human being's aspiration in life is to have a shelter of his own, the inauguration of this complex has in a way fulfilled one of my most cherished ambitions of providing the AGWU with a complex and a seat of its own before my retirement from active trade union activities. Right away, I would like to avail myself of this opportunity to express my appreciation to the Hon. Prime Minister and Hon. Ministers for having kindly accepted to grace our function, despite their tight work schedules. Your presence, among us, Hon. Ministers is in itself a living testimony of your interest towards the social partners and honours in some way the letter and spirit of tripartism.

Historically speaking it is a matter of pride for the AGWU to have as founder the pioneer of the trade union movement in Mauritius, Emmanuel Anquetil and as leader Joseph Guy Rozemont, two prominent political figures who have left an inestimable legacy in the social and political fields by paving, in the early forties the way for the democratisation of workers' rights and political emancipation of the country.

Mr ...., Mr Khalid Buddoo Vice-President AGWU, Dr the Hon Navinchandra Ramgoolam Prime Minister, Pt Shyam Daiboo and Daughter, Dr James Burty David Minister of Local Govt , Raj Allgoo President AGWU & Mr Allen Bhugmoneea Treasurer AGWU on the occasion of laying foundation stone of AGWU

The organisation of this historic event on a Labour Day bears a significant meaning. As workers, we cannot ignore the contribution of our late leader and prominent member of the Mauritius Labour Party, Mr Guy Rozemont who was instrumental in having May Day proclaimed a Public Holiday, some fifty years ago.

On the Other hand, in order to keep the legend of our founder alive and blowing and in recognition of his dedication to the working class, the AGWU has unanimously decided to honour, in its humble way, the founding father of our organisation by naming our complex, the *Emmanuel Anquetil Labour Centre*.

It is with great pride, after 60 years of existence, that AGWU has been able to put up its own building as its Headquarter at Smith Street, Grand River North West, Port Louis. A wish of its founders, the late Emmanuel Anquetil was accomplished by me. To honour the memory of the father of the labour movement in Mauritius, the building proudly bears the name "Emmanuel Anquetil Labour Centre".

The construction of such a building was not easy task for a medium Union. It was a real challenge for me to build an office complex of one story on a land of 30 perches with 4 offices; one waiting room, two W.C, one Bath room, Mess room and Kitchen and a large Conference Hall/ Workers Education Centre fully furnished with Chairs, Tables for 50 participants with all the necessary equipments. My heartfelt thanks go to members of AGWU who greatly contributed financially through their monthly subscriptions and support. In 1975, when I was appointed negotiator there were only 452 members, with Rs10, 000., remaining me from the sale of the AGWU Building at Guy Rozemont Square Port Louis, which were insufficient for the payment of union staff.

The fight was fierce with, on the one hand; the meteoric rise of Paul Bérenger, Leader of the UASI, SILU and GWF, and on the other hand Alex Rime, Minister of Employment and founder negotiator of the OAU. Both unions together grouped the vast majority of the artisans of the sugar industry, had managed to shape the destiny of AGWU by attracting a greater number of union members. In the 1990s', AGWU was the most representative union of the artisans in the sugar industry and had more than 3,000 members, an eloquent figure despite the escalation of other unions.

AGWU Workers' Education Centre

The Emmanuel Anquetil Labour Centre ' at Grand River North West is the pride of Artisans to possess an Education Centre and a conference room that can accommodate a hundred delegates. The project required an investment of Rs1.5 millions. One of the main preoccupations of the AGWU was Workers Education. Today who cares about the education of its members and are workers using this centre for the promotion of workers' education?

The AGWU has always encouraged and continues to encourage people to stand on their own feet not to become slaves to the politicians for their political gains. A trained worker knowing his rights is more valuable to the country; politicians have always taken the workers for a ride. After the fabulous promises, these same politicians have changed their language on the issue of 40 hours after coming to power and speak of "prudence". It should therefore be wary of new union politicians who try to lure workers.

As regards the 2nd activity; in view of the challenges awaiting us in the wake of the globalisation process and increasing pace of development being registered locally, and in line with the concept that an educated worker is an asset both to the country and the economy, and that education and training is the root of progress and development, the AGWU feels an urgency to equip its rank and file members with the necessary knowledge and skills for them to respond positively to the changing environment.

Besides, the role of a trade union in the modern society is not limited to the promotion of worker's rights and interests only; the AGWU could not remain complacent. With the present infrastructure, the union is now in a position to cater to the educational needs of its members on systematic and on-going basis and I am pleased to inform this assembly of the establishment of an Educational Centre in the new complex.

On the other hand, with the policy of mechanisation and centralisation of the Sugar Industry, we are witnessing a gradual erosion of trade union membership. I therefore feel that it is high time for unions catering for the interests of Artisans to start thinking of redefining their philosophy and actions for a common playing field which may ultimately culminate in a merger of the three main non-agricultural workers' union into alone strong union.

CREATION OF THE MTUC
OF EMMANUEL ANQUETIL

Another decision that is likely to affect the Industrial Relations *landscape is my effort to revive the MTUC which was merged with the MCTUC in 1963 to form the MLC.* Democracy being what it implies; and at times power leading to dictatorship, it is regretted that when democratic principles are shattered and the rules of the game changed to suit the players, the only alternative left is the exit door. History only can justify whether our action was good or bad.

As a concluding remark, from a strictly personal point of view, I have a mixed feeling over to-day's function. Shakespeare has rightly said in one of his plays that there is an entrance and an exit on a stage". To-day's function is perhaps the last important one of my career at the helm of this organisation since 1975, and taking stock of what has been achieved for the last past decades it cannot be said that the long path covered so far has been an easy one.

I have experienced my ups and downs; joys and sorrows. While much has been achieved for the upliftment of the working class, yet still more has to be done. My time has come to leave the stage and pass on the banner to a new generation. My successor has already been identified and I am certain that he will be able to face the tide of the time through a pragmatic approach and adjust himself to changing circumstances.

I would wish to express my heartfelt thanks and gratitude to my close collaborators, the International Trade Union Secretariats namely the IMF, the ICEF, and IFBWW for their continued support to the AGWU; the Sugar Authority for its financial support as well the Ministry of Housing & Land for the lease of this plot of land; and to the various organisations which in one way or other contributed in the materialisation of this project.

My thanks go above all to the members of the union who have renewed their confidence in me for the past two decades and to you Hon, Ministers and distinguished guests for you presence.

My dearest wish at the dawn of the third millennium, is to see the workers' dream become a reality. In my opinion the best way is the merging of unions, by keeping the movement independent of the political parties, and use this Emmanuel Anquetil Labour Centre to better the lot of the working class.

On 20th August 1997, I requested the Executive Committee to allow me to retire, as President and Negotiator of the Union on reaching my retirement age. The Committee members wanted me to stay longer. Finally they proposed me a post as Adviser which I accepted, to guide the Acting President until he be mature, which I accepted to do for one year. I handed over the new MLC car bearing No 1604 MY 97, which I was using despite the fact that Mr Dewnath was an employee of St. Felix S.E. and attending office once or twice weekly.

Anyway, it was very unfortunate for me to learn, through the Treasurer Mr Allen Bhugmoneea, about mismanagement of union fund. The Treasurer started complaining that Mr Dewnath was claiming too much money for petrol and other non authorised payments. During my term of office I did my utmost to give appropriate Workers' Education to the trade union officials and Branch Representatives.

An Executive Committee meeting was held with two main items on the agenda:
(1)   The Merger of Organisation of Artisans Unity (OUA) with AGWU
(2)   Explanation on petrol expenditure by the acting President.

Mr Dewnath raised objection and asked to remove the merger of OUA with AGWU. He started shouting and did not want to listen to anyone and the meeting ended in disorder and this for the first time during my term of office.

At the request of Executive Committee Members, on 5th July 1998, I wrote to the General Secretary of the Union and the Registrar of Associations that I was resuming my office of President of the union.

The Treasurer Mr Allen Bhagmoneea had no other alternative than to write to the Registrar of Associations to inquire in the above matter. This made Mr Dewnath furious and he planned a *"coup"* at the AGWU with the help of his good friend Mr **Purmanansing Jhoomuck who was suspended. They started propagating false information on the sugar estates by distributing handbills against the** interest of the union. The Committee members requested the General Secretary to convince Mr Dewnath to appear before a Disciplinary committee and be assisted by the union lawyer Mr Madan Dulloo.

Mr Lall Dewnath was convened, by registered letter dated 28th August 1998, to appear before the Executive Committee of the union on 3rd September at 10.00 hours, to answer a charge under regulation 11 of the Rules of the union, for acting in a manner detrimental and/or contrary to the interests of the union, in the presence of Mr Madan Dulloo. He was also informed, in case he is not satisfied with the decision of the disciplinary Committee, of his right of appeal to the executive committee within one month according to the union Rules.

Unfortunately the Executive meeting was postponed by the General Secretary on the advice of the Registrar of Associations, as the Branch of Mon Loisir S.E. was not properly constituted. It was over represented by one additional Executive member. In the meantime Mr Dewnath, with the help of his good friend Mr Jhoomuck, had canvassed a few members to attend the same committee which the Secretary General had postponed.

On the 3rd September morning Dewnath, Jhoomuck and few members gathered near the office Gate and requested Mrs Ruby Batterie to open the office. Mrs Batterie politely refused to open the office under the pretext that she was on leave and is going to hospital. So the office remained closed.

MISE EN DEMEURE

The very next day, to our great surprise, Mr Rajcoomar Sydamah and myself received a *"mise en demeure" which was* served by the Attorney H. A. Rujobally – informing us that an executive committee met on the 3rd September 1998, under chairmanship of Mr Lall Dewnath and Mr Lutchmeeparsad Ramsurn acting as General Secretary. They have decided to expel Mr Rajcoomar Sydamah as General Secretary and Mr Rajpalsingh Allgoo as Adviser and ordered us to return office keys and union belongings.

The General Secretary had no other alternative than to refute the fabricated false meeting which never took place as the office was closed. The case was defended by union Counsel Mr Madan Dulloo and union Attorney Mr Dev Cowreea.

JUDGE LAM SHANG LEEN'S RULING

The Judge Lam Shang Leen gave Ruling in favour of the President Allgoo and General Secretary Sydamah and ordered Mr Lall Dewnath, Mr Lutchmeeparsad Ramsurn and Mr Purmanansing Jhoomuck to return the keys and all union belongings to the General Secratary. It is important to note that the office ladies did not want to work in the main office at GRNW, as they were previously being ill-treated by them. They were forced to work in the old office at the MLC at 8, Victor de la Faye Street, Port Louis.

Le Mauricien of 11th September 1998, reported the following: on the Case "Après avoir écouté l'homme de l'AGWU, Me Dulloo, et après avoir pris connaissance de la plainte et celui de l'affidavit en date du 4 septembre, le Juge s'est déclaré satisfait que le cas nécessite une intervention urgente « *of the application is served on the respondant* »

Dans son jugement interlocutoire comportant deux parties et quatre points, le Juge Lam Shang Leen écrit à l'encontre du défendeur, « *restraining, forbidding and prohibiting (a) the respondents either personally or through their agents, servants and or preposes from convening, holding or proceeding with any executive committee meeting including the purported meeting scheduled to take place on Monday 7th September 1998 and any other meeting or gathering in the name of the union.*

Le deuxième point de jugement interlocutoire interdit à Lutcheepasad Ramsurn d'agir comme secrétaire-général de l'AGWU et il lui est demandé de cesser d'exécuter les tâches reprochées au plaignant. Toujours dans la première partie de l'injonction, il est fait état de l'interdiction de « *respondent No. 2* (ndlr : Lall Dewnath) *from passing himself off or from acting as President of the union* » Dans la deuxième partie du jugement, la Cour ordonne à MM. Dewnath et Ramsurn de procéder à un « *hand over* » des clés du siège de l'AGWU, situé à l'Emmanuel Anquetil Labour Centre, Grande – Rivière-Nord-Ouest, aux plaignants « *and not to obstruct the access thereof more particularly to applicants Nos 2,3&4* (ndlr : Rajcoomar Sydamah, Rajpalsingh Allgoo et Allen Bhugmoneea) *and other executive committee members* ».

Elaborant son argumentation dans son affidavit, le plaignant Secrétaire- général Rajcoomar Sydamah soutient que lui-même et Rajpalsingh Allgoo sont respectivement le secrétaire-général et président en exercice de l'AGWU, alors que les respondents Nos 1 et 2 sont vice-président et assistant- secrétaire du syndicat. Il souligne le fait que Lall Dewnath avait été convoqué à comparaître devant le comité exécutif « *to answer a charge under regulation 11 of the rules of the union by way of motion..* » et pour avoir « *acting in a manner détriment and /or contrary to the interest of the union"*. Ainsi, le plaignant annonce que l'exécutif de l'AGWU a pris la décision d'expulser Lall Dewnath. Ce dernier, informé de cette décision, a un délai d'un mois pour faire appel, indique-t-il.

Par allures, dams son affidavit, M. Sideman soiling queue les « *respondents have illegally and unlawfully retained the keys of the official seat of the union (...) and are refusing access to the applicants, and other members of the executive committee of the union.* (Georges Alexandre)

Despite the ruling of the Judge, they did not stop creating problems. They broke the lock of the main door twice and replaced it by a new one just to prevent the union officials from performing their normal duty. Mr Lall Dewnath and Mr Purmanansing Jhoomuck were prosecuted on charges of disobeying the Judge's Order by causing "Contempt" by breaking lock of main office and harassing the union officers. The union officers had made several complaints to Police against them in this regard.

By the time the case was taken by the Supreme Court, I had already left the union Position. Mr Dewnath was already elected as President of the AGWU. The Union Counsel asked me what stand he needed to take as the case of contempt was coming for trial at the Supreme Court. And also suggested me, it would be a shame for the prestigious union created by the Father of Trade Union in Mauritius that its President could be going to jail. So I was convinced by the lawyer's stand, and taking into consideration the advice of the union Lawyer that **one successor of Emmanuel Anquetil would go to jail on charge of contempt.** It will be dishonour for history and I agreed to withdraw the case.

It is also important to draw the attention of the members and authorities concerned, that in the Balance sheet ending December 1998, a sum of Rs 68, 435.- appeared as expenditure for Legal Assistance. But there was no case needing any legal assistance in

1998 and moreover no receipt was produced! How did the auditors check this account? If need be I can help to trace out where the money might have gone.

It has been brought to my knowledge that some officials of the AGWU Provident Fund had embezzled several hundred thousand rupees and the case is still under consideration by Police and the ICAC. I hope the above Institutions will be able to find out the person/s that had taken the money fraudulently and they will be punished. My earnest wish is that the AGWU Provident Fund could claim back the money from those who have embezzled it.

Chapter 32

NOMINATION ON
LOCAL GOVERNMENT
SERVICE COMMISSION

It was just a few days prior to my retirement which h was scheduled for the 31ᵗ August, 1997. I was on leave I got a surprise telephone call from Hon Kailash Purryag, the Acting Prime Minister at home. He told me that he urgently needed to talk to me. He also said it was a very important issue and that he could not tell me on the telephone. It was around 1.30 p.m. He requested me to meet him the same day; he told me that he would remain in the Prime Ministers' Office up to 8.00 p.m. I met the Acting Prime Minister at around 5.30 p.m.

He told me that he got good news for me. He informed me that the Prime Minister, Dr the Hon Navinchandra Ramgoolam, had decided to appoint me, the Public & Disciplined Forces Service Commission (PSC). First he needed my approval and then he would submit my name with my C.V. to His Excellency Cassam Uteem, the President of the Republic for nomination to the above Post. I voluntarily accepted the offer as I had retired from the different positions I occupied in the trade Union movements. I thanked the Prime Minister through Hon Kailash Purryag.

It was very unfortunate in my particular case that His Excellency, Mr Cassam Uteem, rejected my nomination upon the objection made by Hon Paul Raymond Bérenger, the Leader of the Opposition was given to understand, according to certain information that Mr Bérenger objected because I was a Trade Unionist. In fact, some time back, I had already retired from my different positions in the Trade Unions and Confederation. It is also important to note that during the time of Trade Union activities, I followed the principle of neutrality to political parties during my terms of office as Trade

Unionist and never campaigned for any political parties. And although I was a born Labourite, my Union the AGWU had adopted neutrality to Party Politics since the time of Mr Rozelmour Vincent in 1971. I am of the opinion that Hon Paul Bérenger was in contradiction with the own President of his Party, who had made a public campaign in favour to nominate a Trade Unionist at the PSC.

The nominations remained pending for about one month until I met Dr Navinchandra Ramgoolam on a Sunday at a wedding of my close relative at the Arya Sabha Mauritius. There he officially informed me about the objection made by Hon Paul Raymond Bérenger regarding my nomination. He told me that he was going to nominate me somewhere else. The Prime Minister also told me that he had already made up his mind to nominate me on the Local Government Service Commission because in those days the nomination to LGSC was made by the Minister of Local Government.

The following year on 6th November, 1998 the Minister of Local Government appointed me on the Local Government Service Commission, under section 5 (1) (b) and 6 (2) of the Local Government Service Commission. I served the Commission for a period of two years.

At the commission we had a good team who gave their full cooperation and this made us work in a very condicive working environment, especially at a time when we had to interview about a hundred applicants daily.

Prior to the individual interviews of the applications and the documents submitted were scrutinised by a team of Senior Officers, and then the Board Members had the responsibility to check all the applications and documents. This exercise is one of the most important and we had paid much attention to the criteria laid down by the Board and the Regulations. As a retired Trade Unionist I was very careful before accepting or rejecting an application.

When general elections took place on the 11th September 2000, the MSM and MMM won the election with a very large majority. Just a few weeks after the new Minister of Local Government took Office, he terminated our contract of service by giving one month notice, with immediate effect by paying one month wage in lieu of notice.
I can proudly say, that during my term Office, I served as Commissioner, no complaint was made about our work at the level of the Board.

I would like to say, although there exists the perception that the Board members of the Commission can be influenced, I can proudly declare that I did my job in all honesty, without fear and favour.

Chapter 33

THE
MAURITIUS LABOUR PARTY

In February 2001, Mr Moorthy Sarassee the Ex. Minister of Industry, and Treasurer of the Mauritius Labour Party, sent me message informing me that the Leader of the Labour Party wanted to meet me. A few days later, I met him, in his Office at SSR Street Port Louis (Ex SSR Residence). We had cordial and fruitful discussions. He requested me to give a helping hand to the Labour Party, particularly in relation to the Labour Movement. I had joined the Labour Party after I retired from trade unions, not to get a ticket from the Labour Party, but to serve the working class. As I was born in a Labour family, my uncle Partab Allgoo was a Trade unionist and equally the General Secretary of the Party I felt it my duty to help the Labour Party. During 2000-2005 my main mission was to re-establish the relations between the Trade Union Movements and the Labour Party.

Right away, Dr Ramgoolam phoned the General Secretary Mr Sarat Lallah and requested him to give me the required facilities at the Labour Party Office to perform my duty.

I used to spend two/three days weekly at the Labour Party office until September 2005, on a voluntary basis. This had given me opportunities to help the General Secretaries (Mr Sarat Lallah, Dr Vasant Bunwaree and Mr Dharam Gokhool)

Sir Seewoosagur Ramgoolam

Renganaden Seeneevassen

Sir Veerasamy Ringadoo

Dr. Navinchandra Ramgoolam

CREATION OF THE TRADE UNION WING

A Trade Union Wing was created, with the following members: Raj Allgoo, Alain Laridon, Fritz Thomas, Yatin Varma, Satish Faugoo, Etienne Sinatambou, Dhanraj Boodhoo. I was nominated as coordinator and Dr James Burty David supporter. The aims of the Trade Union Wing were to study the conditions of work and salary and to suggest amelioration, better labour legislations.

The Executive committee of the Labour Party in April 2002, decided to celebrate the 117th Birthday Anniversary of Emmanuel Anquetil. Dr Vasant Bunwaree the Secretary General, requested me as Coordinator of the Labour Wing to write a Biography of Emmanuel Anquetil which would be distributed on the occasion of the 117th Birthday Anniversary Celebration which was to be held on 18th August, 2002. A drafting Committee was set up with the following members: Yatin Varma, Satish Faugoo, Alain Laridon, Fritz Thomas and myself as coordinator – but it is regrettable to note that none of the Committee members gave a helping hand except Dr James Burty David, who did the editing of the book which was solely written by me, the logical support and messages were written by the General Secretary Dr Vasant Bunwaree and the book was forwarded by Dr Navinchandra Ramgoolam Leader of the Party. I am thankful for the advice given by Dr Burty David and Dr Vasant Bunwaree to produce the book. I am also thankful to Mrs Roma Babooram, officer responsible of the Labour Party Office and Eddy Jacquette, the handyman, for their support and collaboration.

LAUNCHING OF BOOK
"HOMMAGE A EMMANUEL ANQUETIL 1885-1946

The launching of the book entitled "Hommage à Emmanuel Anquetil 1885 -1946 Père du Syndicalism Mauricien" was done by the Dr Navin Ramgoolam, the Leader of the Labour Party and leader of the Opposition at the Centre Social Maire Reine de La Paix on the 117th Birthday Anniversary Celebration. The Hall full of the Labour partisans, this was for the first time that the Labour Party had organised the celebration outside the Labour party Headquarters.

Since then it became a regular feature annual, the last function, I had the opportunity to organise the 120th Birthday Anniversary Celebration which was held at the Town Hall of the Municipality of Quatre Bornes. The previous held at the Farmers' Centre of Riviere du Rempart also was a real success and it was difficult to accommodate the large number of people attending. The Labour Party has never forgotten to pay homage to the Leaders such as Dr Maurice Curé, Joseph Guy Rozemont, Pandit Sahadeo and several others. On these occasions the Trade Union Leaders were regularly invited and this had given a better understanding.

At the Labour Party, particularly Dr Navin Ramgoolam had promised the Trade Union Leaders during meetings, that he will make necessary changes to the Labour legislations, particularly to Industrial Relations Act 1973 and Labour Act 1975. The General Secretary requested the Trade Union Wing to prepare the required amendment. I requested the members of the Labour Wing to discuss the amendment, as suggested by the Leader. In the meantime the MSM/MMM Government had presented a white paper of IRA. Meetings were convened few members attended but no one gave me a helping hand to draft the amendments. When I was facing difficulties to take decisions regarding the right to strikes, I informed the General Secretary, who advised me to contact Sir Satcam Boolell, although he was not in good health, he responded to my request and helped me in preparing the documents. I still remember when I asked him whether we need to re-introduce the rights to strikes, *"he replied by saying it is the Labour Party that gave the rights to strikes and it is a fundamental rights guaranteed by ILO Conventions"*.

FORUM-DÉBAT ON IRA

The FTU had organised a Forum-Debate on the Industrial Relations Act and had invited *the three main political parties, the Labour Party, the MSM, the MMM and the Trade unions to the Debate,* at the seat of the Federation in 2005, to give their respective parties' views, particularly on the White Paper on the Industrial Relations Act of 1973, which was presented by Hon Showkatally Soodhun, Minister of Labour & Industrial Relations. No one from MMM and MSM attended the debate. Dr. Vasant Bunwaree, although his foot was plastered due to an accident a few days early, was present. Dr Vasant Bunwaree gave a brief exposé on the stand the Labour Party and gave the guarantee that once in power they will do the needful. The trade union Leaders wanted to know from Dr Bunwaree, if the right to strike will be re-introduced. Dr Bunwaree gave the assurance that Labour Policy adopted the democratic principle as laid down by the ILO *"The fundamental principle of freedom of association and the right to collective bargaining is a reflection of human dignity. It guarantees the ability of **workers and employers** to join and act together to defend not only their economic interests but also civil liberties such as the right to life, security, integrity and personal and collective freedom"*.

Labour Party Government in 2008 repealed the Industrial Relations Act of 1973 and Labour Act of 1975 and replaced them by Employment Relations Act 32 of 2008 and Employment Rights Act 33 of 2008 respectively and the rights to strike was re-established.

METWU WAS CONTROLLING THE LABOUR PARTY EXECUTIVE COMMITTEE

As the trade unions were the creation of the Labour Party, Emmanuel Anquetil was the Leader of both the Labour Party and trade union organisations, which were working hand in hand for the betterment of the working classes in the years 1930 & 40s'. In those days transport facilities was not available in many parts of the country, it was a problem to organise the workers and attend their complaints, there was urgent need for transportation facilities.

The METWU had no other alternative, despite their limited fund, to purchase a New Vauxhall car bearing the number 2020 for the amount of Rs 3,400.- from its fund and repainted the car red which was the party colour and it was also used for the Labour Party activities. Pratab Allgoo bought an Austin car bearing No 2079 from his own pocket to be used for the Party and only petrol was refunded to him. A large part of the Labour Party's activities expenses were met by the METWU fund in the years 1930 – 40s'. *In those days the Labour Party Executive Committee was under the control of the Mauritius Engineering &Technical Workers Union.*

Although the Trade Unions were the backbones of the labour Party but unfortunately, due to certain differences, Mr. Raymond Rault and a few others left the Party and formed "Parti Travailliste des Travailleurs". A number of Trade unions left the Labour Party even the Artisans & General Workers Union under the leadership of Mr. Roselmour Vincent. At certain point in time The AGWU was controlling the Labour Party Executive Committee, as rightly pointed out by Sir Veerasamy Ringadoo in his book " **AN ACT TO SERVE**" I am citing a Paragraph which read as follows:-

Dr S. Ramgoolam and the Mauritius Labour Party

At the end of the war, with the sweeping results of elections in Great Britain, great expectations built up. The British Labour party's stand in favour of freedom in India, Ceylon was not immediately translated into independence. Things were made to drag and in the case of the colonies, we found that the defence of British interests, coupled with the traditional policy of divide and rule, allowed reform to come only piece-meal. In the case of countries with a plural society, the British played the card of vested interests and allowed matters to drag unduly. Here it took more than two years before the British Government made up its mind to give a new Constitution. Those who joined later would on several occasions hear from Ramgoolam and Seeneevassen the way in which the deliberations of the consultative Committee took place. There was more agreement between Ramgoolam and Anquetil than Dr Cure with Anquetil or Dr Cure and Ramgoolam. Ramgoolam has put on record how before the end of 1936, he took Ramkhelawan Boodhun and Rampersad Neerunjun to Dr Cure and offered their co-operation in his struggle. Dr Cure cold-shouldered them and categorically rejected their offer. All the same they gave him and Anquetil all their support. Anquetil was throughout the meeting of the consultative Committee in close consultations with Seeneevassen and Ramgoolam. Dr Cure had on many issues moved away from the stand taken by many political men especially on the question of franchise. It will be recalled that there is still a mystery regarding a letter written by Creech Jones to Anquetil regarding the extension of franchise. The story, which nobody has been able to verify, went to the effect that it was swallowed by Rozemont in presence of at least one witness.

Rozemont like Dr Cure, was also suspicious. The Mauritius Labour party was largely dependent on the Engineering and Other Workers' Union and the membership of the

Executive of the Party was drawn mainly from artisans who were members of the union. This explains, if an explanation is required, why Ramgoolam although accepted as a Labour candidate, had to support Vaghjee and Beejadhur as independent candidates. Pratab Allgoo, the secretary of the Mauritius Labour Party, and Donald Francis obtained the tickets of the Party. The patching of reconciliation came after the elections of 1948 and was crystallised on the occasion of the bye election of 1951 in which I (Veerasamy Ringadoo) was a candidate. The Executive committee of the Party continued to be largely controlled by artisans.

There were brave people one must concede, and some of them were victims of events of 1936 and 1943 and had lost their jobs. There is no doubt in my mind that what happened in 1948 was caused by "mefiancé" of Rozemont. This prevented Parliamentary Labour party to have shadow composition before the elections of 1948. For the sake of history, I may invoke the case of Seeneevassen who, against the advice of Ramgoolam, stood as candidate and failed to get himself elected as President of the Mauritius Labour Party following the death of Rozemont in 1956. Again most of the artisans had cast a hostile vote. I hope that this explanation will settle for good the question of loyalty of Ramgoolam for Mauritius Labour Party.

Ramgoolam had been unfairly made to appear as a hijacker who took control of the Mauritius Labour Party long after 1948. The truth is that it was convenient for the then leadership of the Party to keep him and a few Indo-Mauritians well away from the membership and especially from the Executive Committee. The result of the 1948 Election brought a jolt to this outlook and evidently by the force of events, a new alignment was formed and took shape well before the end of 1950. By 1951, Ramgoolam became the centre piece and remained so until 1983.

Chapter 34

NATIONAL
REMUNERATION BOARD

THE National Remuneration Board (NRB) is a quasi judicial body initially established under S.45 of the Repealed Industrial Relations Act which is now deemed to have been set up under S.90 of the Employment Relations Act [ERA] .The main function of the NRB is to make recommendations to the Minister regarding minimum remuneration and terms and conditions of employment in the private sector. These recommendations form the basis for the Remuneration Order [RO] Regulations. Presently there are 30 distinct sectors governed by ROs with an average of 3,50,000 workers.

The NRB consists of a Chairperson and a Vice Chairperson who are public officers and they are assisted by a multidisciplinary team of technical staff/researchers in the form of Remuneration Analysts, Labour Officers, Accountant and Statistics Officer.

On the 3rd November 2005, the Prime Minister of the Republic of Mauritius Dr the Honourable Navinchandra Ramgoolam GCSK, FRCP, nominated Mr. Marion Hélène, a Barrister-at-law as Chairman of the NRB and Mr. Rajpalsingh Allgoo M.B.E., M.S.K as Vice-Chairman a Retired Trade Unionist at the NRB which was a quasi judicial body. The Chairman and Vice-Chairman were appointed by the Minister of Labour & Industrial Relations on the recommendation of the Prime Minister, under Section 45 of the Industrial Relations Act of 1973.

The Chairman and the Vice-Chairman had to study the administration of the NRB. The NRB was not completely new to me, because since its inception, I had the opportunity, regularly to represent the different affiliated Unions of the MLC and to depose on their

Caption

behalf and very often having the opportunity to discuss a number issues regarding the function.

As the NRB is a Judicial Institution Mr Marion Helene and I took the commitment to work in complete independence from the Government – Employers – Workers and had a Customer Focus objective to be fair to all parties in the Recommendations to be submitted to the Minister.

On the 3rd November, I was given an office which seem like a meeting place – composed of one large Colonial office table, one executive chair; an old computer not properly functioning; no internet; one set of sofa; 8 chairs.

On the following day I went to work, and called the officer in charge and requested him to arrange the Vice-Chairman's office properly. The officer, who was well known to me, did not hesitate to tell me "why you are worrying about the office equipment? Why you are not doing just like your predecessor, come to office on and off whenever there are meetings?" I was surprised to hear the way this office was functioning. I told the officer that he is paid to work from 9.00 a.m. to 4.00 p.m. and as a matter of principle he cannot do otherwise than to work according to law. It took a few months before the Ministry gave me all necessary required facilities for Vice-Chairman's Office. There was a backlog of Remuneration Orders to be reviewed at the NRB. In the beginning the Chairman placed much confidence in the Head of Remuneration Analyst (HRA), assuming that he would do his level best to help the Board, as he had been at the NRB for more than one and half decades.

I observed that few top officials seemed to adopt a conservative attitude at work, whenever you asked them to work out a document; it took much more time than required, especially compared to other departments or the private sector.

It was unfortunate that the Head of Remuneration Analyst miss guided the Chairman and the Board members on an important issue. The Chairman proposed that Drivers and the Guides of the Travel Agent and Tours Operators should work up to 18 hours per day, whenever their service would be required in the final recommendation of the Travel Agents & Tour Operators Workers Regulations, which were to be submitted to the Minister shortly. I tried to explain that it was contrary to Labour Act of 1975 and the ILO Conventions, Finally on the advice of the HRA, the Chairman agreed to reduce 18 hours work to 16 hours. I was in an ambassassing position and was forced to abstain in the final recommendation, so as not to say opposed.

Fortunately the Minister while making the Travel Agents & Tour operator Remuneration Order GN No. 38 of 2009 had rejected the recommendation of 16 hours work daily for the Drivers and Guides as recommended by the Board.

A Nasty Incident

Sometimes later National Remuneration Board had undertaken the review of Public transport (Buses) Workers R.O. I requested the HRA to prepare a document regarding the lost of the cost of purchasing power (CPI) of the Transport Industry workers since the last review. After several days, I went to the office of HRA to collect the relevant document. The HRA gave them to me, but they were not accurate. When requesting further information from him, HRA replied in an arrogant manner to me. I was not satisfied with the answer given and asked for clarification. He was very angry and he said that never at the NRB, any Vice-Chairman had questioned him, regarding his documentations and said "you have to accept what I am giving to you". As I was quite well versed in this subject since long as a Trade Union Educator, I told the HRA that according to him the percentage was quite low. The HRA even had the gut to say that "you are a layman in this field."

Needless to say how angry I was, and went directly to the Chairman to inform him of the incident. I informed the Chairman that I write to the Higher Authority about this case of subordination. The chairman pleaded in the favour of the HRA, as the HRA was retiring in a few years. Due to the respect I had for the Chairman, I agreed to drop the case on the promise that the Chairman will reprimand and call him to order. Eventually since that day he was moderate.

Later I had to search for relative documents and I worked out the real lost of purchasing power for all categories of transport workers and basing itself on that document the Board gave its recommendations for a wage increase of more than 20% and other benefits The Minister of Labour & Industrial Relations made the R.O. accordingly and the workers were happy.

During our term of office, we have always tried to be just and fair to Employers and Workers while making the recommendations to the Minister. We have always been guided by the principle of Section 47 of the Industrial Relations Act of 1973 and subsequently by Section 97 of Employment Relations Act No 32 of 2008. (Principles to be applied by Tribunal, Commission and Board)

Since the implementation of the New Legislations, the Employment Relations Act 2008 and The Employment Rights Act 2008, the employers were more reluctant to cooperate with the NRB saying that the philosophy of the new legislation should be Collective bargaining.

REQUEST TO REVIEW OF AGRICULTURAL & NON-AGRICULTURAL R. O.

After the Joint Negotiation Panel (AGWU, SILU, and UASI & OUA) had declared a deadlock with the MSPA on the issue of calculation method of the Overtime was requested the Minister was to refer this to the NRB.

On the 5th August 2008, the Minister of Labour & Industrial Relations, acting under section 94(1) of the Industrial Relations Act 1973, referred to the NRB the Sugar Industry Agricultural Remuneration Order of 1983 and the Sugar Industry Non-Agricultural Remuneration Order of 1985, to make necessary amendment.

The Terms of reference were as follows:
(1)   The notional calculation of hourly rate for the computation of overtime on a daily basis i.e. whether the daily basic wage should be divided by 8 hours as it was generally the case for the 45 hour week or by 7 hours with the introduction of the 40 hour week (Intercrop crop 5 day week and Crop season 6 day week)

(2)   The hours of work of the Watchmen who, during intercrop season, are required to work 5 days of 12 hours week in the context of the implementation of the 40 hour week.

The Board had invited the interested parties through Press Notices on 22nd August 2008, to submit written representations. The following trade Unions AGWU, SILU, UASI, PWU, SIWA, and Employers Association MSPA and Cane Growers' Association submitted written memoranda.

The Board held public hearings during which parties deposed in support of their respective written proposals.

In the meantime, with coming into force of the New Employment Relations Act 2008, on the 2nd February 2009, a new Board was constituted and the Board had to issue fresh Press Notices on 30 March and 7 April 2009 which were published in the Government gazette and two daily newspapers following the advice of the State Law Office to proceed anew.

EMPLOYERS STAND

The MSPA members had already implemented the PAT Award as from 2007 crop season. However, they were against any change in the hours of work of the watchmen and the notional calculation of the daily and hourly rates due to its additional finance impact on the MSPA members.

On the other hand there was a good gesture on the part of the Cane Growers' Association, who said in a spirit of fairness, that they were in favour of the extension of the 40 hour week over six days during the crop season to all workers in the industry, so as not to create any discrimination and frustration among workers performing the same job for different employers. But at the same time, the members would not agree to end up in a situation of increasing the cost of production.

The Workers and Employers Representatives had deposed before the Board on their memorandum for and against. The next step was for the technical team to prepare a comprehensive paper on the issue.

In this particular case the Accountant should prepare a document stating the additional financial cost and the ability to pay. But unfortunately the Accountant had already left since long and had not been replaced. In such a situation I had no other alternative but to request the Advisor of the NRB who was an Economist and also the retired Head of Remuneration Analyst, but the latter refused by saying that "this issue does not fall under my schedule of duty".

The technical team was composed of only two persons: one Remuneration Analyst and one Ag. Senior Labour Inspector and the following posts were vacant: Head of Remuneration Analyst; Accountant; Senior Remuneration Analyst; two Remuneration Analysts and a Senior Statistical Officer. I tried to convince the only Remuneration Analyst who was expecting to be promoted but nothing was done, she was so frustrated that she gave the same reply that "this is not in my schedule of duty."

Needless to say, the Board had to make a fresh request regarding the above issues to the Ministry. The Ministry replied that the post of Accountant was advertised but no one was interested.

On the other hand the trade unions were putting pressures accusing the NRB for the delay; I found that there was no other alternative, I voluntary offered my good office to the Chairperson and asked permission to do the job !

I had to make necessary research from Employers, Mauritius Sugar Authority, Trade Unions and Statistical Office and work out the additional cost the employers would have to disburse on this particular issue. The Board wanted to know how I had reached the figure and approved the final Recommendation to be sent to the Minister of Labour and Industrial Relations on the 16 October 2009.

The Board also recommended the following:

Following the reduction of working hours from 45 hour week to 40 hour week in the sugar industry, the watchman's working week should be reduced to the same number of hours in the intercrop season that is from 72 hour week to 60 hour week. In addition, it recommended correction of the anomaly in the computation of the watchman's hourly rate.

The Minister of Labour and Industrial Relations made the G.N. No. 80 & 81 of 2010:

Notional Calculation of hourly rates (Amended GN 80 of 2010)

For the purpose of calculating remuneration –

(a)   for work done in excess of a normal day's work;

a month shall be deemed to consist of 22 days during intercrop season and 26 days during crop season and the basic hourly rate shall be calculated according to the formula –

(I) $W/260$, in the case of a watchman;
(ii) $W/173.33$, in the case of any other worker,

Where in "W" means the monthly basic wage of the worker.

I am pleased to say that the workers and their trade unions were satisfied with the Recommendation –even the Employers who were opposed to additional increase in their wages Bill in the beginning accepted it, because it was just and fair. I would like to remind those concerned that the NRB has always taken into consideration Section 97 of the employment Relations Act No.32 of 2008.

THE NRB FACES SOME ADMINISTRATION HURDLES

Since 2009, the NRB started facing difficulties regarding shortage of staff, Mr Helene the previous Chairperson had made several requests asking additional staff and to replace those who have left but unfortunately no action was taken by the Ministry. After the decease of Mr Marion Helene the Chairperson on the 3th May 2010, I was appointed Ag. Chairperson, I wrote a lengthy letter to the Minister of labour, Industrial Relations on June 2010 in the following terms: *"I would like to inform you of the problems faced by the Board, regarding the shortage of staff and the resource-constraints being faced. In order for the Institution to deliver, it has at least to have a proper team to assist the Board in its investigations, analysis and deliberations on which to rely to make timely and appropriate recommendations to you Mr Minister. Although there has been a lack of proper planning in the past regarding the institution, I strongly believe it is high time to correct this situation which has been persisting for quite some time now and is putting much pressure on the meagre resources at our disposal."*

The NRB technical team was working with only two persons: one Remuneration Analyst, Acting Senior Labour Inspector and a Clerical Officer. The following posts were vacant since some time: Head of Remuneration Analyst; Accountant; Senior Remuneration Analyst, two Remuneration Analysts; Senior Statistical Officer and administrative staff and this hindered the normal work process.

Needless to say the trade unions on several occasions made complaints through the Minister and Press that the NRB was taking far too much time than required to deliver Recommendation.

THE SAGA OF THE SUGAR INDUSTRY JNP -MSPA

The Joint Negotiation Panel (JNP) composed of AGWU, SILU, UASI and OUA started negotiation for a New Collective Agreement with the Mauritius Sugar Producers with the intention to sign a new Collective Agreement since July 2008. Unfortunately they could not reach an agreement on several points. The JNP declared a Trade Dispute under section 64 of the Employment Relations Act of 2008. The matter was taken by the Commission for Conciliation and Mediation on the 3rd March 2010.

The JNP and MSPA could not reach a consensus on their main item, on the percentage of Salary increase. The MSPA had stuck to their previous proposition before declaration of the Trade Dispute under section 64 (1) of the ERA 2008 of 16% and the JNP 35%. The CCM with a view to reaching an agreement suggested 20% increase. It is unfortunate the Commission could not recommend any figure because Section 65 (5) (a) of the Employment Relations Act 2008, does not specifically grant the forum the power to make any formal recommendation.

The CCM finding was as follows:

" Where no agreement is reached after 30 days of the date of the receipt of the labour dispute under section 64 or after the expiry at such extended period as agreed under subsection (4), the commission shall:
(a)   within 7 days submit a report to that effect to the parties to the dispute; and
(b)   Advise the parties to refer the labour dispute for voluntary arbitration under section 63.

The Commission therefore advised the parties to find redress, as provided in section 63, by referring the unresolved disputes for voluntary arbitration to the Tribunal or to an arbitrator appointed by them.

After a negative report of the CCM, the JNP refused to refer the dispute to the Employment Relations Tribunal. The JNP said that they do not found other solution to the dispute than to go on General strike. They had started mobilising their respective members for general strike throughout the country. They had requested the CCM to assist the Balloting according to section 78 of ERA 2008 which had already started.

Thanks to the good office of the Prime Minister, Dr the Hon Navinchandra Ramgoolam, after studying the tense problems of the Industrial Relations in the sugar Industry which had lasted for several months and the report of the CCM, he had considered the prevailing situation not conducive for harmonious for the economic development of the country. He could not keep quiet as our previous Prime Minister as in the case of Sinotex (Mtius) and let the economic go to doom.

The Prime Minster, after having all the necessary information, on the 12 June 2010 through a Press Conference, took a positive stand against the attitude of the MSPA and publicly declared that he did not appreciate the stand taken by the MSPA.

The Prime Minister requested his Minister of Labour and Industrial Relations Hon Shakeel Mohamed to call the MSPA and the JNP Representatives to discuss the above issues. After a few meetings an agreement was reached on 23 June, 2010 and a Collective Agreement was signed on salary increase of 20% between MSPA and SILU – UASI – AGWU, OUA, which was contained in the CCM report and this was done in presence of Hon Shakeel Mohamed. Needless to say, the MSPA signed this agreement against it will, to prevent general strikes in the sugar industry and to keep an industrial peace. Revision of the Sugar Industry Agricultural and Non-Agricultural Workers Remuneration Order Regulations.

On the 21st August 2010, the Minister of Labour and Industrial Relations, acting under section 91 (1) of the Employment Relations Act 2008, referred to the National Remuneration Board for making appropriate recommendations on 21 issues which were not settled at the level of the CCM.

Once I received the letter requesting the NRB to review the 21 issues which were not solved at the level of CCM, I called the Director of Labour and informed him that according to my opinion the above issues should not have been referred to the NRB but rather to the Employment Relations Tribunal under section 63 of the ERA 2008, as suggest by Professor Torul (i.e. advise the parties to refer the labour dispute for voluntary arbitration under Section 63 the parties to the labour dispute may jointly refer such dispute for voluntary arbitration to the Tribunal or to an arbitrator appointed by them) the reply was that he got no directive).

It is important to note that the NRB was bound to proceed with the above case, as per section 91 (3) of ERA, upon a reference under this section, the Board shall submit to the Minister a recommendation on the minimum remuneration and specific terms and conditions of employment.

So, the Board proceeded with the normal procedure according to section 92, by publishing in the Government Gazette and in at least 3 daily newspapers a notice requesting a written memorandum from concerned parties.

On 13 September 2010, the JNP submitted a collective memorandum on behalf of SILU, UASI, AGWU and OUA within the time limit and SIOA and PWU submitted their respective documents a bit later.

On the other hand the MSPA requested the Board a delay of 3 months to submit counter proposals. The Board in it wisdom gave 2 additional weeks. In spite of the delay granted no memorandum was submitted by the MSPA, which was not a normal practice of the MSPA.

Contrary to usual normal common practice of the MSPA, 14 individual sugar companies submitted memorandums individually to the NRB after the deadline for submission of 13 September 2010.

The Chairman called the first public hearing of the above 21 issues to be reviewed by the Board on 27 January 2011, It is sad to note that this public hearing started in a tense atmosphere due to thin difference of the two social partners JNP/MSPA regarding the 21 issues which were not solved by the CCM and was referred by the Minister to the NRB to be reviewed. The JNP was represented by Messrs. Ashok Subron; Devanand Ramjuttun; Lall Dewnauth and others and the MSPA were represented by Mr Jean Li, the MEF by Mr Dursun.

The Chairman welcomed the representatives of employers and workers and thanked all the parties who had submitted their respective memorandum and he said that he was happy that Mr Li and Mr Dursun were present, although they had not submitted any memorandum. The Chairman made an appeal to all present for their cooperation and assured them that he would do his level best to do justice to all parties concerned.

STATEMENT MADE BY
MR PRADEEP DURSUN AG. DIRECTOR OF MEF

The first speaker was Mr Dursun the representative of MEF, who wanted to speak in Creole as he did not want to embarrass anyone due to language problems.

His main argument was that whenever there was a Collective agreement duly signed by the employers and trade unions there is no need for the NRB intervention, in very polite and diplomatic manner.

According to him this goes against the philosophy of the ILO Convention No. 87, the Freedom of Association and particularly the ILO Convention No 98 (4) of the Collective Bargaining.

Mr Dursun drew the attention of the Board that the 21 points the NRB was reviewing had been discussed during negotiation and an agreement had been signed between JNP and MSPA, which was binding and hope that the NRB would take it into consideration. He further added, in his plea, that the NRB is an Independent Judicial Body. It functions according to the Employment Relations Act.

According to Mr Dursun, whenever there exit a Collective Agreement it should be protected and consolidated. He further said, if this sector under review was not organised and had no Collective Agreement, then the NRB would have the legitimate right to review and make recommendations. He even mentioned while the NRB is reviewing this sector, it should also take into consideration not to put the principle of Collective Bargaining in peril. "We need to take into consideration that there exit a Collective Agreement between the parties concerned".

In summing up the Representative of MEF made an appeal to the Board. Please while reviewing this case take into consideration the power conferred upon the NRB and the philosophy of section 97 of ERA 2008. Before ending his intervention, he said that he hoped that the Board in its wisdom would take into consideration all the points raised. The Chairperson assured him that would always under the parameter of the laws.

RELATIONS MSPA/JNP

Mr Ramjuttun gave a brief expose on their relations in the above issues between JNP/MSPA – he wanted to enlighten the Board regarding their apprehension and anxiety why MSPA had refused to represent it members as usual. He explained that all the trade unions form part of the JNP are recognised and do have a Procedural Agreement duly signed with the MSPA. Furthermore, historically speaking, since its' creation for more than 60 years , the MSPA has always negotiated with the recognised unions on behalf of its members on salary and conditions of work and just a few months back the MSPA negotiated with them and signed an agreement on behalf of its members. It is regrettable to note for the first time the MSPA was changing the rule of the game by asking us to negotiate with individual Sugar companies and the MSPA refused to submit memorandum to the NRB. Mr Ramjuttun said that he failed to understand the reasons why MSPA had asked its members to submit individual a memorandums to the NRB. According to Mr Ramjuttun, it was the CCM who had requested the Ministry of Labour to refer the 21 points, which were not settled at the CCM level to be referred to the NRB. He continued saying, they still had a "Protocol d'Accord" duly signed in 1994, which was still in force with the MSPA. The Award of the TAP of 1999, 2002 and 2003 are still in force. He made an appeal not to do anything which would go against the ILO Convention No. 100, which Mauritius had already ratified and incorporated in section 20 of the Employment Rights Act 2008.

Request for Clarification

Mr Lall Dewnath wanted to have a clarification regarding the Chairman statement; he said that he was worried because the chairman had accepted individual written memorandums from the sugar estates companies. The chairman explained that it was according to law and also a common practice – the NRB since its creation has always accepted individual representations, to be more precise, the NRB in it publications in Government Gazette and Newspapers has always, request the interested parties to submit written memorandums for a particular Remuneration Orders to be review. Moreover it has never been said in the notice that only recognised Trade Unions of employees or Employers associations could submit memorandums and hope it has cleared the doubt now.

I wish at this stage to put on record the problems faced by the Board. There has been a fundamental difference in the interpretation of the above issue. Was the Board the proper institution to review this case? The Board received several memorandums submitted by individual sugar companies under protest and reserve.

The main points of employers during NRB public hearing which were as follows:-

(1)   Employer made strong objection at the Board sitting that this case should have been referred to the employment Relations Tribunal and not to the NRB. The CCM recommended, in its report, the two parties to refer the case for joint voluntary arbitration to the Employment Relations Tribunal (ERT) or to an independent arbitrator as provided in the ERA Act No 32 of 2008. The trade Unions jointly referred the case for voluntary arbitration and threatened to organise a general strike in the industry;

(2)   The employers and their Federation, MEF reminded the Board that Mauritius has ratified the ILO Convention No 98 which is fundamental one and has an obligation, arising from the very fact of its membership in the Organisation, to respect, to promote and to uphold in good faith and in accordance with ILO Constitution the principle concerning the fundamental rights, namely, the rights to collective bargaining which are the subject of this Convention;

(3)   The MSPA and the MEF believe that there has been a procedural flaw and that the reference to the NRB was unwarranted in the circumstances and have drawn the attention of the Board to that fact;

(4)   Federation, NRB is a minimum wage fixing institution with is clearly defined under the law. Its jurisdiction is limited to unorganised sectors and where adequate collective bargaining arrangements do not exist.

(5)   The state has an obligation to fully promote collective bargaining and thus should not have recourse to a procedure which will undermine the entire collective bargaining process. This constitutes a bad precedent and breeds uncertainty regarding the fate of duly signed collective agreements.

(6) The Cane Growers Association on other hand, though they have not submitted any memorandum, have challenged the Board that in case the Board makes any recommendation on this issue, they will have recourse to the Supreme Court in this matter;

Due to objection raised by the employers and in the light of the above, the Chairman, with the Board's approval, did not have other alternative than to write to the Solicitor-General and request a legal advice regarding whether it is legally correct under the Employment Relations Act No 32 of 2008 and its philosophy regarding Collective Bargaining as provided for by the ILO Convention 98 (with all required documents attached).

The Board had to face a terrible problem which might happen for the first time the reason was that the trade unions leaders could not see each other eye to eye with the Employers Representatives.

During a Board hearing meeting of 17th February 2011, the chairman suggested the parties to postpone the meeting until a ruling is obtained from the State Law Office in the above matter. Following this suggestion, the members of the Joint Negotiation Panel objected strongly and showed their disapproval in terms of language, high tone and gestures which may be considered as "misbehavism" and as a contempt to the Board. The negotiator even threatened to do a sit-in and spend the night in the Board room, if the calendar of meetings set earlier was not adhered to. To quote from the argument *"ou pe dire nou ou pe postpone? Be nou pou dormi lamem e nou pou fer tou travayer lindistri sikrier debark isi. Pa ena simin ou postpone sa. Ena demokrasi dan sa pei la, se pa MEF qui roule sa pei la, pa tablisman ki roul sa pei la. »*

The Board was thus forced to allow the JNP Representatives to continue their depositions.

In order to have a clear picture of the law, the Board members requested the Chairperson to write to the Solicitor General to receive its view on the above matter. The Chairperson wrote to the state law Office on 23rd February 2011, in the following terms:

REQUEST OF ADVICE FROM STATE LAW OFFICE

The Board would appreciate if the Solicitor General could advise the Board as to whether such behaviour could be considered as an offence under paragraphs 22 and 24 of the Second Schedule of the ERA 2008, if affirmative, which measures could be taken against the person who committed such offence and whether in such a situation the Board can still proceed with hearing the party/parties?

On the 4th March 2011, SLO sent a reply to the Chairperson in the following teams:

It would be a matter for the Board to determine as to whether the conduct and behaviour of the Joint Negotiation Panel at its meeting of 17 February 2011 were of such a nature as to constitute a breach of the relevant sections of the Second Schedule of the Employment Relations Act.

The Board may wish to consider the suitability of referring the matter to the police, which may enquire into the whole issue and seek the advice of the director of Public Prosecutions as to whether prosecution may be initiated for any alleged offence/s which may have been committed. It is unfortunate that in some cases the legislators have written the law which I am of the opinion that it is not complete taking for example above case and there are several others. The Industrial Relations Act 32 of 2008 stipulates the following:

21. The President or Vice-President of the Tribunal or of the Commission shall not be called upon to give evidence relating to proceedings held before them in any other proceedings.

22. (1) *There shall not be included in any publication relating to any order, award, report, recommendation or other statement made or authorised by the Tribunal, the Commission, the Board, or by the Minister, any information disclosed during the course of proceedings under this Act by any party or witness in proceedings before the Tribunal, the Commission or the Board which was made known to the Tribunal, the Commission or the Board only by the disclosure, and in respect of which the party or witness has made a request during the proceedings that the information be withheld from publication, and no person concerned in or present at any proceedings of the Tribunal, the Commission or the Board shall publish or disclose the information to any person not concerned in or present at those proceedings, except with the consent of the party or witness.*

    (2) *Any person who publishes or discloses any information in breach of subparagraph (1) shall commit an offence.*

    (3) *Subparagraphs (1) and (2) shall be without prejudice to the power of the Tribunal, the Commission or the Board to take such other steps as they may consider necessary or desirable to safeguard national or industrial secrets or other information appearing to the Tribunal, the Commission or the Board to be deserving of confidential treatment.*

23. *subject to any other enactment, it shall be at the discretion of the Tribunal, the Commission or the Board to admit or exclude the public or representatives of the press from any of their proceedings.*

24. (1) *In relation to proceedings before the Tribunal, the Commission or the Board –*
    (a) *where the public or representatives of the press are excluded, no report or summary of the proceedings shall be published; and*
    (b) *where the public or representatives of the press are permitted to be present, a fair and accurate report or summary of the proceedings may be published.*

    (2) *Until the order, award, report or other result of the proceedings has been published in accordance with this Act, no comments shall be published in respect of the proceedings or any evidence adduced in the course of those proceedings.*

(3)   Any person who, before any award, order or other result of any proceedings before the Tribunal, the Commission or the Board has been published in accordance with this Act, publishes –

      (a)   the terms of the order, award or report of other result; or (b) any comment on the proceedings or any evidence adduced thereat, shall commit an offence.

POWERS OF TRIBUNAL, COMMISSION AND BOARD

25.   at any sitting of the Tribunal, the Commission or the Board, any person who –

      (a)   subject to paragraph 20(2) refuses to answer any question to the best of his ability;

      (b)   insults any member thereof;

      (c)   wilfully interrupts the proceedings or misbehaves in any other manner; or

      (d)   commits any contempt of the Tribunal, the Commission or the Board, shall commit an offence.

I am of opinion that the legislators should have clearly stated, in case someone commits any contempt of the Tribunal, the Commission or the Board, shall commit an offence. Who will judge the case and fix the penalties? As suggested by the state Law Office, if it goes to Police it will take years –suspend the revision of the R.O. concern, in the means time what will be the fate workers? The Judge Harris Balgobin in the case Sinotex (Mtius) had politely drawn the attention of the Commissioner of Police and DPP, it was not an industrial matters.

Training of the
Technical Staff of the NRB

The Workers, Employers and Government recognised the work done by the NRB since the last four decades, to keep industrial peace and harmony in this country. Having been at the helm of the NRB for a number of years, I am of the opinion that the Technical Staff should be given the opportunity to follow specialized courses locally and Overseas to better serve the institution.

These employees are recruited with their Academic Qualifications, but without any training. During my term of office at the NRB, I got the opportunity to assess the Technical Staff, they do a great work, and they are the lifeblood of the Institution. According to my information no one at the NRB had the opportunity to follow any Advanced Training Course for the last 15 years. I am of the opinion, that the Technical Teams should be given further training opportunities, to acquire general knowledge such as: Job Classification and Job Evaluation; Risk Assessment; IT; The National Pension Scheme; Private Pension Fund; Occupational Safety, Health and Welfare; Job to people with disabilities, etc.

On the other hand the employers are represented by highly qualified professionals in their respective fields; even some Trade Unionists do have good knowledge in their respective domain.

One of my recommendations to the Decent Work programmes was that the Technical Officers should be given training. Fortunately the ILO Representative was an old friend of mine. Once he was back to Geneva he informed me that an appropriate Course is due to start within 3 weeks at the ILO Turin. The application was made through Email and was accepted within a week. In this particular case the Permanent Secretary of the Ministry was very helpful, within 10 days, he managed to get finance to purchase air ticket and the Senior Remuneration Analyst attended the Course.

The Technical Teams are the lifeblood of the NRB; I wish to suggest the Permanent Secretary of the Ministry to pay particular attention by providing opportunities to the Technical staff, also the Chairperson and Vice-Chairperson just to keep pace with the changing modern industrial society. This of course will benefit the NRB, thus promoting better industrial relations in Mauritius.

Chapter 35

REPLACEMENT OF THE NRB
BY COLLECTIVE BARGAINING
IN MAURITIUS

SINCE the National Remuneration Board (NRB) has been set up, to determine the wages and conditions of service to be applied to the private sector workers, the employers claimed that the system has inherent weaknesses and it is not conducive to productivity growth and too much rigidity. Consequently, there had been suggestions to scrap the National Remuneration Board or apply it to unorganised sectors, and promote Collective Bargaining in the Wage Determination Process. More precisely implementation of the new Employment Relations Act 32 of 2008 and the Employment Rights Act 33 of 2008, the trade union leaders are complaining that the employers feel stronger.

In a recent case of JNP/MSPA the Minister of Labour & Industrial Relations had referred the Remuneration Order of agricultural Workers and Non-agricultural Workers Remunerations; the Minister had asked the NRB to review the above R.O. The Mauritius Employers Federation made a strong complaint to the ILO in the following terms:

* The NRB is a minimum wage fixing institution with clearly defined powers under the law. Its jurisdiction is limited to unorganised sectors and where adequate collective bargaining arrangements do not exit.

* In the case of the sugar industry, the recent collective agreement has been signed between employers and trade unions.

- Mauritius has ratified ILO Convention No 98 which is a fundamental one and has an obligation, arising from the very fact of its membership in the organisation, to respect, to promote and to uphold in good faith and in accordance with the ILO Constitution.

- The State has an obligation to fully promote collective bargaining and thus should not have recourse to a procedure which will undermine the entire collective bargaining process. This constitutes bad precedent, breeds uncertainly regarding the fate of duly signed collective agreements.

So, according to workers organisations this piece of legislations is not favourable for the workers. If applied to the letter "the NRB should only review the unorganised sectors and where there are no adequate collective bargaining arrangements, and then the NRB will have its jurisdiction to make Recommendations.

Is it possible to get Industrial peace without the NRB RECOMMENDATIONS? I am of different opinion; with more than 300 trade unions for an organised labour force 119,000 out of total working population of more than 550,000 proper Collective Bargaining would not function properly.

Let us see how the labour force are organised according the Registrar of Associations: Trade Unions Membership in Mauritius divided in groups as at 31.12.2011

No of members	No of Trade Unions	No of members
0-30	10	184
31 to 100	128	6,972
101 to 500	105	23,450
501 to 1000	34	25,121
1001 to 5000	21	43,732
5001 to 10,000	0	0
10,000 +	1	10,071
In process of dissolution	1	0
Not available	9	0
	309	109,530

Number of Trade Unions Sector -wise as at 31.12.2012

Sector	No of Unions
Civil Service	89
Para statal Bodies	75
Local Authorities	10
Private Sector	143
Total No of Trade Unions	317
Number of Trade unions Federations	29

Are the conditions for collective bargaining fare and reasonable, and does conducive atmosphere exist in general for the promotion of collective bargaining? The literature in the 4th schedule of the Employment Relations Act 2008 is nicely written, somebody reading it has a very good impression that Collective Bargaining might be functioning quite well just to mention a few:

(i)   Good human relations between employers and workers are essential to good employment relations;

(ii)   Basic employment relations principles and harmonious employment relations;

(iii)   Management shall, in consultation and co-operation with workers and their trade unions, aim at improving the minimum standards of working conditions specified in any enactment;

(iv)   Workers' Participation in decision making;

(v)   Every enterprise having a labour force of 50 or more workers shall establish a joint Consultative Committee;

For the good functioning of the Collective Bargaining, there are 162 subsections which detail the different steps needed.

Now the question arises how many of the nice wordings in 4th Schedule, of the employers are implemented, and who are adhering to. What steps is the Ministry of Labour taking to redress and establish them a better working environment?

•   According to newspapers very often, we read that workers are victimised because they belonged to a trade union.

I am of the opinion that it was a mistake to remove section 49 (5) of the IRA in the new ERA: Any employer who fails to comply with subsection (2) shall commit an offence and shall, on conviction, be liable to imprisonment for a term not exceeding six months and to a fine not exceeding two thousands rupees.

Will Collective Bargaining be successful in Mauritius and replace the NRB?

According to trade union Experts:

Collective Bargaining Means Equality with employers

In order to engage in successful collective bargaining workers must become and remains a united force

If the employer knows the union has the strength and unity to call a 100 per cent effective strike, he will bargain with the union leaders and try to reach a fair agreement or compromise.

- if the unions are not united, or if they are weak, the employers will not treat them with seriousness and will either refuse to bargain or will force the union leaders to accept a poor settlement. Therefore, anything which weakens the union destroys effectiveness of collective bargaining.

There is no effective collective bargaining if:-

- the union lacks organisational strength (a union that has no power to oppose the employer cannot bargain: it can only beg, and beggars have to be satisfied with whatever is given to them – most of the time they receive nothing).

So, I leave it to the the readers to make their own judgement.

Chapter 30

DEFINITION
OF WAGES

THE definition of wages is complex. Wages are defined as return to labour. This simple economic definition, however, has to be considered in the context of terms and conditions of employment. Employers define wages as all costs incurred for the recruitment and use of labour in their enterprises. This includes direct wages, fringe benefits, social security benefits paid to the employees and other costs incurred for occupational safety and health and human resource development. Employers are therefore concerned with the total cost of labour.

Workers usually define wages as the direct payments received for work done. They consider wages as a means for an acceptable quality of life in the context of the standard of living in their country. Wages are, therefore, classified as follows:

Subsistence wage is a quantum which provides for basic subsistence needs;

Living wage: - a quantum which provides for subsistence and means for a quality of life which is acceptable in society.

Fair wage: - a quantum which is determined through negotiations based on opportunity cost of labour, labour market conditions and cost of living.

The quantum is usually above the subsistence wage and close to the living wage. Workers are concerned with the immediate quantum of disposable income, although they recognize that fringe benefits associated with terms and conditions of employment which include paid weekly days of rest, paid public holidays, paid medical leave and treatment, paid annual leave, quarters or rent in lieu, free amenities of water supply and electricity, transport, etc

There are some universal features in payment systems for all the above categories of workers. The main components in payment systems are as follows:

Basic wage: this is a fixed payment for a wage period which is the consideration for the contract of service. The quantum is determined based on market conditions of supply and demand of labour, entry qualifications, cost of living, level of experience based on service in the enterprise and critical nature of responsibility held by the worker.

The quantum varies with each enterprise.

Productivity Incentives: this component in the remuneration system is subject to the workers level and quality of productivity. This is usually measured in terms of physical output or revenue brought in through the workers efforts. The actual quantum's fixed as productivity incentives depend on the nature of industry.

Special Incentives: these are payments made where workers are scarce or conditions of work are difficult. (Example Bus Industry payment of a risk allowance)

Prosperity Payments: this component is often referred to as bonus payments. This is subject to the prosperity of the enterprise which is measured in terms of net profit. The quantum of bonus for each worker is according to his level in the hierarchy of the management of the enterprise.

Social security payments towards gratuity, provident funds, pensions, contingent payments for occupational hazards, occupational rehabilitation in the event of occupational injuries and survivors' pension.

These 5 important components feature under various designations in remuneration systems. The Basic wage per unit time is paid as an unqualified fixed payment or in some cases with qualifications to turn out for work and completion of duties. Employers are conscious that this component is a fixed cost obligation and, therefore, resort to ensure that work is performed before payment is due and disbursed. In some instances, such as in the case of agricultural workers, the basic wage is based on basic income security through a Guaranteed Minimum Wage per unit time for a level of output and turn out. In the manufacturing sector similar models are also implemented for production workers to ensure that wages are paid only for work done.

Productivity incentive payments are usually tied to performance measured in terms of turn out for work and levels of output. Both these measures are modified and adapted according to the nature of work in the context of the enterprises concerned. Productivity must be evaluated in the context of realities of working conditions especially technology and human capital of workers. Productivity is, therefore, "working smart and not merely working hard".

Special incentive payments are paid to workers in order to cope with the hardship involved in the work and to attract and retain workers in occupations occurring at odd hours during the day, and/or are hazardous, or in remote areas. These payments are also made when the nature of work becomes difficult due to uncertainties such as weather conditions and normal productivity cannot be achieved. For example, productivity of plantation workers are affected by adverse weather conditions and as wages depend on output of workers, a special incentive is necessary to ensure they cope with difficult work conditions caused by adverse weather conditions and are able to earn a reasonable wage.

The selection of remuneration system based on payment by results, productivity linked wage system and productivity gain sharing systems depend on the nature of enterprise, types of employment, organization and methods of work, level of technology used and labour market conditions. While employers retain their prerogative to determine organization and methods of work, workers need to organize themselves into viable and strong trade unions so that they will be able to negotiate effectively during collective bargaining on wages and terms and conditions of employment.

Collective bargaining is only effective when both parties i.e. *employers and trade unions negotiate from a position of equal level of knowledge and understanding of the economic circumstances of the enterprise and the industry.* Trade unions must have the total support of the workers so that trade union leaders can make effective representation and decisions on behalf of the workers they represent. Principles of good governance viz. democracy, transparency and accountability are crucial for the conclusion of successful and meaningful collective agreements. An effective social dialogue between employers and trade unions based on mutual trust can strengthen a process of co-operation and collective bargaining based on an objective understanding of the realities of economic circumstances in the enterprise and industry. The trade union priority is sustained employment and social justice while the employer is focused on sustained economic viability, competitiveness and returns on capital. Both are mutually dependent on each other to achieve their objective.

The process of collective bargaining is therefore not acrimonious between the two social partners as both recognize that meaningful income distribution in society in a free enterprise based economy can only be achieved through collective bargaining.

Chapter 37

FUNCTION OF THE NRB

INTRODUCTION

In recent years, there were lengthy debates about the relevance of the Remuneration Order regulations in our pay determination system. The employers claimed that our system has inherent weakness and it is not conducive to productivity growth and contains too much rigidity. Consequently, there have been suggestions to scrap the National Remuneration Board and promote Collective Bargaining in the Wage Determination Process.

The regulation of wages and Conditions of employment Ordinance, (No. 71 of 1961) provided for the appointment of "Minimum wage Boards'" and the establishment of Wages Councils' for the regulation and conditions of employment of Workers in the colony of Mauritius. Under that Ordinance, the Minister, from time to time, appointed minimum wage boards to inquire into the wages and conditions of employment of workers and submit recommendations for the determination of basic minimum wage. The Minister also established wages councils when he was satisfied that no adequate machinery exited for the effective regulation of wages and other conditions of employment, in any trade, industry or occupation. Other ordinances which covered the field of Industrial relations were the trade Union ordinance, 1954 and the Trade Disputes Ordinances 1965. In 1973, all such existing legal enactments were repealed and replaced by the Industrial Relations Act No. 67 of 1973, which was presented in Parliament on the 18th December, 1973 which came into force on the 23rd February

1974; all existing legal enactments were repealed and replaced by the Industrial Relations Act 1974.

For this purpose various bodies have been established under the IRA and one of such body is the National Remuneration Board set up in 1974 to fix a minimum remuneration and other conditions of employment for private sector Workers.

THE NATIONAL REMUNERATION BOARD (NRB)

The National Remuneration Board (NRB) was established under section 45 of IRA the Board composed of:-

Chairman and vice-Chairman and not less than four and not more than ten other members who shall be appointed by the minster, after consultation with such organisations representing employees and employers as he consider appropriate.

The Chairman and the members of the Board shall be appointed for such term as the Minister may determine.

1. (a) where the minister refers any maters to the Board under section 94, the Minister may appoint such even number of assessors as he thinks fit, half to represent employees and half to represent employers, interested in the particular matter as he considers appropriate and if, after consultation, the Minister is unable to secure the consent of suitably representative persons for appointment as assessors whether to represent employees or employers or both, the Minister may appoint assessors to represent employees only or employers only, or may refrain from appointing any assessor.

The National Remuneration Board (NRB) was established under section 45 of the repealed IRA to fix a minimum remuneration in respect of any category of employees in the private sector, has been deemed to have been established under the Employment Relations Act No. 32 of 2008.

Chapter 38

THE MINIMUM WAGE DETERMINATION PROCESS

UNDER section 90 of ERA, the chairperson and Vice-Chairperson of the NRB shall be public officers.

The shall be reconstituted and shall consist of-
(a) A Chairperson;
(b) A Vice-chairperson;
(c) A representative of the Ministry responsible for the subject of economic development;
(d) A representative of the Ministry responsible for the subject of industry;
(e) 2 representatives of workers;
(f) 2 representatives of employers;
(g) 2 independent members.
 * The Chairperson and the Vice-Chairperson shall be public officers.
 * The independent members shall be appointed by the Minister on such terms and such period as he may determine.
 * The representatives of workers and of employers shall be appointed by the minister for such period after consultation with the most Representative organisations of workers and employers.

The Board function with the back-up of a technical bureau headed by the Head Remuneration analyst, one Senior Remuneration Analyst; two Remuneration Analysts, one Accountant, a Statistical Officer, a Senior Labour Officer and a Labour Officer and the supporting staffs.

The Board usually acts upon a reference from the Minster (in case of the IRA the Chairman could have done on his own) to submit recommendations regarding revision of wages and other conditions of employment to the Minister.

Decisions on minimum wage levels are reached after an intensive hard exercise which starts with the hearing sessions, with all the parties concerned, that is representatives of employers and employees assisted by legal and Technical Advisers as well as members of the public may make their submissions to the Board. Thereafter, the technical staffs accompanied by Board Members, conduct its own investigations through a series of site visits and interview with both employees and employers.

(Please note the information obtained during interview the workers, Employers and public remain confidential)

Additional information may be called for in order to enable the technical staffs to prepare a comprehensive report concerning the economic, social and financial aspects of the sector under review.

- Subsequently, the Board holds a series of meetings to discuss the findings of the investigating and examine the report submitted in order to reach a decision regarding the Recommendations to be made.

- Once a decision is reached, the Board publishes in the Gazette and in at least three daily newspapers a notice specifying that copies of the recommendation, it proposed to make may be obtained at the office of NRB. Interested parties are hereby invited to submit written counter representations within the time of not less than seven days or more than fourteen days from the date of the publication. The Board considers any written representation made within the time specified in the notice and makes such further inquiries or gives such further consideration to the matter as it thinks necessary.

- It then submits its final recommendations to the Minister not later than twenty eight days after the publication of the notice. The Minister may accept, reject, amend or refer the recommendation back to the Board with a request to reconsider them in the light of observations he may make.

The NRB is the only legal authority set up to fix minimum wages. However, this does not preclude employees in any sector from reaching an agreement with their employers to fix terms and conditions of employment as long as they do not contravene the existing order. Such collective agreement has been reached in sectors like the sugar industry, Construction Industry, etc.

The statutory minimum wage coverage touches practically all the workers in the private sector from the level of Chief Clerk downwards. Wages for the managerial staff and other professionals are negotiable. There is a long standing tradition of fixing minimum wages on a sector by sector basic rather than on a national basis as is the practice in most countries of the world. Within four years after the establishment of the NRB , 23

Remuneration Order Regulation were made and to date there are 30 such regulations which cover almost all sectors/industries except for employees in extremely lucrative business such as banking, insurance, gambling activities and emerging sectors in the offshore and ICT. As at to date, some 275,000 workers who account for almost 50% of the total labour force are estimated to be covered by minimum wage regulations in the 30 different sectors.

CRITERIA TO DETERMINE THE LEVEL OF MINIMUM WAGE

In establishing Minimum Wages and determining the criteria for the purpose of fixing minimum wage levels, the Authority has not lost sight of the main objectives of ensuring that wage earners are given the necessary social protection in order to overcome poverty and satisfy their basic needs and of providing an instrument of macro-economic policy. When fixing minimum wage levels in Mauritius, each sector is assessed on its own merits and on its importance in the national economy. Thus, the criteria applied need not be the same for all sectors. The following criteria of minimum wage fixing are spelt out under section 97 of ERA.

(a) The interests of the persons immediately concerned and the community as a whole;
(b) The need to promote decent work and decent living;
(c) The need to promote gender equality and to fix wages on the basis of job content;
(d) The principles of natural justice;
(e) The need for Mauritius to maintain a favourable balance of trade and balance of payments;
(f) The need to continued ability of the Government to finance development programmes and recurrent expenditure in the public sector;
(g) The need to increase the rate of economic growth and to protect employment and to provide greater employment opportunities;
(h) The need to preserve and promote the competitive position of local products in overseas markets;
(i) The capacity to pay of enterprises;
(j) The need to develop schemes for payment by results, and as far as possible to relate increased remuneration to increased labour productivity;
(k) The need to prevent gains in the wages of employees from being adversely affected by price increases;
(l) The need to establish and maintain reasonable differentials in rewards between categories of skills and levels of responsibilities;
(m) The need to maintain a fair relation between the incomes of different sectors in the community; and
(n) The principles of best practices of good employment relations.
(o) These criteria are not exhaustive but have been generally followed at the initial stage of minimum wage fixing.

Above all, due consideration was given to the need to increase the rate of economic growth and to create greater job opportunities and to alleviate the problem of unemployment. Thus, there have been crying disparities in the minimum wage levels in different sectors. The sugar industry, for instance, had been for quite some time the leading sector with far advantageous terms and conditions of employment because the industry was flourishing and the sugar magnates had the capacity to pay. When the EPZ was launched in 1970, wages were fixed at a very low level in order to absorb the available pool of unemployed labour.

The initial level of minimum wages has evolved from *"Orders"* made by the **Wage Councils** and the **Minimum Wage Boards** and there are no records to show whether it has been the result of empirical studies of basic needs of an individual worker or of a household. As already pointed out, each sector has been assessed on its own merits and its importance in the national economy in terms of employment creation, foreign exchange earnings and contribution to the gross domestic product and most important of all the ability to pay. It is also most probable that minimum wage levels have been determined with a spirit to strike a reasonable balance between the employee's demands and the employer's proposals. Initially, there was quite an important gap between public sector and private sector wages for the same occupational group of workers. Wages in the public sector were higher except for the sugar industry and labourers or field workers in the public sector wanted their wages to be aligned with those obtained in the sugar industry. But there has been a reversal in the situation following the PRB revisions in the public sector. Labourers in the sugar industry are now claiming for the same terms and conditions of employment as their counterparts in the public sector.

The Permanent Arbitration Tribunal (PAT) was set up under section 39 of the repealed IRA; to settle industrial disputes has also been deemed to have been established under the Employment Relations Act 2008. The Employment Relations Tribunal is composed a President who is required by law to be of the level of a Judge; two Vice-Presidents and not more than ten other members.

Apart from those two institutions, the Tripartite Committee met once yearly to adjust the cost of living which has also influenced the level of pay in both the public and private sectors. It has been one of the most important bodies set up where the Government consults representatives of both employers and employees in granting salary compensation to adjust increases in the cost of living to employees both in the public and private sector.

It is important to say that the first legislation concerning wage adjustment concerning the lost of purchasing power was introduced in July 1977 by Sir Veerasamy Ringadoo, the then Minister of Finance under the special Wage Increase Act. Since then wages and salary compensation have been adjusted every year except for 1978 and 1989 when the meeting of the Tripartite Committee was chaired by the Minister of Finance.

In 2007, the Government had referred the issue of salary compensation to the National Pay Council which was chaired by Mr Poonoosamy to encourage tripartite negotiations and make recommendations to the Government for an annual minimum salary compensation adjustment. Most of the Federations were against the setting up of the National Pay Council and disapproved the nomination of worker representatives to the Council.

It is important to note that there is no Collective Bargaining Process in the Public Sector including the Para Statal Bodies, Municipalities/district Council and Private Secondary Schools Authority (PSSA).

In the public sector the terms and conditions of employment for employees which account for around 15% of the labour force, their Salaries and conditions of Service have always been revised by salary Commissions headed by expatriates until the establishment of the Pay Research Bureau (PRB) which was established in 1977. It functions as an independent and permanent organisation. The review of salaries and conditions of employment and grades in the public service, all Para Statal bodies, Local Authorities and the Private Secondary Schools Authority is headed by a Director of the Pay Research Bureau and the Bureau is under the direct responsibility of the Prime Minister.

has caused great changes in the lives of workers throughout the world. Contract of service has been subject to the law of hire and fire. Dismissal without justification should be a thing of the past and that is the main move behind this piece of legislation.

"In working the principle of this Bill we have been inspired by discussions which have taken place in Geneva at International Labour Organisation in 1962 and 1963 on termination of employment at the initiative of the employer. We have been fortunate in reading a very interesting supplement of the review in comparative legislation on this question of dismissal". We have been fortunate to compare legislation in Germany, France and Belgium. And we know countries where provisions already exist against arbitrary dismissal. In France the law has existed for a fairly long time, and it applies to everybody. So it does in Germany and Belgium. In England from where our laws are borrowed, unfortunately the Britishers have been very conservative on the side of the public and on the side of Government. They will always believe in collective bargaining in this matter, except for this year when a Bill on employment is actually before the Parliament containing such clauses which depart from the principle of allowing parties and unions and the employers to settle the terms of service.

The aim of this Bill is to provide security for our employees. It is not possible with the development of trade unionism in Mauritius to imitate the situation in England. It will be a very long time before the bargaining power of the unions will be such as to be able to exact fair and reasonable conditions from the employers. That is why Government has found it necessary to intervene and within the general pattern, Government has set to provide for the workers fair wages and good conditions of employment."

Chapter 40

TERMINATION OF
CONTRACT SERVICE BOARD

I had the honour and privilged of serving as workers Representative on the Termination of Contract Service Board under different Chairman: such as Mr Harold Glover former Chief Judge of the Supreme Court, Dr Bhagiruttee and Mr D. B. Seetulsingh Former Judge of the Supreme. I can assure that the workers were better treated in those days and had guarantee regarding their security of employment. Section 30 of the Labour Act 50 of 1975, provided a security against dishonest employers.

Reduction of work force: - Employer means an employer of not less than ten workers. (2) Any employer who intends to reduce the number of workers in his employment either temporarily or permanently shall give written notice to the Minister, together with a statement of the reasons for reduction. (3) on receipt of a notice under subsection (2), The Minister shall refer the matter to the Board (TCSB) for consideration. (4) Notwithstanding any other provision of this section, no employer shall reduce the number of workers in his employment either temporarily or permanently- (a) before the lapse of 120 days from the date of the notice under subsection (2); or (b) pending the decision of the Board, whichever is the later.

Where an employer (a) reduces the number of workers in his employment either temporarily or permanently without giving to the Minister the notice required under subsection (2); (b) acts in breach of subsection (4) he shall, unless good cause is shown, pay to the worker whose employment is terminated a sum equal to 120 days' remuneration together with a sum equal to six times the amount of severance allowance specified in section 36(3)

Where the Board finds that the employer's reduction of the number of workers in his employment- (a) is justified, the employer shall pay the workers whose employment is terminated severance allowance; (b) is not justified, the employer shall pay the workers whose employment is terminated an amount equal to 6 times the amount of severance allowance specified in section 36(3), or reinstate the workers in his former employment.

The TCSB has been repealed since introduction of the Employment Rights Act 200since then, the Workers and Trade Unionists have been complaining that employers are abusing the workers' rights. They argue that it has been very easy for employers to get rid of workers specially those who want to join a union or help their trade union to recruit members. There are a number of Businesses, which are closing down on their own will.

Furthermore I am of the opinion, if section 49 (5) of the Industrial relations Act 67of 1973 should have been maintained, which read as follows; - (5) Any employer who fails to comply with subsection (2) shall commit an offence and shall, on conviction, be liable to imprisonment for a term not exceeding six months and a fine not exceeding two thousand rupees (the fine could have been increased).

Chapter 41

AS A MATTER OF
CONCLUSION

THE world today is at a turning point. We have made such tremendous advancement in technology that even the layman has the world at the tip of his finger through the internet access of his mobile. Hence, the world seems to become smaller. We are talking of a global village. Even now, a group of scientists are working on ways and means of making Mars a habitable place after the Earth is engulfed by the overwhelming Sun in future.

The coming decade's will definitely usher a new world order, where the law of the jungle will prevail. Superpowers will control the market and weak economies will grow weaker with the result that workers will ultimately bear the brunt of structural adjustments within their enterprises. With globalization, guaranteed markets, preferential tariffs, quotas and fixed market prices will disappear. Cut-throat competition between superpowers like Canada, China, Japan and USA and weak economies will highly affect workers the world over.

There will be an economic war where fragile economies will have to stand united if they don't want to be the first casualty on the battlefield. Unity will be the sole means of resistance. Already, trade blocs grouping small economies are emerging to strengthen their bargaining power. Even rich European countries are working on strategies geared towards a common European Constitution.

In such a precarious context, the trade union movement is also expected to undergo structural reforms. We have to rise above the established mindset that has governed trade unionists of late. We need trained union officials who understand market trends and who can make genuine proposals in favour of workers. In Mauritius, the Trade Union Trust Fund which was set up to promote the interests of workers' organizations is conspicuous by its absence on the scene. It's high time for it to shake off the lethargy and act. It should organize training programmes for trade unionists which will help them to keep abreast of latest technologies and learn new economic trends.

Secondly, we have to stop the fragmentation of the trade union movement. We must allow big and International unions to emerge in the interest of workers in general. The IFCTU was divided on the base of political ideology. International Confederation of Free Trade Unions (ICFTU); founded in London in 1949 by unions opposing growing communist control of the World Federation of Trade Unions (WFTU) in the initial phase of the cold war; the breakaway was triggered by the WFTU's aim to absorb the hitherto autonomous International Trade Secretariats (ITS) and its rejection of the Marshall Plan. With this background and the American Federation of Labour (AFL) as an affiliate, the ICFTU in the first two decades of its existence strongly identified with Western democratic values and strictly refused contacts with communist and Eastern European state controlled unions; it closely cooperated with the sixteen ITS's; shortly establishment its founding the ICFTU established a regional network.

A meeting of International Confederation of Free Trade Unions (ICFTU) and of the World Congress of Labour (WCL) took place on Vienna in 31 October 2006. Both the ICFTU and WCL merged to form the International Trade Union Confederation (ITUC), which includes almost all members of the two former internationals as well as a number of non-aligned national centres. Now they claim a membership of 124 million, to ensure more effective representation of workers and pursuits of their rights and interests in the global economy.

The World Federation of Trade Unions (WFTU) represents the Communist tradition of union internationalism, and was in *ideological/political* competition with the ICFTU during the Cold War era.

In order to better defend the interests of their members in a politically unstable and deteriorating environment, the Nepalese teacher organizations have amalgamated to create the Teachers Union of Nepal last year. This year, the International Confederation of Free Trade Unions (ICFTU) and the World Confederation of Labour (WCL) will merge in order to ensure more effective representation of workers and pursuits of their rights and interests in the global economy.

Therefore, unity will constitute our only weapon against merciless profit-minded multinationals and ultra-liberal governments which surrender too easily to the instructions of the IMF/World Bank and the World Trade Organization which encourages private sector competition, putting profit before public benefit. More than ever, trade unions require safeguards to ensure that public services such as education and other services of general interest be not undermined by WTO support for privatization.

Sources of information
1   Commission Truth & Justice

2   Aapravasi Ghat

3   Book written by Miss Mathilde de Plevitz

4   Le Mouvement Syndicale de l'Ile Maurice

5   Report on Trade Unions in Mauritius by Kenneth Baker

6   Ramnarain – Life & Struggle

7   Personnel Interview Years back– H. Ramnarain & M. Jugdambi

8   Newspapers:- Le Mauricien; Week- End; L'Express – Le Socialiste

9   Report Commission of Inquiry in the Sugar Industry by Dr Dragoslav Avramovic

10   Labour Relations in Mauritius by A.K. Gujadhur

11   Indradhanush

Chapter 42

ANNEXURE I

Paper presented as a Resolution by Rajpalsingh Allgoo M.B.E., M.S.K. at the 29th IMF World Congress – San Francisco, California U.S.A. 25-29 May 1997.

Dear Brothers and Sisters,

Today with the Globalisation and Liberalisation of Trades, Workers, Employers and Governments in developing countries are faced with numerous challenges. It would be impossible for me to deal with all the related issues in a short period of time. But I will rather try to analyse the challenges which the workers and the unions will have to face.

1. *Global labour market competition*

   The new global labour market has put workers into an increasingly fierce competition with each other. Growing cross-borders flows of jobseekers are posing serious problems for sending as well as receiving countries, and the new mobility of capital allows it to take advantage of differences in wages and social conditions. Indeed, low production costs and repressive labour laws are becoming more and more the means by which governments appeal to International capital. As a result, the most basic goal of the organised labour at national level – taking wages and working conditions out of competition – is under direct attack by transnational Capital, and labour's principal strategy – of showing solidarity – is undermined by growing labour market competition.

2. *The collapse of communism and the of system competition*

The end of the political competition between economic systems has had another important consequence for unions and workers. As long as there were competing systems, the economic and political power wielders on all sides needed to ensure that the workers and communities governed by them really benefited from economic growth and that at least the appearance of social equity was preserved.

Now that this competition has ended, this motivation has also disappeared, and victorious global Capital feels much freer to take the gains workers and unions had won, and to dismantle progressive social and economic institutions.

3. *Continuing underdevelopment*

Exports are a normal part of economic activity and development. But the type of export-led development which was and is being promoted by neo-liberal policies, the technology and resources, and made them overly dependent on fickle external International Monetary Fund and the World Bank, destroyed economic activities that had allowed the target countries to meet many of their needs with available markets instead of developing the purchasing power of domestic workers.

Prevailing development policies also perpetuate the dependence of many developing countries, particularly the least developed, on primary materials exports, whose price fluctuations cause severe economic difficulties in the exporting countries. Moreover, the private capital driven development, by turning national economies over to global Capital, restricts domestic capital accumulation thus perpetuating permanent dependency, especially in the least developed countries.

4. *The marginalisation of labour in world governance*

The preceding forty years have seen the development of the United Nations System, the Breton Woods institution of economic governance, GATT/WTO, regular summits of heads of states and governments to deal with global political and economic issues (i.e. the G7) and the proliferation of regional structures. Nevertheless, given the scope of the task, institutions of the global governance remain weak.

Labour has long supported these international institutions because the critical issues of war and peace, economic development and workers' rights require strong international institutions. But our problem is that virtually all these institutions are now dominated by political forces hostile to Labour's aspirations and strategies. This is particularly clear in the economically oriented bodies, but Labour is marginalised even in bodies with political and social orientation, such as the UN and the ILO. Aside from the fact that the latter are often paralysed by disputes between states, it is increasingly difficult to have labour's view represented, much less made prevalent, in part because of weakening of labour influence on national governments.

5.   *Potential gains*

Much has been said about the actual and potentially negative impact of the economic trends but that is not to say that there are only negative consequences. Globalisation, for example, creates both winners and losers. The question for Labour is whether this is more than a zero-sum game and whether there are sufficient gains for workers and their communities.

In the developed world, the more highly skilled workers may benefit. The service industries – particularly those servicing global capital are growing strongly. Unfortunately, this is only small comfort for organised workers. Many of the groups that gain, such a professional or financial service workers, have a low degree of unionisation and are resistant to organising efforts.

In developing countries, the arrival of transnational corporations brings jobs and usually better wages and working conditions. Some of these jobs have, of course, been shifted from already existing workplaces, but in many cases additional jobs will be created to fill growing demand in these emerging markets. Obviously, capital inflows, including those from private investors, under certain conditions can contribute to improving living standards in developing world.

In addition, globalisation allows some traditional agricultural and craft producers to access niches in the world market. This provides much needed income and may allow preservation of local cultures and social structures.

These examples show that globalisation could benefit workers throughout the world but, as already noted, inequality is growing and it is not uncommon that the gain of globalisation and economic development go primarily or entirely too transnational corporations or local elites. Moreover, much of the profit from investment inflows is repatriated right back to the investing countries thus impeding capital formation in the developing regions and putting them at a permanent disadvantage.

As a result it is clear that the promise of globalisation will not be realised simply by following some deregulation agenda according to the ruling market ideology. The globalisation process must be shaped to a social equity and a lessening of dependency for the weakest economies in the world. Let us see what is happening in a country where Labour Laws were supposed to be among the best Labour Legislations of the World, according to IMF News: AUSTRALIA *legislations introduced on January 1, 1997, were designed to reduce trade unions' rights and introduce further flexibility into the labour market, by strengthening legal constraints against illegal or unauthorised industrial action, as well as shifting the focus of collective bargaining from the national or regional level to individual company contracts. However, the Minister for Labour Relations, Peter Reith, was quoted as publicly stating, while visiting Hong Kong on April, 10, the Australian government is aiming to improve trade and investment prospects by introducing "sweeping reforms to its labour laws".*

6. Union priorities and principles

In the current political context, the labour movement will either learn how to live and act effectively in the new arena of economic globalisation to build its own strength and global regulatory institutions, or it will face increasing losses. Most fundamentally, it is crucial that democratically decided policies instead of profit driven markets determine our collective social and economic futures. To achieve this, globalisation must be slowed down.

From a trade union perspective, globalisation involves risks but it also offers opportunities. We must harness the latter to establish new rules to restrain the abuses of deregulated globalisation and to further the interests of the working people. We need an action program that will help us to more effectively defend our achievements, to restore the confidence of our membership, and to win new gains for working people. The global challenge we face requires global responses – an action framework that transcends national boundaries.

7. **Our Program should build on the following priorities:-**

Strengthening of international co-operation in the economic and monetary field through the co-ordination of-

- Industrial policies aimed at boosting productive investment and creating jobs;
- The regulation and stabilisation of financial markets;
- the Fiscal policies to prevent the dismantling of social security systems, to smooth Economic cycles and assure sustainable economic growth.

Promotion of fair trade among nations, prohibitions of social dumping and respect of core labour and environmental standards;

- Integration of developing countries into the world economy through the establishment of a fair commodity prices, the access to international markets under equitable terms and a socially responsible policy on the part of international lending institutions to foster economic and social advancement.

8. **More jobs and environmentally sustainable growth.** For us, full employment is a basic priority and governments have to put the creation of adequate and fairly remunerated jobs to do away with the reduction of unemployment at the centre of their action in full respect of workers' and trade union rights. A worldwide co-ordination of economic and monetary policies is needed to prevent unsustainable payment imbalances and exchange rate fluctuations and create more and better employment for all.

9. Economic policies must also incorporate stringent rules and measures aimed at securing an environmentally sound and sustained development. Environmental protection and development are interlinked and have to be dealt with as such. We cannot accept that workers throughout the world are exposed to inadequate environmental standards and that health and safety norms are sacrificed on the altar of international competition.

Thank you

Chapter 43

ANNEXURE II

RAJPALSINGH ALLGOO
M.B.E, M.S.K

Rajpalsingh Allgoo has had a very rich career in the Trade Union movement, both locally and at international level. In fact, he was still at school when he engaged himself in Union work, giving a helping hand to his uncle, Rampertab Allgoo, a well-known trade union leader of his time.

Essentially a self-made man, he has followed a vast number of training programmes and courses, and participated in countless workshops and seminars abroad, starting g with a Monitors' Course on workers' education in 1976 in Monrovia, Liberia. The course was initiated by the ICFTU and aimed at forming trainers to train Trade Unionists in workers' education.

In 1984 he obtained a Diploma in Advanced Trade Union Leadership from the District of Colombia University in Washington, USA. The course was organized jointly by the World Bank and the International Monetary Fund.

In 1978, he participated in a workshop in Cooperative and Credit Unions in Maseru, Lesotho, organized by ACOSCA. Since that time Rajpalsingh Allgoo has participated in a lot of other conferences, workshops, seminars, study tours organized in dozens of countries in the five continents, including the United States of America, Great Britain,

Bulgaria, France, Portugal, Sweden, Germany, Switzerland, India, Iraq, South Africa, China, Japan, Singapore , Australia and most African countries.

From 1988 until his retirement in 1997, he attended the Annual General Meetings of different International federations to which the AGWU the ITGLWF were affiliated. He has also chaired several international meetings as Executive member of organizations. On the local front, Rajpalsingh Allgoo has occupied the following positions:

- President, Artisans and General Workers' Union
- President, Mauritius Labour Congress
- Director of Organisation Textile & Garment Workers' Union
- Negotiator, Transport Employees Union
- Educator/Advisor, Mauritius Labour Congress
- Deputy Chairman, Sugar Industry Labour Welfare Fund
- Member, Board of Directors EPZ Labour Welfare Fund
- Member, Advisory Board of Occupational Health & Safety Welfare
- Member, National Economic Development Council
- Member, Advisory Board of Mauritius Sugar Authority
- Member Termination of Contracts Service Board
- Member, I.V.B.T. Advisory Board
- Commissioner, Local Government Service Commission
- Vice Chairman, National Remuneration Board
- Councillor, National Economic & Social Council
- Acting Chairman, National Remuneration Board
- Member, Termination of Contracts Service Board

Rajpalsingh Allgoo has also authored a few books:

1. Movement Syndical de L'Ile Maurice

2. Golden Jubilee of Artisans & General Workers' Union

3. Hommage a Emmanuel Anquetil (1885-1946) Pere du Syndicalisme Mauricien

4. Occupational Health Safety & Welfare Handbook

5. A brief History of Trade Unionism in Mauritius

He has also published several magazines for the AGWU and the MLC, as well as documents on IRA, Labour Act 1975, Occupational Health Safety and Welfare, Workers' participation, etc.

www.ingramcontent.com/pod-product-compliance
Lightning Source LLC
Chambersburg PA
CBHW080619030426
42336CB00018B/3021